TONY STARK, ODYSSEUS, AND THE MYTHS BEHIND MARVEL

TONY STARK, ODYSSEUS, AND THE MYTHS BEHIND MARVEL

ANCIENT HEROES IN THE MODERN WORLD

PETER MEINECK

wm

WILLIAM MORROW
An Imprint of HarperCollins*Publishers*

HarperCollins books may be purchased for educational, business, or sales promotional use. For information, please email the Special Markets Department at SPsales@harpercollins.com.

hc.com

FIRST EDITION

Library of Congress Cataloging-in-Publication Data has been applied for.

ISBN 978-0-06-338264-0

25 26 27 28 29 LBC 5 4 3 2 1

For Desiree, Sofia, and Marina — My Heroes

CONTENTS

TONY STARK, ODYSSEUS, AND THE MYTHS BEHIND MARVEL

PROLOGUE

THE NEW ANCIENT MYTHOLOGY

We all have a sense of what mythology is: stories of heroes, gods, and monsters, impossible quests to fantastic lands, epic wars, endless cycles of bloody revenge, and extraordinary tales of magic and the mysteries of life and death. We tend to think of myths as stories told by ancient peoples, such as the Greeks, Norse, Egyptians, Sumerians, or Maya hundreds, even thousands, of years ago. Yet I see mythology alive and well, thriving on our movie and TV screens, and in the pages of our books and comics. One of the most prevalent myth-making machines operating today is the pop cultural behemoth known as the Marvel Universe. How do these modern stories relate to the ancient myths, and what might they reveal about us today?

Humans have been telling myths for at least as long as we have been able to speak—some eighty thousand years and possibly for much, much longer. The more paleontologists learn about Stone Age caves, the more they realize that these sites were used not only as shelters but also as ritual performance spaces. Stone Age people would journey deep inside to experience elaborate art on undulating cave walls that seemed to move in the flickering firelight. They encountered masked shamans performing mesmerizing stories and heard the rhythms of drumming and the sounds of music, chanting, song, and spoken word.

Even before humans developed the ability of sophisticated speech, people were transforming their physical environments and creating performance spaces. Then they artificially illuminated them with fire and created their own abstract mythic worlds. As the oldest human-made fire yet found—at the Wonderwerk Cave in South Africa—is over 1 million years old, we can imagine how our *Homo erectus* ancestors who gathered there shared their dreams in the firelight and even envisioned the realms of their gods. Mythmaking is as old as humanity itself.

A Stone Age cave in southern Germany provided an incredible example of very old mythmaking, dating back some forty thousand years. In 1939, right as World War II was about to start, a geologist helping to excavate a cave at Hohlenstein-Stadel discovered something truly remarkable: around two hundred tiny fragments of a carved mammoth's bone. It wasn't until 1982 that the fragments were reassembled to the point where the figure's facial features could be made out and 2012 when additional fragments were added to complete the figurine. What was revealed was truly incredible. Not only was this twelve-inch ivory figurine the oldest representation of a human yet found, it had the head and face of a lion. What was this extraordinary carving? A masked shaman? A mythical beast? Or perhaps the world's oldest superhero, a very ancient version of the mythic big cat–human characters like Herakles (Hercules) of Greek and Roman mythology or Marvel's Black Panther?

We do not know the purpose of the Löwenmensch (Lion Person) Figurine or its gender. For the people of Aurignacian culture who brought down a great woolly mammoth, retrieved its highly valuable tusk, and then painstakingly carved it with a flint tool, there must have been an epic story associated with it. That myth was more than likely played out in the dark recesses of that prehistoric cave, lit by a glimmering fire.

In many ways, the movie theatre is our modern equivalent of those ancient caves. We still encounter myths in the darkness. We watch images animated by flickering lights and "shaman" movie stars wearing costumes and even masks acting out narratives before us. The images may now be digital, but the electricity that powers them is still the spark of divine fire.

The Greeks told a myth that fire was stolen from Olympus and gifted to mortals by the Titan Prometheus. For that, the gods punished Prometheus by chaining him to a mountain, where his liver was pecked out by an eagle every day. With fire humans had the potential to transform their lives and perhaps even challenge the gods. To counter this the Olympians devised a plan: they had Hephaestus, the ingenious god of technology, create something never before seen—a woman. Her name was Pandora, which means "all giving" because each of the gods imbued her with an almost divine quality. They dressed Pandora in the finest clothes and gave her a jar filled with all the things that could plague humanity. The plan—to distract the mortal men so much that they would never be able to really harness fire in the way that the gods had—was a superdestructive divine thunderbolt. We all know the story: Pandora's jar (or box, in some versions) is opened because humans can't help being naturally inquisitive, and out flies every trouble that will forever affect humanity. Except hope—that remained. Was hope another evil, the feeling of delusion, or was it a divine spark intended to keep us all going? This is what myths can do—offer us a divine spark of hope, when things otherwise seem completely lost.

We can set, for example, the story of Pandora and her connection with divine fire alongside modern Marvel myths such as the plot of the 2015 movie *Avengers: Age of Ultron*, where an AI machine created by Tony Stark and Bruce Banner to protect the Earth ends up deciding that the most effective way to do so is by destroying humanity. Both myths ask us to consider the limits of our imaginations and how far we choose to open the Pandora's Box of technology to solve our problems. In each example we have a myth about tampering with "divine" fire.

For all the fantastical stories myths relay, the ones that adapt and survive contain actualities told in a way that ensures they stay memorable. Myths are not false. In fact, when we analyze their meaning, we often see that they communicate very real events, social tensions, important rites of passage, and the deepest concerns of the culture within which they are told. This is another reason why Marvel has been so effective—the memorable characters, their distinctive masks and costumes, gripping narratives, fantastical interstellar beings, the expansive multiverse, they all help us to receive the stories metaphorically. The Marvel Universe is never perceived as real, even though it often brilliantly reflects our most pressing realities.

I have spent my career teaching, translating, staging, and writing about ancient myths and how they were expressed in antiquity. I am fascinated by why these stories were told, who did the telling, how they did it and who for, and how they changed depending on who was receiving them. If myths survive and continue to be handed down, then they contain something essentially important to the people who tell them. In short, we can tell a good deal about an ancient society based on the myths they articulated. What then might the myths of Marvel reveal about us? Are they completely new creations, or are they based on much older archetypes? How do we receive our myths differently from ancient peoples? Is Marvel a new kind of ancient mythology—an American mythos?

To answer these questions, let me start at the beginning:

April 2018: The opening weekend of *Avengers: Infinity War*. I am seated in my local movie theatre with my eleven-year-old daughter. She is already a huge fan of the Marvel Cinematic Universe. This is a new experience for me, and I have been late to the MCU party, which started in 2008 with the release of *Iron Man*. Sure, I had heard the buzz about the movies. My students in my mythology class at New York University, many of them studying film, had been comparing the ancient myths we were discussing to Marvel stories. But this was my first foray into the whole Avengers phenomenon, which up until now had been an alien world to me.

A few months prior, my daughter and I saw *Black Panther*. At the time I didn't register it as a Marvel movie, but a brilliant piece of superhero storytelling not afraid of tackling some contemporary hot button issues head-on. As a scholar who specializes in ancient performance, I enjoyed the scene in the "Museum of Great Britain" in which the supervillain Killmonger took the African Igbo mask. I delighted in the portrayal of the female warriors the Dora Milaje, and the use of ancestor worship. At that tumultuous time in American culture, *Black Panther* felt cathartic: a new legend made from ancient myths.

I admit that my expectations for *Avengers: Infinity War* were not particularly high. These were comic book characters, after all, and so I could understand why my daughter was into the whole thing. I felt the same way lining up outside a cinema in the south of London early in 1978 to see *Star Wars*. I have never forgotten the feeling of exhilaration when that massive Imperial Star Destroyer swept across the big screen. Back then I knew Spider-Man from the animated show that aired in the afternoon on British TV. I had seen *The Incredible Hulk* with Lou Ferringo in green body makeup and that wig. Still, I was more of a *Six Million Dollar Man* kind of guy back then. I knew about the Marvel comics, but I couldn't afford those glossy color booklets I saw on the rack at the corner store. I instead read the British sci-fi comic *2000 AD* with characters like Judge Dredd,

Robo-Hunter, and Nemesis the Warlock. So, despite being thrilled by *Black Panther,* I came to *Infinity War,* popcorn in hand, thinking I was going to be watching a very expensive kids' movie.

By the end of the film's 149 minutes, I was blown away.

I was *moved* by *Infinity War.* A story of a monstrous yet strangely philosophical purple villain called Thanos, hell-bent on exterminating half the world's population. The movie gripped this cynical, overanalytical, and hypercritical classics professor. I knew that Loki was a Norse god but not why he died in this incarnation. I was unaware of the history of Dr. Strange and Wong. I had yet to meet the fantastic Guardians of the Galaxy. I did not know the backstory of Wanda Maximoff and Vision. I was really confused about the guy with the metal arm, an assault weapon, and a mullet, and what he was doing in Wakanda. Despite all of this, I was enthralled.

Then at the movie's end, the heroes failed! Thanos was victorious! How refreshing in a superhero movie, no less. I got up to leave and my daughter told me to stay put: "There's always end credit scenes, Dad." But even those piled on the misery. Samuel L. Jackson (I didn't know about Nick Fury yet) disintegrating. An Avenger watching his family crumble into ashes before his eyes. Had Marvel done the unthinkable and produced a true American tragedy? I was completely hooked.

Driving home from *Infinity War,* it struck me that the concept of superheroes failing was like one of the greatest myths of antiquity, the *Odyssey.* In that epic story, the Greek mythic hero Odysseus is a kind of Tony Stark figure—a master of ideas, a "man of twists and turns." The classicist and translator Emily Wilson calls him "complicated." Odysseus uses his intellect, charm, good looks, powers of persuasion, and whatever technology had to offer to achieve his hero's quest. He is also a famous trickster, and the ancient Greek version of a great cosmic battle involving countless heroes and supernatural entities, the Trojan War, was won by a plan of Odysseus's.

This was the false gift of the wooden horse, whose belly was full of Greek warriors.

In the Greek mythic tradition Odysseus was portrayed as a compromised or damaged hero. We see him making bad decisions, losing all the men under his command, and unable to get home for ten long years. When he does finally return, disguised as a beggar, his house is overrun with greedy suitors trying to win over his wife and murder his son. The *Odyssey* shows us that the hero must find a new way to exist in the world if they want to find their way home. Marvel also deals with the same kinds of issues. What does it mean to be a hero? Can anyone achieve anything meaningful alone? How should great power be wielded? What kind of society do we want to live in?

As a professor who teaches ancient mythology, I became intrigued by what Marvel was communicating to us and what it all might mean. So, I set out with my daughter to watch every Marvel movie in chronological order at home. I spent a year devouring the old Marvel comics going all the way back to 1939. I came to love the striking artwork, complex story lines, cross-character pollination, and retconning. I watched several MCU TV shows like *WandaVision, Loki, Daredevil, Punisher, Luke Cage,* and *Echo*. I read about Marvel and the MCU and its creators. I interviewed Marvel screenwriters, worked alongside directors. Then I offered a class at NYU on Marvel and mythology, and I think I learned more from my students than they did from me. I saw the passion these stories provoked and how similar they were to myths I knew from all across the ancient world.

The ancient Greeks called their stories about gods, monsters, legendary figures, and folktales, *muthoi,* which means "a spoken account." These performed stories of the divine or distant past helped ancient peoples understand the world they lived in, explain uncertainties, and bind them together in a shared culture. Was Marvel doing something similar? Was it developing a new mythic universe based on existing ones? Does this help account for its epic success?

Like Odysseus winding his way through the Mediterranean all those millennia ago, I took a roundabout route to becoming a classics professor. This is a scholar of Greek and Roman literature, history, and culture. Growing up working-class in South London, I had always been fascinated by the past. Perhaps it was an escape from the realities of everyday life. England is knee-deep in archaeological remains, and at ten years old I was allowed to help on a small dig in southern England. I'll always remember the thrill of uncovering a large piece of a Roman vase that had been thrown down a well by someone two thousand years ago. I was struck that the last human to touch that vase was a person who lived in Roman Britain. Even then I wanted to know how they lived and what stories they told.

Comic books also spoke to me at this time, in the form of the *Asterix* series by the French artists Goscinny and Uderzo. These were the epic adventures of a Gaulish superhero, made invulnerable by a magic potion, who went up against the invading legions of Julius Caesar. I'm sure I became a classics professor because of Asterix, and I bet I'm not the only one. I first engaged with the *Odyssey* at that time too, not as a literary text, but a storybook full of arresting images of gods, storms, and monsters. This is the power of graphic art that Marvel knows well. It is one of the oldest forms of mythic and ritual communication, stretching back some fifty thousand years to the paintings that adorned Paleolithic caves. The Greeks really loved *graphai*—drawing and writing. They illustrated their vases with scenes of gods and heroes, epic combat, and monsters. Marvel comics stand in this age-old tradition of mythic graphic communication.

Perhaps those tales also inspired me to get out of the south London suburbs, seek my own adventures, and look for heroes. As a teenager I joined the Marine cadets inspired by Ray, a former Royal Marine who had landed in Normandy on June 6, 1944, and spent the next year or so fighting through Europe. Ray ran a small corner shop, and I worked a paper route on my bike early in the mornings.

Once Ray found out I wanted to join the Corps, he confiscated my bike, doubled the size of my load, and had me run it with two large bags of newspapers slung over each shoulder. Sunday was a particularly hard run with those huge copies of the *Sunday Times* and the *Observer* weighing me down. To me Ray was an almost mythical figure, and I wanted to emulate him. The stories he told of his time in the Marines sounded like epic myths.

Ultimately, a military career was not in the cards for me, although I did serve as a Royal Marine reservist while I was in college. There the power of mythology was palpable. Every recruit had to learn the famous battles of the Royal Marines since their founding on October 28, 1664. Woe betided the hapless "nod" (a commando trainee) who got a date or detail wrong. A lack of knowledge of Royal Marine history meant a "beasting," which pretty much sounds like it was, a horrific ten to twenty minutes of intense physical fitness usually involving a very rugged landscape, thorny bushes, or excessive amounts of mud. But the corps history was learned and loved. These real historic events became myths, and—this is key—myths are not untruths, they are "hypertruths" in that they contain essential elements of what is valued by the culture that tells them. The mythology of the Royal Marines is a large part of what makes them an effective unit, and it was what I still saw in Ray thirty years after he left the service. This is the lasting power of mythology.

One day in the mideighties, I was on parade for a visiting general when he stopped and asked me what I was studying at university. "Ancient World Studies, sir," I crisply replied, standing at attention. "Well, that will certainly be useful fighting the Russians in the snows of Norway, won't it!" On reflection the general was right, and my path took a sharp turn into my studies, then to a career as a technician, producer, and director in the theatre, before landing in academia. Yet I have never lost my deep respect and affinity for people who serve in the military and first responders, which is probably why I still volunteer as a firefighter, an EMT, and a rescue technician. In fact, a good deal of this book was written at the firehouse between calls.

So, at the same time I was having my Marvel mythological epiphany, I was working with a group of American military veterans on the *Odyssey* for a program that used Greek myths to frame their experiences. This saga of a warrior returning home after twenty years of war and wandering struck a chord with these veterans of Iraq, Afghanistan, and Vietnam. We created performances and public discussions about big themes in American culture that were also in the ancient stories: democracy, leadership, heroism, trauma, and homecoming among them. This work reinforced my sense that these old myths held an intrinsic power to get to the heart of a matter. They are our equivalent of Black Panther's Ancestral Plane—the place where we meet our ancestors and share in their wisdom.

The program was called The Warrior Chorus, and the vets took their works to the Obama White House, the US Capitol, the Metropolitan Museum of Art, Federal Hall in New York City, and other venues across the United States. In one gig in a public library in Mississippi a leather-clad Vietnam vet, the leader of the local chapter of Rolling Thunder, a veteran bikers' group, stood up to speak. He had just watched a scene from the *Odyssey* where the hero is reunited with his wife, Penelope. At that heightened emotional moment, she tests him, to make sure he knows the secret of the making of their marriage bed. She also wants to know if the man who has returned home after so much war and suffering is the same man she married.

The story tells how at that moment, Odysseus feels like a drowning man reaching out to her to be saved. The vet turned to his wife, who was sitting beside him, and said, "I've never told you this before, but that's exactly how I felt coming home from Vietnam. There was so much killing, I didn't know if I could ever love or be loved again. I was drowning, but you reached out." She clasped his hand, and everyone there knew they were witnessing an incredible moment of truth. In my own twenty-year marriage I have been surprised how myths like the *Odyssey* can be incredibly useful in helping to articulate and navigate some of the stormy seas that any relationship needs to cross. This is another power of myth: its ability to communicate something essential across generations, like the wisdom of our ancestors enshrined in a story.

Marvel's Stan Lee knew the power of mythology, so much so that he has become something of a mythological figure himself. The story is well-known: Lee rose from scrappy inkwell filler and lunch boy to creative genius and publisher. Every time Stan "the Man" Lee popped up in one of his many cameos in the Marvel Cinematic Universe, he was presenting a mythical persona. Lee offered a nostalgic connection to the world of Marvel comics and the equally mythic Marvel bullpen, the imaginary "boiler room" in New York where artists and writers diligently toiled together. Lee understood that to create fan loyalty, his brand needed to become mythic—not only the characters but the people who created them.

Ancient myths can sometimes seem confusing. There are often many different versions of the same story from different times and places. For example, Homer tells us that Aphrodite, the deity of erotic love, was a daughter of Zeus, but the poet Hesiod says she was older than Zeus and born from the castration of Kronos, whose genitals fell into the sea and birthed the goddess.

Likewise, the modern myth of Stan Lee has multiple versions. His role at Marvel is constantly debated by fans, particularly who created which character and when. However, Lee understood that regardless of who created the characters, they had to be distinctive and reflect familiar archetypes. Then the stories themselves needed to be accessible and entertaining. What made them mythic is that Lee knew they should provide some deeper meaning to the lives of Marvel's readers.

Stan Lee is something of a paradox. Was he the creative genius who built Marvel into an international powerhouse, or—to use Marvel artist extraordinaire Jack Kirby's words—was he a "double-dipper" whose reputation was built on the work of others? Either way, Lee understood the mythic proportions of the material he was publishing.

The term "mythology" is also an oxymoron and something of a paradox. On one level, it means the study (*logos*) of stories (*muthos*), but for the Greeks, *muthos* and *logos* were oppositional concepts. *Muthos* meant anything spoken and came to denote a traditional story, a term derived from the Latin *tradio*, meaning "hand down." But *logos* indicated something far more rigid or fixed, like a law, a rule, a formula, or a specific argument or theory. In Greek, *logos* is often translated as "the word" in the sense of an authoritative statement, while *muthos* is a story that is told. Simply put, *logos* is logical, and *muthos* mythical.

Myths are not fixed versions of a particular story; they are fluid, flexible, ambiguous, and sometimes complex and nuanced. In effect, a myth must convey meaning to act as a *muthos*. If the story told has no meaning, it probably won't be told again. When we see the same kind of myth cropping up in different cultures at different times, we should ask, Why is that story being retold, and what does it mean to the people who hear it?

The ancient Greeks were well aware of the significance of their myths. The philosopher Aristotle said that making up stories is one of the first things that humans do as children. We fixate on characters by playing with stuffed animals, action figures, and dolls, and we work out the world around us through creative play. This is what Aristotle called *mimesis*. This does not really mean "imitation" because mimesis involves another basic human cognitive function: "Theory of Mind"—our ability to project onto another what they might be thinking. For instance, babies know very early on that smiling will provoke a reaction from their caregivers. Theory of Mind seems to be an innate quality among humans, and it is key to the act of myth-making, which involves having us care about the stories being told and the characters who inhabit them.

In the fourth century BCE Aristotle called *muthos* the soul of drama. In 1970 Stan Lee wrote that a story "without a message, however subliminal, is like a man without a soul."[1]

• • •

Marvel stands on a foundation of ancient mythological traditions from the peoples of Mesopotamia, the Near and Middle East, Africa, India, China, and the Americas, the Norse, the Celts, and others. In this book I set many of their stories next to Marvel as either the basis of them or working in the same kinds of ways. However, there will be a focus on the ancient Greeks in these pages for a few reasons.

First, I am a professor of classics. I specialize in and teach the drama, mythology, literature, history, and culture of the ancient Greek world. With that being said, I do not see the Greeks as a monoculture, but a deeply interconnected group of peoples, sharing a common language, with a multiplicity of influential cultures arrayed all around them.

Second, because the Greeks were situated amid the Mediterranean Sea, they soaked up a plethora of different mythic traditions from the Near and Middle East, Africa, the Black Sea and Balkans, Western Europe, and across the existing trade and festival routes to India and even as far as China.

Third, the Greeks happened to write many of their myths down at a time when the production of books became much more widespread. Greek also became the language of literature in the Hellenistic and Roman worlds. This means we have a lot of Greek myths, and they, in turn, have had a great deal of influence on us.

This is what makes ancient Greece so fascinating, particularly classical Athens, which was the New York City, Shanghai, or Nairobi of its day. In Athens's harbors were the constant exchange of goods, the babble of commerce, and the to-ing and fro-ing of artists, emissaries, and festivalgoers. The ancient places of exchange like Athens were not at all dissimilar to the exhilarating atmosphere of cultural ferment that greeted Marco Polo in the massive Chinese port of Quanzhou, or what Shakespeare heard from seafarers at the taverns near the docks in Elizabethan London.

In those bustling port cities myths were told and retold and then spread across different cultures at different times. This means there are no canonical versions and no singular texts that later adaptations must adhere to. This is called the "fidelity discourse"—the notion that there is one original version that all others can be traced back to. But oral transmission and mythic performances simply don't work that way.

Like us, myths adapt to survive. Why and how they adapt tells us so much about their purpose. When Marvel creatives "retcon," or create new, retroactive continuities between old story lines and new ones, they are standing in the same mythic tradition as the Sumerian *Gilgamesh*, the Indian *Mahabharata*, and the Greek *Iliad* and the *Odyssey*. All these texts borrow from similar mythic tropes and even each other. Consequently, when the Marvel cocreator Jack Kirby introduced a character known as Gilgamesh (or "The Forgotten One") in the 1977 comic *The Eternals*, he was part of an age-old practice spanning at least four thousand years, back to the Sumerian myth of Gilgamesh, the oldest surviving written story in the world. In this way the artists and writers of the Marvel comic books and the screenwriters and directors of the MCU are our modern mythmakers.

I have been fortunate to work closely with these new mythmakers as a consultant on several movie and TV projects. On one of those movie gigs, I found myself sitting on a plush bench by the elevators in an achingly hip film production office owned by two prominent Marvel directors. I watched a group of cool hipsters make elaborate espresso-based beverages, play pool, crouch over a retro Pac-Man table, throw darts, and grab organic snacks from what looked like an endless supply cupboard. It was mesmerizing. I was eventually ushered into a large conference room plastered on all sides with images of Greek mythological characters, movie stills, and actor headshots.

There I met some of the most successful and creative people who have worked as MCU screenwriters, directors, and producers. We spent the next two days delving deep into Greek mythology and I got to watch how the brilliant minds of these movie professionals operated. It was a thrilling, caffeinated, ancient Greek joyride as I experienced these mythmakers at work. I saw firsthand how at the root of the creative process of developing a superhero movie screenplay is a desire to understand what that story meant to the people it was originally created for.

The project I was advising on was a non-Marvel live-action retelling of a beloved mythological character. The opportunity to be in the bullpen of narrative creativity on such a project at this early stage was a rare gift for a scholar of the performance of ancient myth. The movie artists first wanted to hear more about the Greek myths they were interested in recreating. They often seemed quite shocked by what I revealed to them—irrational and sudden slaughters, despicable child-killing, terrifying manic rages, brutal spousal abuse, deep depression, chilling curses, and ritual defilement—the Greek heroes we tend to encounter in children's stories, cartoons, or as a fun toy in a Happy Meal were often deeply damaged.

This idea of the broken hero struck a chord with the writers who had developed incredibly successful past MCU movies. "We could go there if this was a Marvel project" was a refrain I heard several times whenever we talked about a particular knotty, violent, or disturbing aspect of the character's story. This returns me to my first response to *Infinity War*: those heroes were damaged and volatile, and they made mistakes. The Marvel superhumans were in fact very *human*, just like many of the characters we encounter in ancient mythology.

I hope that this book offers Marvel fans a new way to approach the characters and stories they love and perhaps even learn some new things about them from a different perspective. I also hope the lover of mythology or the ancient world might come to appreciate how Marvel stands in a long and vibrant tradition of mythmaking and how many of the stories are complex, compelling, and quite revealing about our own society. In many ways these twentieth- and twenty-first-century comic book and movie characters are ancient heroes still living in our modern world.

CHAPTER 1

CAPTAIN AMERICA: THE *ETHOS* OF MARVEL

The word "hero" is derived from the Greek *hērōs*, which means "protector." In ancient Greece certain mortals who had achieved *kleos* (glory or fame) in life were venerated in death. Their burial places were viewed as offering protection to the community, and they were honored like saints with festivals and religious rites. Yet a hero was not divine but a mortal whose larger-than-life acts, both positive and negative, had been remembered and preserved in myth. Those myths were conveyed through performance, sung in the great halls of the elite, recited at festivals all across the ancient world, staged at the theatre to large audiences, and displayed on wall paintings, mosaics, vases, and sculptures that adorned both sacred sanctuaries and city-states. The manners by which stories of heroes were conveyed in antiquity were not so unlike the comic books, movies and TV shows, games, and high-profile PR events of the Marvel Universe.

If a hero was remembered, they were said to live on after death in the blessed fields of Elysium, a place of beautiful meadows in the underworld. If forgotten, the hero became just another shade in Hades. Mythic memory offered the closest thing a human could get to immortality. To be sung, and now written, about was to achieve a kind of mythic divinity.

For the Greeks, being a hero did not necessarily mean that you did something good or noble, more that the deeds you accomplished during your life achieved *kleos*—fame or glory. The most famous Greek hero was Herakles (Hercules), whose name contains the term *kleos*. Herakles was the son of Zeus and the mortal Alcmene, and he was celebrated in many cities all over the Greek world, from Spain to Anatolia. Though a son of Zeus and incredibly strong, Herakles was human. At his death he was the only mortal to achieve divinity. Yet Herakles led a very troubled life. He was despised by Hera, the queen of Olympus and goddess of childbirth and marriage, because she saw his almost-divine powers as a threat to the fragile relationship between the gods and mortals. If a mortal hero was this powerful, why would the humans even need the gods?

Herakles was most famous for completing twelve impossible labors imposed on him by his cousin Eurystheus ("broad strength") who ruled the ancient city of Tiryns, a fortified citadel where Herakles was supposed to rule. Instead, Hera held back Herakles's birth so his cousin, now born first, would inherit the crown instead. Since then, Eurystheus did all he could to get rid of his powerful rival, fearing he would one day be overthrown. So far, this sounds like an archetypal heroic tale—the protagonist denied his rightful place and forced to undertake impossible tasks to win it back. But the Herakles story takes a much darker turn: Each time he tries to marry and start a family, Hera drives him insane. In a fit of madness the hero does that which we consider the most unheroic—he slaughters his family. In many mythologies the hero is a troubled character, and their stories can leave us with the sense that none of us would really want that kind of fame.

At least with Herakles we can feel sympathy for him as his madness is inflicted by a god. But then there is another famous hero, Oedipus, and his tomb at Colonus near Athens protected the city from its enemies. He was famous for unknowingly sleeping with his mother and fathering children with her, then railing against the gods when he found out the truth. Not very "heroic" by our definition. But having Oedipus's reputation protecting your land is a lot like having the Hulk as a border guard. On the face of it, the Hulk defies the heroic stereotype due to the damage caused by his uncontrollable anger, but when directed by the Avengers he becomes a force for good.

Herakles fulfills a similar heroic role in Greek myth. He doesn't turn green and inflate in size, but he is a terrifying berserker, a warrior who goes into a rage-fueled, altered state when fighting, and his eyes twist in his head and blaze like fire. Herakles uses his great powers for good, defeating monsters and tyrants, but he also destroys what he loves, including his own family.

While the kind of protection offered by Herakles or the Hulk comes with the risk of uncontrollable rage and indiscriminate destruction, and Oedipus seems more of a supervillain than a benevolent guardian, there was a kind of Greek hero that was seen as a defender. This was the *Alexandros,* which means "a protector of others" in the sense of repelling enemies. Alexander the Great is the most famous bearer of this illustrious name, but it was also given to Paris, the prince of Troy and lover of Helen, even though his actions brought war. More than any other Marvel superhero, Captain America fulfills this role.

Captain America was introduced in December 1940 by Timely Comics, the forerunner of Marvel. At that time Britain had been at war with Germany for seventeen months. Adolf Hitler's forces had swept through Europe. The Nazis were setting up concentration camps for Jews, Romani, queer people, academics, political prisoners, and anyone whom the regime considered "degenerate." Britain was being relentlessly bombed by the Luftwaffe, Germany had invaded France, Belgium, and Holland, and the concentration camp at Auschwitz had opened. America was still a year away from entering the war.

From the beginning Marvel was defined by its superhuman characters set against the background of the coming war. Its first comic book, *Marvel Comics #1*, had been released by Timely in August 1939 and introduced several characters. There was the Human Torch, the Angel, Namor the Sub-Mariner, the Masked Raider, and a Tarzan-like figure called Ka-Zar. By issue #2, the Angel was shooting down Nazi bombers over Poland. Then in issue #3, Namor was sinking German U-boats. Right from the start Marvel's characters were responding to real events in the world—and what's more, they were taking a stand.

At the foundation of the Marvel universe lies something essentially heroic. Almost two years before America entered the war against the Axis powers, Bill Everett was telling stories about a superhuman figure from Atlantis doing battle with the Nazis. Then came Captain America in 1940, a new hero billed as "against those who would conquer the United States" and the "sentinel of our shores." Readers were encouraged to sign and become one of Captain America's United States Junior Sentinels. Then they would receive a membership badge and an ID card. The Captain was introduced bedecked in his red, white, and blue stars-and-stripes costume. He carried a kite-shaped shield, which resembled the one on the great seal of the United States, and wore a blue half mask emblazoned with a distinctive white "A" and edged with small wings.

Captain America's creators, Jack Kirby (born Jacob Kurtzberg) and Joe Simon (Hymie Simon), were sons of Jewish immigrants from Europe and aware of the dangers of the Nazi regime. In *The Human Torch #3*, released in December 1940, a story by Carl Burgos

(Max Finkelstein) already has the Torch battling a Hitler look-alike named "Hiccup." In one brilliant panel a tendril from the Torch's fiery wake singes off Hiccup's Hitler moustache. In that same issue Namor helps the US Navy defeat a surprise seaborne attack by the Germans and is rewarded with a ticker-tape parade in New York City. It's clear Captain America was introduced for one incredibly urgent purpose: to galvanize American youth against the Nazi regime.

When Captain America burst onto his own comic book cover that December, Kirby and Simon did not hold back. Now there were no euphemisms for Germany's leader. Steve Rogers the supersoldier from Brooklyn is punching Hitler in the face with a mean right hook. The Nazi dictator falls on a map of America and a book marked "sabotage plans for U.S.A." There was no doubt what Captain America was fighting for.

The publication of *Captain America Comics #1* was a heroic act. In early 1941, in addition to the isolationist movement, there were others who were politically sympathetic to Hitler's far-right government. The America First Committee had more than 800,000 members and 450 chapters across America. This organization included highly influential figures such as automaker Henry Ford and aviation hero Charles Lindbergh. Kirby and Simon must have known that Captain America was going to piss off a lot of very powerful people.

Jack Kirby described how the Timely office regularly received anonymous death threats against its staff because of *Captain America*'s anti-fascist content. One Nazi sympathizer buzzed threats through the intercom. Kirby said he rushed down to the lobby to confront him, but the man was gone. The story itself is emblematic of the real risks the early Marvel creators faced by introducing *Captain America* at such a politically charged and divided time. Things got so bad that the mayor of New York City, Fiorello La Guardia, gave Simon and Kirby police protection. Once the USA entered the war,

Simon, Kirby, Burgos, and many other Marvel artists enlisted and went on to see combat. Not all heroes wear capes.

Captain America would develop from WWII anti-Nazi fighter to the leader of the Avengers. With his round American star shield, he epitomizes the archetype of the protector. Steve Rogers grows up in Brooklyn as a puny but resolute child. He stands up to bullies but does not have the physical strength or stature to defeat them. When World War II begins, he is determined to join the US Army despite successive medical rejections. Then he agrees to be injected with the superserum and is transformed into a much stronger, more athletic version of his former self. From then on, both in the comics and the later movies, Captain America stood as a symbol of American ethical behavior, even if sometimes that role edged the character toward the Greek philosopher Aristotle's warning in his famous treatise on drama, *Poetics*, that a character should possess a mixture of both virtues and flaws.[1]

Despite what Aristotle says, there are times we have needed Captain America's ethical certainty and inherent goodness. A poignant reminder of this occurred in the 2012 movie *The Avengers*. Loki, the brother of Thor, has crashed a high society party in Germany. After a bold show of violent domination, he forces the fleeing guests to kneel before him. He tells them that this is their natural state and that he will be their ruler. But one elderly man resists Loki and refuses. Although not explicit, the implication is that he is a Holocaust survivor. Loki responds by aiming his mace to obliterate the old man, ready to snuff out his act of defiance. He fires—and the blast is suddenly deflected by Captain America's Vibranium shield. Steve Rogers has arrived in the nick of time. He tells Loki that he's seen this kind of thing before in Germany. Here is the defender in action, protecting humanity against harm, while reminding us of Marvel's own genesis in the bold stories of its Nazi-busting heroes.

Jack Kirby imbued the characters he created with traits that spoke to him directly, saying in an interview in the late 1980s, "I feel that my characters all have some part of my character. I feel that they are in me in some way." Later in 2011 he said, "A character can't be contrived, they have to have an element of truth."[2] There's no doubt that Kirby would've loved to have swung that powerful right hook at Hitler on the cover of *Captain America Comics #1*.

Characters are at the heart of Marvel. The ancient Greek word *charassein* contains an element of what Kirby was taking about—that the creation of a character is in some way one of personal transference, a kind of mythological wish fulfillment. In Greek the term *charassein* means "to carve out" or "to engrave something distinctive." This could be a sign on an embossed seal or coin, or the features of a dramatic mask carved by a highly skilled mask maker and worn in the Greek theatre. *Charassein* is to make a recognizable visual signifier, which was for Kirby and other Marvel creators the first step in realizing a new character, before any narrative was worked out. When Jack Kirby talked about "feeling" for a character and then sketching them out and creating a recognizable iconography, he was operating within the realm of ancient mythical *opsis* (spectacle). It is notable too that Captain America is masked, as are so many Marvel (and other) heroes, an important mythic element we will return to later in this book.

Marvel was always a visual medium, from the first illustrated comics in New York to the international blockbuster movies that are viewed all over the world. In *Poetics* Aristotle said that it was the visual element (*opsis*) that was the best conveyer of *muthos* in the theatre. As "theatre" means "seeing place," this makes sense, but he goes on to say that *opsis* is the element that can't be explained as an art form or technique. Instead, it is the preserve of the mask maker, implying something mystical, ancient, and almost sacred.

The other definition of character is also derived from a Greek word, *ethos,* which means "the inherent quality of a person." Kirby instinctively placed *charassein* and *ethos* together, seeking to communicate what his characters stood for through their visuality. There's a vivid portrayal of this in the 2014 movie *Captain America: Winter Soldier.* The *ethos* of Steve Rogers won't allow him to participate in SHIELD's massive new surveillance program as he feels it is depriving people of their personal freedom. When he learns that the Nazi organization Hydra has infiltrated America's government and counterterrorism programs, he knows he needs to embody the character of Captain America to inspire people to follow him. "If you're going to fight a war, you need a uniform," he says, before stealing his vintage, WWII-era red, white, and blue mask and costume from the Smithsonian Museum.

In *Poetics* Aristotle tells us that a character should be consistent, but even if they are inconsistent, they should at least be consistent in their inconsistencies! As Captain America transformed from a hero created to respond to the threat of Nazi domination to the leader of the MCU's Avengers, those character consistencies, stronger in Captain America than perhaps any other Marvel character, seemed antiquated in the ethically challenging and increasingly culturally divided America in the 2000s. Captain America's ethical constancy then became a dramatic foil for conflict over how a hero should conduct themselves in the modern globalized world.

In *Winter Soldier,* screenwriters Christopher Markus and Stephen McFeely emphasized Steve Rogers's mythic status as a man out of time, a member of the "Greatest Generation" in his nineties, but with the biological appearance of a man in his prime and the strength, speed, and power of a supersoldier. Here America's iconic warrior fights not only the deeply embedded conspiracy of Hydra, but also the growing use of AI technologies for surveillance and warfare. The film reflected contemporary fears about our dependence on technology and the power of an algorithm to decide the fate of millions of people at a swipe on a touchscreen. Initially Nick Fury, the director of the US counterterrorism agency SHIELD, extols the advantages of "Project Insight" as he shows Steve the massive new Helicarriers and their incredible firepower. He explains that this new technology will allow SHIELD to neutralize terrorists before they strike. Steve asks about due process. "We can't afford to wait that long," replies Fury. "Who's we?" responds Steve.

Winter Soldier deliberately sets the individual ethics of Captain America in direct conflict with the relegation of human responsibility to a machine, which, as we see in the movie, can be co-opted and abused by hostile forces. In this case it's Hydra, but now the Nazis are among us, embedded within the ranks of SHIELD and even in the highest tiers of the American government. For Hydra's plan to work, "humanity needed to surrender its freedoms willingly." *Winter Soldier* asks us if this is really the world we want to live in. Captain America has other ideas.

This same theme is explored in *Captain America: Civil War*. Hydra has been manipulating world events to ferment chaos and allow for the implementation of Project Insight, due in large part to the work of Hydra's own superwarrior, the Winter Soldier. But this most repellent of enemies turns out to be Steve's childhood friend and WWII commando comrade, Bucky Barnes, who has been brainwashed to carry out these atrocities. Steve does not hesitate to protect his friend, even when it seems Bucky has killed the king of Wakanda and Tony Stark's parents. This brings Steve deeper into conflict with Iron Man, with the Avengers already divided over the United Nations' insistence that they be controlled by the new Sokovia Accords.

This is Marvel at its most meta: the Avengers are being condemned for the very violence that we, the audience, have all enjoyed in the movies. Even mythic heroes are not exempt from the human cost of collateral damage. The villain of *Civil War* is a man whose entire family was accidentally killed by the Avengers in *Age of Ultron*. Tony Stark, racked by guilt, agrees with the boundaries set by the

Accords: "If we can't accept limitations, we're boundless, we're no better than the bad guys." On the other hand, Steve, having just dealt with the effects of SHIELD's unknowing overreach and infestation by Hydra, advocates for taking responsibility for one's own actions. From then on, Captain America becomes an outlaw. For Steve Rogers it is faith in the individual and his own ethical compass that rules him, not the government. Here, Captain America is most like his ancient mythical counterpart, the hero of the Trojan War, Achilles.

Marvel's meta mythology is highly effective and immerses us in both an epic story that unfolds around the world and a deeply personal conflict between two famous heroes who were once on the same side. However, this is not new. We see the same narrative elements operating in one of the most famous ancient epic tales, Homer's *Iliad,* which takes place during the final year of the decade-long Trojan War. *Winter Soldier* and *Civil War* took Marvel Golden Age and Silver Age characters and placed them in stories that reflected American tensions over government surveillance, the rise of AI, the wars in Iraq and Afghanistan, and the US culture wars. In archaic Greece in the eighth century BCE, the *Iliad* did the same thing, taking famous heroes from the past and placing them in an epic story that reflected a rapidly changing world.

The *Iliad* opens by asking the spirit Menis, or "Rage," to inspire a story of Achilles's own rage, "dark and murderous that cost the Greeks thousands sent to Hades, their corpses as feasts for dogs and birds." As with screenwriters Markus and McFeely's approach to violence in *Winter Soldier,* so too the audience of the *Iliad* is asked to experience a story of their heroes at war and confronted with the resulting carnage.

And what an epic story it is. The Greeks have been laying siege to Troy for ten long years, determined to recover Helen, who had absconded with the Trojan prince Paris, leaving her husband, the king of Sparta, Menelaus. His brother, Agamemnon, whose name means "resolute" or "steadfast," viewed this as an insult to the Greek kings and a threat to the way power was traded by aristocratic marriages. Troy must be punished, and the city must fall. So, Agamemnon and Menelaus gathered a huge force of warriors and sailed across the Aegean Sea to the northwestern coast of modern-day Turkey. Troy was located at the mouth of the Dardanelles, a highly strategic region that controlled shipping in and out of the Black Sea.

Unable to topple Troy, the Greeks have been violently plundering the surrounding towns and villages. One of Agamemnon's "war prizes" is a captured young girl named Chryseis, and her father, a priest, comes to beg for her return. Agamemnon refuses and kicks the forlorn old man out of the Greek camp. These kinds of war prizes were symbols of power and status, and Agamemnon cannot appear weak before the other Greek war chiefs. Then the old priest calls down a plague on the Greeks and they begin to die. The only way to stop it is to give the girl back, but nobody dares order Agamemnon to do it—no one, that is, except the greatest single warrior at Troy, the hero, Achilles.

A version of Achilles's name is found written on clay tablets in Linear B, a pre-Greek language dating to 1450–1200 BCE, the Greek Late Bronze Age. At this time Greece was studded with hill forts ruled by warrior chiefs and their close retinues of fighting men. The stories that were told about these warriors grew into local legends and, in some cases, myths that came to be known across the Greek world. Achilles could have once been one of these war chiefs, although his name, which means "he who brings pain to many," suggests that even as far back as the Bronze Age he was a mythological hero. The question is, which of the "many" receives the pain? In the *Iliad* it is both the Greeks and the Trojans.

Achilles is also uncannily similar to one of the oldest heroes we know of, the Sumerian warrior-king Gilgamesh, whose stories date back to 2800 BCE. Both young men have divine mothers and mortal fathers, they are both obsessed with their own mortality, they can be brutal and reckless, and they were known for their close relationships with a best friend. For Gilgamesh this was the wild man Enkidu; for Achilles it was the warrior Patroclus. Both friends are killed, and Gilgamesh and Achilles suffer the loss. The name Gilgamesh means "the ancestor is a hero," and with the close cultural connections between Bronze Age Greece and the Near East we can view Achilles as a kind of mythological warrior descendant of Gilgamesh. In much the same way, while Captain America was created in the 1940s and then re-created in different story lines since, the character type itself looks back toward other *Alexandros* archetypes such as Achilles and Gilgamesh. Bucky Barnes, even in his guise as the Winter Soldier, and Steve Roger's loyalty to him, stands in the same tradition as Enkidu and Patroclus.

Most Greek myths have their roots in the Bronze Age (3000–1000 BCE). The journeys of Jason and the Argonauts, Theseus and the Minotaur, and Perseus and Medusa were probably based on a time when seaborne raiding across the Mediterranean was one way in which these warrior communities increased their wealth and prestige. The spirits and monsters they faced were mythic metaphors for unknown lands and peoples. The real Bronze Age warrior kings wanted to pass on their wealth to their sons, which was another way in which their names could be preserved and their deeds remembered. Elaborate funerals provided a means by which the people accepted a continuity of power between generations, and the bodies were buried in prominent tombs filled with precious objects, weapons, and armor. These tombs were sites of local worship as the ancient warrior buried there had become a semidivine protector of that society—a hero. Rituals and festivals grew around these figures and their tombs, which scholars call hero-cults, and people would come to appeal to them for protection, not at all unlike the later Christian

Saints. This was the *kleos* of the hero transformed into a protective power for the wider community.

There's a great example of modern heroic *kleos* in *Winter Soldier*. Steve Rogers has infiltrated the Triskelion, SHIELD's headquarters, and is speaking to the staff over the intercom. He informs them that they are unwittingly participating in a Hydra plot by launching the new Helicarriers. Several start to ignore their commands and say they are acting under "Captain's orders." The reputation of Captain America is such that just his voice is enough to inspire resistance and then a full-on battle.

Kleos is why Agamemnon cannot return his war prize to her father in the *Iliad*, and *kleos* is what Achilles has been promised in return for dying young. Just like the oppositional positions of Iron Man and Captain America in *Civil War*, Achilles and Agamemnon represent two divergent ways of being a warrior and a hero. Like Tony Stark and Steve Rogers, both Greeks represent attitudes that come from totally different times.

Achilles stands up to Agamemnon, who is the supreme commander of all the Greeks at Troy, and demands that he stop the suffering and return the girl. A colossal public argument ensues. As the greatest single warrior at Troy, Achilles could have easily drawn his long bronze sword and struck Agamemnon a death blow. But he can't: he has sworn an oath to fight against Troy, and to be an oath breaker is the worst ethical violation a Greek hero can make. It would completely destroy his *kleos*.

Agamemnon is no fool. He knows he must return Chryseis, but he also needs to save face and protect his reputation. So he takes Achilles's own war prize, a girl called Briseis, in recompense. This is an enormous public insult to Achilles and a very aggressive show of dominance. Achilles can't fight back—he swore that oath—but he can do something far more damaging: he withdraws himself and his men from fighting, although they do not leave, and then he asks his mother, the divine sea nymph Thetis, to appeal to Zeus to turn the war against the Greeks and destroy his own comrades.

It all sounds very similar to *Civil War* as Steve Rogers becomes a fugitive and actively fights against his former teammates. But Achilles shares other mythical tropes with Captain America: Steve Rogers was given superserum to make him superhuman, while Achilles was dipped into the waters of the underworld by his mother to make him invulnerable. Captain America is given a distinctive round shield made of the almost indestructible Vibranium. Achilles is given armor made by the gods and a wondrous shield that depicts the life in Greece he will tragically never see.

If Agamemnon, the resolute king, and Achilles, "he who brings pain to many," were once real or based on real figures in the Bronze Age around 1250 BCE, how did their story change by the time the *Iliad* was written down around 750 BCE? This was in the Greek archaic period, a time of tumultuous change. Something cataclysmic happened around 1200 BCE that pushed the Greeks into decline. There are many theories—wars, famine, mass migration and invasions, disease, climate change, or a combination of them all. Whatever the cause, the Bronze Age kings in their fortified citadels no longer ruled and their palaces were abandoned. In the period from around 1200 to 800 BCE, Greece was comprised of small farming communities, with its people living among the ruins and tombs. It was only through the performance of myth in speech and song, and the enactment of rituals to the gods and heroes, that anything survived of the past.

Things gradually transformed in the Greek world, and by around 800 BCE we see increased trade and cultural connections, more farming, population growth, the development of ironworking, better technologies, and migration. As a result, communities got bigger, and both warfare and politics changed. Far more people had disposable income and could afford their own armor. The old reliance on a few warrior aristocrats for protection began to wane as some cities could now field hundreds of heavily armed infantrymen. A new style of warfare developed involving ranks of men fighting in tight formation and protecting each other with their large, round shields. Now even the aristocrats had to stand in line and serve alongside farmers, artisans, and shopkeepers. This so-called hoplite revolution ("hoplite" means "shielded and armored warrior") might have even been a precursor to democracy as social cohesion and power sharing increased. In fact, the hoplite phalanx (close order line), further developed by Alexander to overtake the Persian empire, was the dominant form of warfare in antiquity until finally destroyed by the Romans in the third century BCE.

Today we might look at Achilles and his incredible fighting skills as a real hero and despise Agamemnon as the original REMF (Rear Echelon Mother Fucker, as high-ranking officers were known during the war in Vietnam). However, those archaic-age Greek hoplites might have had a different idea. In the *Iliad* the old veteran Nestor tries to defuse the quarrel over Chryseis and set both men straight: Agamemnon should certainly respect Achilles because he is the best warrior, but Achilles must obey Agamemnon, because *he has more men*. The *Iliad* then is not only a clash between two great warriors, but it also shows a social and political battle. One side is represented by Agamemnon, who can deploy large numbers of infantry; the other is an old, aristocratic single-combat style embodied by the fighting prowess of Achilles. When Steve Rogers rejects the tenets of the Sokovia Accords and extols his personal ethical code, I see a reflection of Achilles standing up to Agamemnon. We are conflicted by Steve's choices, just as we are by Achilles's—we admire the stand and expression of a heroic code, but we also know the damage it will inevitably cause. Myths ask us to consider what we need from our heroes and whether the status we give them is always a good thing.

Having interviewed Christopher Markus for this book, I know the screenwriters of *Civil War* did not have the *Iliad* on their minds when they created this scenario, but this is another power of myth: while it can react to real events and change, something universal gets communicated to us in a kind of mythical collective consciousness. Markus calls this connecting us to "a web of pasts," both Marvel's many story lines and the ancient myths that still resonate with us today. Mark Twain reportedly said, "History does not repeat itself, but it often rhymes." This can also be applied to mythology, especially when those myths are responding to real-life events.

After World War II, Captain America's popularity waned, and by the mid-1950s the character was retired from Marvel's roster. Then Stan Lee and Jack Kirby revived him after testing out an "imposter," criminal Cap, who fought the Human Torch in *Strange Tales #114* in 1963. The text on the first story page of *Avengers #4*, where Captain America takes his place among his fellow superheroes, advised readers to "save this issue! We feel you will treasure it in times to come!" Good advice, it seems. A copy in very good condition sold for $143,000 in 2017. Although a mint condition copy of 1940's *Captain America Comics #1* sold for more than $3.1 million in 2022! Mythology can sometimes rhyme really well.

Captain America's status as the *Alexandros* of American values has meant that he has been co-opted by people on both sides of the political divide. For example, at the white nationalist Unite the Right 2 rally held in Washington, DC, in August 2018, there was a counterprotestor and former US Marine dressed as the character. When interviewed about his decision to wear the outfit, Patrick Rincon told the *Marine Corps Times*, "This is America, and nobody should feel complacent about countering fascists."[3] The iconic Captain America imagery has also been appropriated by people taking part in the insurrection at the US Capitol on January 6, 2021. This led Jack Kirby's son, Neal, to go on the record against such use of the character. He said it was an insult to the memories of his father and Joe Simon, both of whom were World War II veterans. For some today Captain America is a symbol of almost libertarian independence from government overreach and socialism. For others he represents the spirit of the freedoms that come with democracy and being an integral part of a group.

For Achilles, his quest for *kleos* becomes so entangled with his sense of his own identity and how it was perceived by others that it leads to his downfall. He allows his best friend, Patroclus, to go into battle dressed in his armor as the Trojans advance on the failing Greeks. When the Trojans see who they believe is Achilles back in the fight, they turn and flee. Except the Trojan hero, Hector, who decides to confront the enemy. Patroclus dies that day at the hand of Hector, and Achilles's rage burns white hot. Nothing will stop him from destroying the man who killed his Patroclus. But is that all that is really motivating Achilles, or is it the fact that Hector first thought he was taking on the great Achilles and won? The *ethos* of Achilles turns ugly as his heroic quest becomes not one of *kleos* but personal retribution. Yes, he kills Hector, but once this is done and he buries Patroclus, the story of Achilles is effectively over. It will not be he who conquers Troy.

As for Achilles and Agamemnon, their fates are as diverse as the ways they fight and lead. Achilles is killed with an arrow fired by Paris that strikes him in the only place he is vulnerable, the heel where Thetis held him as a baby when she dipped him in the river Styx. Remember, Paris was also called Alexander, and in this one act he protected his city from one of its greatest threats. But Troy's luck does not last. Agamemnon finally wins the Trojan War, but only with Odysseus's trick of the wooden horse. The fake gift is stuffed with Greek warriors and taken into Troy under false pretenses, an act against the codes of hospitality policed by the gods. The hidden fighters slip out of the belly of the horse at night, open the gates, and let Agamemnon and the army in to completely destroy the city, including all its sacred temples. But the fall of Troy is not the end of Agamemnon's story: he has sacrificed his daughter, Iphigenia, to obtain the winds to sail to war, and now he has to come home and face her mother. We will pick up the thread of this story in chapter 3.

Surely this myth about the death of Achilles has no relationship to real events. Perhaps . . . except in 1960 a group of Swedish archaeologists found an amazing suit of Bronze Age armor at Dendra in Greece that covered the entire body and neck. This would have been an incredibly expensive panoply. Only a very wealthy aristocrat could have afforded it, and the Dendra panoply is the only one of its kind found to date. Imagine then the effect the sight of such an armed warrior would have had on the battlefield. Its wearer would have seemed invulnerable. Except, that is, at the backs of the legs, which would have been exposed. Maybe in one Bronze Age battle a lucky shot from an archer pierced the calf or heel of this warrior and brought them down with a crash, allowing a foot soldier to finish them off. Could Achilles's heel have been based on reality, after all?

Achilles lived up to his name, bringing great suffering to both the Greeks and the Trojans at Troy. Yet all he wanted was everlasting *kleos*, that his fame would be such that someone somewhere would always sing, say, or now read his name. Then he would get to reside in a glorious heroic state in the hallowed fields of Elysium. So I guess we just bought him another day of immortality. Yet even this is later questioned by Homer in the *Odyssey*. In that story of homecoming from the Trojan War, Odysseus journeys to the underworld where he meets the soul of Achilles in Hades. "Surely," Odysseus says, "there will never be a happier man than you, Achilles, during your life we honored you as if you were a god and now in death you are the lord of all you survey." Achilles's shade stares at him blankly and says, "I would rather be a living servant than lord of the dead."[4]

The *Iliad* asks us to consider if Achilles's relentless pursuit of his warrior *ethos* was ultimately a good thing. After all, it cost the Greeks thousands of dead beneath the walls of Troy. There's an inflexibility to Achilles that can make him seem insufferable and even self-righteous. The only time he lets his guard down is when Priam, the father of the Trojan hero, Hector, whom Achilles has killed, comes unarmed to his tent and pleads to be able to bury his son. In this scene at the end of the *Iliad*, the great warrior cries as he thinks of his own father in a similar situation, and for a brief moment, we get to see the power of empathy as Achilles gives Hector's corpse to the grieving Priam.

Steve Rogers has the same kind of ethical inflexibility. In an interview in 1990, Captain America cocreator Jack Kirby said, "I don't think Captain America would do anything wrong. He wouldn't. Even at the cost of his life. I can tell you that's a true feeling." Kirby saw Rogers as a man of principle, not just a comic book character but a man *of* character. Aristotle had something to say about this aspect of *ethos* in a book he wrote for his son Nicomachus. He said that excellence of character is a state concerned with choice.[5] The moral certainty that Steve Rogers exudes has led an exasperated and expedient Tony Stark to say that sometimes he "just wants to punch him in his perfect white teeth." But what has made the Captain America stories so compelling is watching the protector hero make choices and live with them, even at the cost of his status and position. However, like Achilles, sometimes that kind of personal ethical rigidity can become highly destructive to others and even a kind of empathetic blindness. And yet, there are moments when we all dream about making a stand like Achilles or Cap, whatever the cost.

Marvel gets this right about its heroes: the most compelling are also sometimes the most deeply flawed.

CHAPTER 2

TONY STARK: *POLYTECHNES*

Since the rise of the MCU, Iron Man has become the face of technology in Marvel, with his company, Stark Industries, behind so many of the technological advances that occur throughout the stories. This ranges from Captain America's Vibranium shield to the motors of the massive SHIELD Helicarriers, to the arc reactor that both powers Iron Man's suit and keeps Tony Stark alive. Tony is a man unable to exist without total dependency on an external technology, and this makes him the ideal mythological metaphor for the human condition. The simple fact is that humans have all been dependent on one form of technology or another, whether a three-million-year-old flint blade or the latest form of generative AI.

Technology, its use and abuse, has been a major narrative element of Marvel since its beginning. The cover of the first issue of *Marvel Comics* in 1939 featured a synthetic man created in a laboratory by a scientist, who immediately feared his creation. This was the Human Torch, ablaze in flames, and once free from the confines of the laboratory he became a fearsome crime fighter. Then in 1963 in *Tales of Suspense* we first meet another scientist, Tony Stark, and learn how he invents the technology that enables him to transform into Iron Man: a tiny arc reactor that prevents shrapnel moving to his heart and killing him. Without this piece of technology this man of iron would not be able to exist at all, let alone become a superhero.

It might seem as if the Marvel Universe's fixation on technology is a by-product of the technological revolutions of the twentieth century. However, the mythology trope of the technological superhuman is far older. In fact, the ways people have increased human potential through technology is an essential element of what defines us as *Homo sapiens* or what has been called *Homo faber*—the human toolmaker.

Humans are totally dependent on technology to survive and have been since our earliest evolutionary stages. For at least a million years and possibly much longer, humans have been using external technologies for lighting fires, building shelters, making clothes, and processing food. Our brains need so much energy to operate that we rely on tools and cooking to make proteins and glucose easily digestible. The philosopher Andy Clark calls us "natural born cyborgs." Our minds are configured to "seek out a search for non-biological resources, so that we think and feel through our best technologies." Clark maintains that these kinds of "bio-technological unions" are inherently human, from the first honed flint edge used to cut the skin of an animal to Iron Man's Mark LXXXV suit. Clark has it that "our technology is inseparable to who we are and how we think."[1]

"Technology" is derived from two Ancient Greek words—*technê*, meaning "art" or "craft"; and *logos*, meaning "way of" or "the word on." But the term has much older roots deriving from the Indo-European *tek*, which means "to make a house by wattling," which is the weaving of branches to form walls. Yet the Greeks were conflicted about the value of technology and the skilled craftspeople who practiced technical arts. Socrates and Plato thought it was a low form of human expression and could distract from deep thought and virtuous acts. Yet this view is quite elitist and contains the idea that the philosopher can come only from the upper echelons of society. Their material needs would be met by the technical class, the craftspeople who, according to Socrates and Plato, could not achieve the same depths of wisdom. For the philosophers the problem with *technê* is that it could be good or bad depending on how the tool was used. So, while technicians were valued for their ability to make useful items, they were disdained because they ultimately had no control over what they made. *Technê*, then, came to mean "subterfuge" or "trickery," like the way we still might describe someone as "crafty." Such a person was not to be trusted because they possessed an artful, even conniving mind.

Technology was also perceived as a threat to the social order in Greece. Even though for most of the classical period (480–323 BCE) Athens was a democracy, land-owning aristocrats still controlled a good deal of wealth and power. Their social structure was based on birth and land, not the production of material, human-made items. A skilled craftsperson or artist, on the other hand, could amass personal wealth and influence by selling the products they made, which is why we find so many of those distinctive Athenian vases painted with red figures all over the Mediterranean.

Contradictory to their ambivalent attitude to *technê*, the Athenians were perhaps more dependent on it than any other Greek city-state. Not only were they a major producer of fine art, which they exported throughout the known world, but those trade routes and their homeland were protected by a large fleet of warships called triremes. These were very fast, narrow craft with three banks of oars and bronze prows, which meant they were highly maneuverable, fast, waterborne battering rams. This fleet, built in Athens and rowed by working-class citizens, many of whom would have been employed in the technical arts, provided the peace and security that allowed the city to thrive and, ironically, considering the philosophers' negative attitudes to technology, become a vibrant center of learning and culture.

We can see this conflicted attitude in a famous play by the Athenian dramatist Sophocles, *Antigone*. Here's a little of it from Paul Woodruff's excellent American translation:

Many wonders, many terrors,
But none more wonderful than the human race—
Or more dangerous.

This song, performed by a chorus of elders from city of Thebes, lists the technological marvels accomplished by humans: traversing the waves by sail and oar, turning the earth with the plow, taming and yoking horses to do the work, hunting and fishing with clever traps and nets, inventing language and laws, building homes. But for all those incredible achievements the chorus warns:

*He has cunning contrivance [*technê*]*
Skill surpassing hope,
And so, he slithers into wickedness sometimes.[2]

That same sense of tension about the uses and abuses of technology is a recurring theme in Marvel, right from Professor Horton's fears over his creation of the Human Torch to Iron Man's decision to give up making arms and instead turn his skills to serving with the Avengers. But as we are now becoming increasingly dependent on the internet, artificial intelligence, self-driving vehicles, drones, and robots, can ancient myths about technology help us understand where we are going and the dangers that lie ahead? Can Iron Man also help us make our way through the complicated technological world we now find ourselves living in?

We are all a little like Tony Stark. Even if we do not possess a smidgeon of his technical prowess, most of us fully embrace the technologies that purport to make our lives easier, safer, and more efficient. It is now almost impossible to function in modern society without a smartphone, internet access, and a computer, even though there are many who can't afford them. Were the Greeks wrong about the social mobility that technology provides? We tend to idolize the technocrats that have brought us these devices and bestow on them a kind of semimythical status, whether that is Steve Jobs, Jeff Bezos, or Elon Musk. There is a good deal of them, or those like them, in the MCU's character of Tony Stark, who can often be more tech-bro than hero.

Aristotle warned his son about this in *Nicomachean Ethics*. While he accepted that *technê* could be a good thing, he knew that its products were artificial. He placed *technê* in sharp contrast with *episteme*—knowledge about the necessities of life and nature—and *phronesis*—thinking about how to act. With *technê* "the means are separated from the ends" as history of science professor Eric Schatzberg has so well stated.[3] Once a thing is made it can be easily misused despite any good intentions that went into its creation. Weapons developed for our protection can be turned against us; plows designed to produce food can overfarm the land and cause starvation; cities built to offer us shelter and defense can cause disease and plague.

Consequently, the Greek god of technology, Hephaestus, was a truly ambiguous figure. He could make the most incredible robots, automatic devices, armaments, and artistic objects, but he was regarded as ugly, dirty, disabled, cantankerous, and solitary, and he was frequently spurned and bullied by the other Olympians. Even Hephaestus's titles indicate his contradictory nature: *Aithaloeis Theos*—"God of Soot," *Klytometis*—"Famous for Craft," *Amphiguēeis*—"The Lame," *Khalkeus*—"Bronze-Smith," *Kyllopodion*—"Crooked-Foot," and *Polytechnes*—"Many Crafts."

Hephaestus is so despised by Zeus that he throws him off Olympus. This is because he is not Zeus's son but the child of Hera, his wife, who conceived him without a man. Hephaestus lands on

Lemnos, a barren island where he sustains a serious injury that makes it difficult for him to walk. Lemnos was an accursed place, a volcanic island where the women neglected the shrines of Aphrodite, so she took revenge on them by afflicting them with a nauseating smell. Repulsed, their husbands took to having sex with prostitutes and foreign women, and the women, incensed at this shameful treatment, murdered their husbands. It was also the island where the Greek warrior Philoctetes was marooned on the way to Troy when a wound he sustained became so putrid and rank that his comrades could no longer stand the smell. Hephaestus was none too happy about being hurled down to the barren and smelly Lemnos.

I detect a great deal of Hephaestus *Polytechnes* in Tony Stark. Sure, he's überwealthy, charming, and views himself as a hit with women, but there is something ugly about his self-centeredness and arrogance, as well as his obsessive behavior. Similar to Hephaestus, Tony Stark is thrown into a cave and held captive by a group of terrorists. These guerrillas have been at the receiving end of the powerful weaponry that Stark Industries has been selling to the military. Like Hephaestus, Stark is seriously injured. Shrapnel from one of his own weapons threatens to pierce his heart. He must be connected to an artificial power source to survive. Now Tony Stark is very much the visual embodiment of Andy Clark's "natural-born cyborg."

The concept of an iron man, or men, is far older than Marvel and lies at the heart of our understanding one of the biggest technological revolutions in the ancient world. This was the transition from the Bronze Age to the Iron Age, which started around 1200 BCE. It was a very tumultuous time, as the historian Eric Cline has shown.[4] There were several cataclysmic interconnected events including climate change, rising sea levels, drought, plagues, wars, civil unrest, invasions, mass migrations, and even seismic events such as volcano eruptions and earthquakes. The myth of the fall of Troy comes from this period, with one theory suggesting that the story of Odysseus's wooden horse is a mythological metaphor for an earthquake. Poseidon, the god of the sea, was known as the earthshaker, and earthquakes were said to be caused by the thundering hooves of the horse he rode upon the seabed. The horse was a symbol of Poseidon, and the famous tale of the wooden horse could be a mythical way of explaining how Troy was weakened by a seismic event and then destroyed by marauding Greeks.

In Greece the existing Mycenaean society, which consisted of a network of local war chiefs presiding over warrior aristocrats in fortified citadels, collapsed. As a result, the population shrunk and there was significant economic hardship. But then came an astounding technological revolution: the widespread manufacture of iron.

We don't know for sure where this new technology originated. Technical innovations are a lot like myths in that they can seem to spring up in seemingly unrelated places at the same time. However, often the conditions for these new developments are in place because of widespread cultural exchange. Remains of Late Bronze Age iron smelting have been found in central Africa, the Middle East, Anatolia, Siberia, and on the island of Cyprus.

Cyprus was already a major center of copper production, and iron can sometimes be an accidental by-product of that process. Yet with all those Bronze Age maritime trade routes established and the collapse of the Hittite empire in what is now Turkey, it seems likely that our ancient Iron Man (or Men) might have immigrated to Cyprus sometime in the twelfth century BCE. In any event they figured out how to transform the large chunks of reddish-looking rocks that littered the island into an incredible, hard metal that could be easily worked and sharpened. These ancient Iron Men completely changed the world.

Bronze, which up until then had been the dominant metal for tools and weapons, is made from copper, which melts at 1,972°F degrees, and tin, which melts at 442°F. Somebody on Cyprus realized that those red rocks, which were iron ore, would soften if the fire got hot enough. How hot? A whopping 2,796°F, an impossible temperature for ancient kilns to achieve. However, when charcoal was added, the carbon that was emitted transformed the ore into an amorphous hot blob at much lower temperatures. This hot ore could be beaten out with hammers, reheated, and beaten out again, then cooled. In this way, the metal's imperfections could be worked out. Now it was possible to make far more sword blades, spearheads, nails, plowshares, hammers, and other tools that were much cheaper and much, much stronger.

A mythological counterpart to Tony Stark, and in many ways to Hephaestus, is Odysseus. It is his idea to build the Trojan horse that eventually wins the ten-year-long war, and he is known as *polytropos,* meaning "crafty, well-turned, or complicated." One of the first ancient references to the process of iron smelting comes from Homer's *Odyssey,* and it is both vivid and gory. Odysseus and some of his crew find themselves trapped in the cave of the huge one-eyed cyclops, who has sealed the entrance shut with a massive boulder. The cyclops refuses Odysseus's appeal for hospitality and instead begins eating his men. This giant is far too strong to overpower, so Odysseus hatches a plan: he offers the Cyclops a gift of a very fine, heady wine, and tells him that his name is No-one. The Cyclops thanks "No-one" and says in return for the wine he will eat him last. Then he chugs the entire wineskin, and, unaccustomed to such a strong drink, falls into a deep, boozy sleep. As he snores in the corner of the cave, Odysseus and his men take the Cyclops's massive wooden stave and whittle it to a sharp point. Then they heat it in a fire before plunging it deep into the Cyclops's eyeball. Homer says:

That's how we plunged the fiery pointed stake
In the Cyclops' eye. The blood swirled in a whirlpool
Around its searing point. His eyelids and forehead

Were seared by the heat from the burning eyeball
And its roots crackled in the fire and hissed
Like an axe-head or adze a smith plunges into water
When he wants to temper the iron—that's how his eye
Spluttered and hissed around the olivewood stake.[5]

The Cyclops awakens in searing pain, and when other giants come running to see what the commotion is he yells out, "No-one is hurting me! No-one is hurting me!" And so, they depart. Odysseus and his men escape by hanging beneath the Cyclops's sheep as he unrolls the boulder to let them out in the morning. The craftiness of Odysseus defeats the brute strength of the Cyclops. For all that, I do feel a bit sorry for the Cyclops, who wasn't bothering anybody until Odysseus and his men turned up and tried to steal his cheese. Perhaps the first cheese and wine party in recorded history?

Iron is mentioned many times in the *Odyssey*, which shows us how widespread this technology had become by the eighth century BCE, when the story was written down. Yet the myth may also be remembering something important about Odysseus—that this Bronze Age king was an early adopter of the brand-new technology of iron. This might be the significance of the row of twelve iron axe heads that he must shoot an arrow through to prove his identity when he returns home. The *Odyssey* tells us that he must perform an impossible task to win back the hand of his wife, Penelope, and defeat the suitors who have been camped out in his palace. This is to "shoot through iron," which clearly no arrow could do. But Odysseus pulls it off with a trick that rivals the wooden horse—he sends the arrow through the socket where the iron axe head slips onto a wooden handle.

It's a fantastic shot, to be sure, not to mention he had to string a mighty bow too, a mythological trope that is also found in Book One of the Vedic *Mahabharata*, where the hero Arjuna wins the right to marry the princess Draupadi by performing a similar feat. Odysseus's task must be a much older Indo-European myth, but Homer changed it by adding the uniformity of the twelve axe heads demonstrating the innovation of iron—now things could be manufactured consistently and with precision. But like Hephaestus and Tony Stark, it is also the mettle of the man himself that drives his success. During the long voyage home Odysseus's second-in-command turns to him and says:

You're a hard man, Odysseus, stronger
Than other men, and you never wear out.
A real iron man.[6]

Hard as iron he may have been, but when Odysseus finally returns home after twenty years, he seems more like Hephaestus. He is disguised as a beggar, bedraggled and alone. Just as Hephaestus is shunned from Olympus, Odysseus seeks shelter with an enslaved pig farmer, Eumaeus, who nurtures the stranger with his simple hospitality, offering him a staff so Odysseus can limp to his palace, just like Hephaestus. When Odysseus is recognized by his old nurse, it is because of a prominent scar from a leg injury he sustained as a young man. Finally, Odysseus proves his true identity to Penelope by describing how he built their secret bridal bed in vivid technical detail. The spirit of Hephaestus is in Odysseus, just as it is in Tony Stark and his artificial "heart."

As more ancient Iron Men began to spread throughout Greece and take this new technology with them, myths about superhuman ironmongers grew. One said that ironworking was invented by the Telchines, mythical sea creatures with fins for hands and dogs' heads. Like Hephaestus, who worked with them, the Telchines were despised by Zeus and forced deep under the sea. Later on the volcanic island of Lemnos, the place where Hephaestus was discarded, there was a mystery cult sacred to the Kabeiroi. These were Hephaestus's mortal offspring who guarded the secrets of his forge. Like Cyprus, Lemnos was an island rich in iron deposits and a fine powder made from iron oxide called Miltos, which had antibiotic properties and was used for healing. In the *Iliad* Hephaestus says that it was the inhabitants of Lemnos who nursed him back to health. Was this a mythic memory of the famous healing properties of "Lemnian Earth"?

With these almost unbreakable iron tools, Greek farmers could clear, plow, and plant their arid land much more effectively. Weapons became deadlier, cheaper, and more widely available. Ultimately, this led to the development of a new type of hero: the citizen-soldier, a farmer or tradesman who could afford to equip themselves with armor and weapons and fight for their city-states. Now instead of a few heavily armed aristocrats with expensive bronze weapons, cities could field large iron armies in the hundreds and then thousands.

These iron-armed men marched together in a new form of cooperative warfare called the phalanx, which we mentioned in the last chapter. Each man in the shield wall was protected by his comrade at his side. Some scholars have seen the phalanx as helping to create a new middle class in archaic Greece. As more people participated in actively fighting for the state, their share of political power increased. In cities such as Sparta, Argos, and Athens this led to the development of early systems of limited democracy. An Athenian phalanx defeated a Persian invasion force more than ten times its size at the battle of Marathon in 490 BCE. When the Persians returned ten years later with an enormous armada, it was the advanced shipbuilding technology of the Athenians that was able to meet the threat with a brand-new navy crewed by the Athenian working class. This meant that by 480 BCE every adult Athenian male citizen both fought for the state and participated in its government.

On land, the iron-weaponed phalanx remained the dominant

form of warfare. It was used extensively by the Spartans and then employed by Alexander to conquer the East. It stayed the foremost battle technique until devastated by the Romans in the third century BCE. The Romans used the pilum, a short throwing spear with a long iron shank that could pierce armor. Then they developed a short steel thrusting sword for close-quarter fighting called the *gladius*. Soon after the Roman legionaries adopted iron chain mail from the Celts, which was relatively lightweight and flexible but could still offer a good degree of protection. This technology that was now mass-produced in forges throughout the Roman Empire helped its army dominate most of its opponents and control territory of around 1.9 million miles. All of this with an iron- and steel-clad regular force of around 125,000 men, which is fewer than the number of law enforcement officers in the state of New York!

The Romans embraced technology wholeheartedly, and their version of Hephaestus was named Vulcan. He was a beefy blacksmith with huge biceps and a large hammer. Vulcan was revered and rarely shown as disabled. During the Industrial Revolution of the nineteenth century, Vulcan became a symbol of mechanized power. A large cast-iron statue of the god built in 1904 can still be visited in Birmingham, Alabama. That connection between Hephaestus/Vulcan and technology in myth was the reason why Spock, the scientific officer of the USS *Enterprise* in *Star Trek*, was from the planet Vulcan. Since 2006 Vulcan has been a Marvel character, brother of X-Men Cyclops and Havok. He is a "living forge" able to absorb and redirect all manner of powerful energy sources. Today when we think of a god of technology, we see nothing but power and certainty. Vulcan has none of the ambiguities of Hephaestus, and I'm not at all sure this is a good thing. Marvel's Iron Man returns us to a more ambivalent view of technology, one that fits right in with the kind of attitudes we find in the *Odyssey* and the stories of Hephaestus—it offers us wondrous abilities, but for all its advantages technology frequently comes at a price.

Marvel's Iron Man was created in wartime. In the 1963 comic where the character is first introduced, we see the weapons inventor Anthony Stark almost killed by shrapnel from a North Vietnamese booby trap. He is captured by the Communist enemy and forced to build them a devastating weapon. Instead, he makes a bulletproof cast-iron suit, powered by the cutting-edge technology of the early 1960s—batteries, transistors, electromagnetic power, and pressure jets. In his Mark I suit he resembles an iron-clad medieval knight, or Talos, the huge metal robot built by Hephaestus to guard Crete. In the second installment of Iron Man, we see him wearing an iron breastplate and secretly plugging it into the shaver outlet in the bathroom to keep the iron shrapnel from entering his heart. Iron Man is totally dependent on technology to survive; even without his suit, because of that shrapnel, he is always Iron Man, incredibly powerful, brilliantly intelligent, yet deceptively vulnerable.

In the MCU, Tony Stark does not achieve his technological advancements alone. He has the significant help of several sophisticated artificially intelligent assistants. One is the aptly named HOMER—the "Heuristically Operative Matrix Emulation Rostrum." Another is JARVIS—"Just a Rather Very Intelligent System." Then there is FRIDAY—"Female Replacement Intelligent Digital Assistant Youth," a reference to the name of the servant character in Daniel Defoe's 1719 novel *Robinson Crusoe* and the origin of the term "Man Friday." Many of Hephaestus's inventions seem operated by a kind of ancient AI, envisioned as a form of unseen, divine power. These include automatic serving tripods that scuttle around Olympus, fire-breathing horses, singing maidens, bronze bulls, and golden robots. Iron Man's AI laboratory assistants are the modern equivalent of what we find in Hephaestus's forge.

In some Greek myths Hephaestus is credited with the creation of a giant bronze man named Talos, who was built to guard the island of Crete from invaders. In other versions of the Talos story, he is one of the last giants to walk the Earth, or a strange primeval nature spirit that grew from an ash tree and became clad with bronze. In the most famous telling, the journey of Jason and the Argonauts as told by the ancient author Apollonius of Rhodes, he is all of these creatures—a kind of hybrid fearsome monster that hurls rocks at the *Argo* and will not allow the ship to pass.[7] The version of Talos built by Hephaestus is an automaton, a robot powered by a single vein of divine blood, called ichor, covered in a thin layer of skin that runs from his head to his ankle. Talos is a kind of ancient cyborg. The Argonauts cannot defeat Talos; their own bronze weapons do no harm to his massive, sturdy metal body, and they find themselves trapped and unable to get back to mainland Greece.

Traveling with the Argonauts is Medea, a princess of Colchis on the eastern coast of the Black Sea. She fell in love with Jason when he came to steal the golden fleece and used her skill in *pharmakia*—shamanistic healing and magic—to help him. She thinks she can defeat Talos, not by force but by introducing him to the possibility of love. Our ancient sources do not tell us how she achieves this, but the ancient Greek author Apollodorus says that she projects images on Talos's eyes.

Until Talos encounters Medea's magic, he only knows what he has been programmed to do—protect Crete and repel invaders. Medea unlocks his consciousness and the parts of him that are human. This new, overwhelming feeling of desire momentarily "short-circuits" his functionality, and he forgets the Argonauts he is trying to kill. Medea causes Talos to remove a plug in his bronze giant's ankle. The ichor drains away, and Talos dies.

In Apollonius's version of the myth, it is not love that is offered to

Talos but the idea of death. This new awareness of his own mortality freezes Talos's operating system like an ancient version of Apple's eternally spinning wheel. As Talos contemplates death, he staggers, unsure of who or what he is, and in this moment of mortal vulnerability, he tears the skin that holds the ichor on a rock, bleeds out, and collapses to the ground in a useless heap of metal.

It is as if the hope of love or even immortality condemns Talos to accepting his own mortality. This myth might make us wonder what will happen if our newfangled AI systems discover love and even death. In the myth of Talos it is the most human of traits that brings the seemingly indestructible bronze giant tumbling down.

Hope is at the heart of the other famous cyborg created by Hephaestus, Pandora, the first woman. The archaic poet Hesiod tells us that Hephaestus made her from clay and water, and then several gods imbued her with exceptional human qualities. Hesiod's account is meant to be humorous and played for a group of men at an ancient equivalent of a working men's club or a frat party roast, so it's misogynistic, to say the least. Yet it is the spirit of human inquisitiveness that leads to the opening of Pandora's jar, and it serves as a vivid mythic metaphor for the potential dangers of technological innovation.

The parallels between the myths of Pandora and Talos and the main theme of *Avengers: Age of Ultron* are quite uncanny. To be sure, the rise of technology and warning about it getting out of control has been a feature of dystopian science fiction for much of the twentieth century. Think of Aldous Huxley's *Brave New World*, the out-of-control computer HAL in Arthur C. Clarke's *2001: A Space Odyssey*, or Philip K. Dick's *Do Androids Dream of Electric Sheep?*, which became the 1982 movie *Blade Runner.* In fact, the first recorded use of the word "Robot" is from a 1920 Czech play, *R.U.R.* by Karel Čapek. The word is from "robata," which means "forced laborer."

In Čapek's play the robots are made from synthetic biomatter and closely resemble humans. Eventually they revolt and wipe out humanity. The poets warned us, as Marvel continues to, even though ironically there is so much technology deployed in the making and marketing of these modern cautionary tales.

Ultron is created by Tony Stark and Bruce Banner originally as a device to protect the Earth from alien attack. However, it becomes an existential threat to humanity when the machine, following its directive, uses its artificial intelligence to conclude that humanity itself is the biggest threat to the planet and therefore must be destroyed. Like Talos, as Ultron grows exponentially in cognitive abilities and consciousness, it starts to act human and even fear death. Now Ultron can contemplate mortality, his power is limited, and Vision, an android sympathetic to humanity, is able to destroy him.

Vision is a gamble by Stark. The only way he can see Ultron being stopped is by creating an equally powerful artificially intelligent automaton. Banner is initially appalled at Stark's recklessness, but Stark replies, "I know what everyone's going to say, but they're already saying it. We're mad scientists. We're monsters, buddy. You gotta own it. Make a stand." This is where Stark is most like Hephaestus and Odysseus: he uses technology in the most human way, which is often pretty reckless.

The famous Greek myth of Daedalus and Icarus provides a warning about embracing the technological hero too much, to the point where humanity gets lost. Daedalus designed the labyrinth beneath the Palace of Minos on Crete where the Minotaur was imprisoned. He was said to have carved statues so lifelike they seemed to move, and he created new tools like the awl, the drill, and the plumb line. Of course, it was his invention of artificial flight that cost the life of his son Icarus, when he flew too close to the sun. The wax holding Icarus's wings together melted and he fell to his death.

In ancient myth, synthetic technology is always constrained by the limitations of humanity.

The myths of a new technological hero, Iron Man, struck a chord with movie audiences in 2008, with Robert Downey Jr.'s performance effectively relaunching the Marvel franchise on the big screen. For all their craftiness, what makes the stories of Hephaestus, Odysseus, and Tony Stark even more compelling is that they also project a certain vulnerability, and this is what makes a legendary *polytechnes* human. Hephaestus may be divine, but with his disability, his "dirty" job, and his broken marriage to Aphrodite, he is the most anthropomorphic of all the Olympians. As for Odysseus, he returns home in disguise and then outwits and slaughters all the suitors who have been eating and drinking their way through his wealth and demanding that his wife marry one of them. The goddess Athena returns him to his former glory as he stands before his wife, Penelope, home at last after twenty years.

Penelope dares to test Odysseus with the secret knowledge of their marriage bed, which he crafted from the trunk of a great olive tree. When he thinks someone has moved it, he loses his cool and rants like a child about how he made it, for them. In this moment of vulnerability, for all his skill, Penelope sees the true man and they reunite at last.

Craftiness and *technê* can take us only so far, and the myths show us that what matters most of all is to be human, and we humans are vulnerable. That's what makes Tony Stark heroic: for his bravado, quick wit, and opulent wealth, he is always vulnerable. His technology keeps him alive, but it can also destroy him. Perhaps the Greek philosophers were right to be dubious about what technology can and can't do. Even Odysseus, after finally reuniting with Penelope after twenty years, must leave again to make his peace with Poseidon and come to terms with the life he has led. He is told he must travel to a land whose people know not the sea and walk far inland with his oar on his shoulder. When someone mistakes it for a winnowing blade, he must plant it in the earth and make his peace with Poseidon for blinding his son, the Cyclops.

A winnowing blade is a large wooden paddle that looks like the long-handled implement they use to put pizzas in wood-burning ovens. The act of winnowing—separating the wheat from the chaff—was sacred to the Earth Mother goddess, Demeter, and was part of a ritual of *catharsis*, or cleansing, when the bad was separated from the good. Before one could be cleansed they had to refute the bad things they had done and own their mistakes in a kind of ritual purging. Only then can Odysseus hope to find peace. Those old wrongs can't be fixed—the Cyclops will still be blind, Odysseus's men are still all lost, the city of Troy stays destroyed—but the ritual of *catharsis* produces self-realization and the letting go of hate, rage, fear, and lies. Only then will Odysseus be blessed and no longer the *polytropos*, the man of "twists and turns."

Christopher Markus, one of the screenwriters of the *Captain America* movies and *Infinity War* and *Endgame*, among other MCU films, talked to me about the importance of these human moments of realization and how they become all the more important among the incredible technologies of the Marvel Cinematic Universe:

> *At the end of* Civil War *when Tony Stark has found out that the Winter Soldier has assassinated his parents, he understands all the sci-fi nonsense, the mind control, that it wasn't really him, it was Hydra, but he says, "He killed my mom." It's a bizarre situation to be in, but when you get down to it, this incredibly smart, powerful, rich superhero, who's fighting his friend, who's dressed as an American flag—there's an insoluble problem. I love that about this whole situation*—it can't be fixed. *They eventually agree because there's a greater threat, but Steve's best friend murdered Tony's*

parents and Steve didn't tell him and there's nothing you can do to fix that. And to have gotten to a place where that's a canonical fact, and it has to be lived around rather than solved—that's where I want all stories to go, to a place where they don't get fixed.

Technology holds out the promise that everything can be improved and "fixed," yet as Markus explains, we are enthralled by the things that can't be fixed. He went on to tell me how hard it was to keep that story line unresolved and how it resulted in a brilliant moment in *Endgame*: Tony Stark drives up to the Avengers headquarters, having decided to join them despite his considerable differences with Steve Rogers. Tony looks at Steve and says, "Resentment is corrosive and I hate it." The line was apparently an ad-lib informed not just by the narrative Markus and McFeely had created but also Robert Downey Jr.'s own personal struggles. Markus explained that to him this is one of the most incredibly heroic moments in the MCU, when Tony sets aside the will to win, exert revenge, or undo a past wrong, and chooses instead to let it go for a far greater good.

In these times of increasingly accelerating technological advancements, when the algorithm is by now certainly out of Pandora's jar, myths can offer us a path back to our humanity. They can show us what happens when we get too close to the sun and, like Odysseus, remind us that for all our inventiveness, we are only as strong as the earth we live on and where we choose to plant our oar.

CHAPTER 3

BLACK WIDOW: AMAZONIAN QUEEN

The previous two chapters have dealt with characters who are defined as heroes, but what about heroines? Where do they fit into both the Marvel Universe and mythological traditions in general?

Marvel today is largely dominated by male characters. Even though since the 1970s Marvel has consistently added more female characters and women writers and artists, only around 25 percent of Marvel characters are female. The first Marvel Avengers comic in 1963 featured four male team members—Thor, Iron Man, the Hulk, and Ant Man—and one female, the Wasp. By issue #4 Captain America had replaced the Hulk. Then in 1965, the Avengers welcomed another female member, the Scarlet Witch; and in 1966, Black Widow joined. In the MCU's Avengers, Black Widow has been there from the start. We will analyze the fascinating mythological context of the Scarlet Witch in a later chapter, because here I want to explore how Natasha Romanova (later Romanoff) as Black Widow develops into the Marvel version of a mythological Amazonian female warrior, even more so than DC's own famous Amazon, Wonder Woman.

Black Widow began her graphic life as a Cold War–era Russian seductress who distracted Tony Stark while another Soviet agent tried to sabotage Stark Industries. As the character developed, she became one of the most independent Marvel superheroes and the most well trained. Black Widow relies on her skill and ability more than the Soviet's superserum that imbued her with added strength and speed. Stan Lee is credited for the name Black Widow, although the term was already well known in popular culture as a moniker for a "femme fatale" killer who lured lovers to their deaths. There had been a 1954 Hollywood film noir of the same name starring Ginger Rogers and George Raft, and the term frequently featured in newspaper headlines for stories involving sex and murder initiated by women.

Female black widow spiders are, of course, said to devour their mates after sex. While this is rarely true, black widow females can be up to one hundred times larger than the males. When they do mate, the smaller male must situate himself between the fangs of the female. So, if she happens to be hungry at the same time, well . . .

In Greek mythology Clytemnestra, the wife of King Agamemnon, the commander of the Greeks during the Trojan War, was perceived as a female spider trapping her mate and destroying him. Agamemnon had sacrificed their daughter Iphigenia to get fair winds to sail on Troy. In the version of the myth told by the Athenian playwright Aeschylus, when he returns home ten years later, Clytemnestra welcomes him back by rolling out an expensive red (crimson really) carpet, and she praises his glory and invites him in to take a cleansing bath.[1] Agamemnon knows that treading on these incredibly expensive woven and dyed fabrics would be seen as an act of extreme arrogance, as if he were an Eastern potentate, and he demurs. But Clytemnestra cleverly draws him into her web by appealing to his own sense of masculinity and pride and even making him relive his decision to sacrifice their daughter, without ever mentioning her name. Agamemnon is outclassed and outwitted, and so he agrees to step on those woven threads.

Mindful of the value of these crimson tapestries, Agamemnon removes his war boots, a sign that he is now defenseless. He steps down from his chariot and onto the fine fabrics, and as he walks carefully toward the great open doorway of the house of his father, Clytemnestra prays to Zeus to fulfill her plans "once and for all." Watching this scene as Aeschylus staged it in Athens in 458 BCE, the audience saw this legendary warrior king stepping in what looked like blood and knew this was a dead man walking into a spider's web.

Once inside, Agamemnon removes the rest of his armor and clothes and slips into a warm bath infused with delicate aromatics and fine exotic unguents by his doting wife. As he rises to leave the soothing water, she wraps him in a new robe she has woven specially for him. Immediately something feels wrong to Agamemnon. The robe grips and tangles around him. He struggles to move his arms, and the more he does the more the robe tightens its grasp like a spider's web. This is not a robe but an entangling net that he cannot escape from. As the conqueror of Troy stands up in his bath and desperately struggles to break free from this web, he slips and falls back into the water. He looks up to his wife for help, confused and bewildered, and sees the flash of metal as Clytemnestra raises a great bronze double-headed axe above her head.

A woman is not supposed to be able to wield such an implement, which was used by the priests to slice the head from a great cow or bull as a sacrifice to the gods. As the massive sharp blade comes hurtling toward him, Agamemnon realizes that he is the offering, not to the Olympians above but to the age-old ancient female spirits that reside deep beneath the earth. Agamemnon is being sacrificed to the Furies, female demons that punish all those who dare to spill their own kin's blood. Now the great king is paying the price for his sacrifice of his daughter Iphigenia. It takes three great blows to kill Agamemnon. Until the last he writhes in the bath screaming for help, but nobody rushes in to save him. He has left his men at the shore, so keen he was to reconcile with his wife and return home like nothing had happened. The elders who gathered outside the palace hear those terrifying screams, but they debate and dither, feeling like they do not have the right to intervene. They are, after all, subjects to the king and queen and not used to acting without their orders.

When the old men of Argos finally resolve to enter the palace, it is far too late. Clytemnestra emerges from the great doorway splattered in her husband's blood, her eyes dark and steely. She shows them Agamemnon tangled in her spider's web. Agamemnon has been killed as if he were a sacrificial bull, slaughtered at a great festival when the Athenians marked the transfer of power from one administration to the next. Normally that bull would have then been butchered, cooked, shared among the people, and eaten. Not Agamemnon's corpse, although his body is emasculated—his genitals cut off and hung around his neck and his corpse buried upside down, a ritual act meant to signify the erosion of his male line. All the elders can do is mourn their slain king and sing, "Oh my king, lying there in this spider's web, such a sacrilegious death!"

In many ancient mythic traditions, spiders are associated with women's weaving as a form of craftiness, strategic thinking, and weaponry, like Clytemnestra's bathrobe mantrap. The concept of the seductive spider is fairly widespread in mythologies. For example, Japanese folklore has Jorōgumo, a shapeshifting *yokai*, or spirit, that appears with the body and head of a beautiful woman and the legs of a spider. She was said to entrap men with her beauty and the promise of marriage, ensnare them in her web, and drag them to their deaths.

Like Marvel's Black Widow, female mythic spider figures can

be protectors. There are many women spider characters in Native American mythology, including the Navajo Na'ashjé'íí Asdzáá and the Hopi Kokyangwuti, who are weavers and protectors of humanity. The Chippewa (Ojibwe) have a female spider protector called Asibikaashi who taught the people to make weblike dream catchers to protect children as they slept. For the Greeks there was Arachne, who bequeathed her name to the entire species. Her myth as told by the Roman author Ovid is particularly illuminating.

Arachne was from Lydia, a region on the western coast of Turkey. She came from a family that had grown very wealthy by selling an expensive purple dye made from the Murex shellfish, the same dye Clytemnestra used on the tapestries that lured Agamemnon to his death. It was the Phoenicians who were best known for manufacturing and trading this dye, hence the meaning of their name "the purple people." The Phoenicians came from a cluster of cities in what is now Lebanon, Jordan, Syria, and southern Turkey, and they founded colonies in North Africa, southern Spain, Sardina, and Sicily. Arachne's father was called Idmon, meaning "the knowing," so what we see in this myth is a character who came from a very prosperous, well-connected, and knowledgeable people.

Ovid connected his Arachne to sheep farming and said she learned the arts of collecting, spinning, and weaving wool from an early age. Her tapestries became famous, and she boasted that she was a better weaver than Athena. You can see where this story is going. Athena, the goddess of strategy who is usually represented armed for battle, also presided over the craft of weaving. The production of woven fabric required a great deal of technical skill to sort, spin, and dye the wool, work a loom, and preplan the intricate patterns that the Greeks were able to weave. The most highly prized woven works were clothing, blankets, or tapestries that depicted mythological scenes related to the family who owned them. It is not hard to understand why the art of weaving became associated with the spider and their ability to make intricate webs and spin long threads.

Arachne's reputation and fame are outshining Athena's. Not good. So, Athena does what the Olympians always do—she moves to prevent a mortal from becoming too godlike. Athena first gives Arachne a chance. She approaches her disguised as an old woman, compliments her handiwork, but advises her not to compare herself to a god. Arachne laughs and repeats her boast. At this Athena appears in her true divine form and challenges Arachne to a weaving contest to settle the matter once and for all. Arachne should have known better, but she's become obsessed with her own abilities and fame, and so she accepts. The goddess and the mortal immediately start weaving away, quickly darting their shuttles through the upright strands and pulling through their variously dyed threads, like a pair of spiders spinning their intricate webs.

Athena creates four designs, each depicting a famous moment from myth where the gods punished mortals for claiming they were their equals. There was Queen Rhodope and King Haemus, who said they were like Zeus and Hera; Athena depicts the moment they were transformed into mountains as punishment. The next shows Gerana, who claimed she was as beautiful as Hera, being turned into a crane. On the next panel is Antigone, the sister of King Priam of Troy, who compared herself to Hera and was turned into a bird too, in this case a stork. Finally, bringing the point very close to home, is another daughter of a wealthy Phoenician named Myrrha, who was transformed into a tree after her father had challenged the gods to a musical contest and, of course, lost.

It is a trope of Greek mythology that women fight with fabric. We have already seen how Clytemnestra uses crimson tapestries and a netlike gown to bring down the powerful war chief Agamemnon. Medea uses a poisoned robe and crown to kill Jason's new bride and her father, and Philomena reveals that she has been raped by her sister's husband, King Tereus, in a tapestry after her attacker cuts out her tongue and imprisons her. Arachne counters Athena with more than twenty beautifully woven scenes depicting the times when Zeus, Poseidon, Apollo, Dionysus, and Kronos disguised themselves as mortals, animals, or plants, and either raped, assaulted, or falsely seduced mortal women.

Athena is both amazed at the exquisite workmanship and furious at what Arachne has chosen to depict. She destroys the tapestry and strikes Arachne with her shuttle. Mortified at upsetting the goddess, Arachne hangs herself. But Athena takes pity on her and transforms her into a spider, allowing her to climb back up the thread she is dangling from. Hence in Greek the word for spider is *arachne*.

Marvel's Black Widow possesses similar traits to the independent and highly skilled Arachne and Clytemnestra, who was from Sparta, a city where women had a great deal of personal agency, could own property, and take lovers. Yet Natasha is also a warrior, a woman who uses skill, deception, and her martial abilities to best her opponents. This relationship between weaving, battle tactics, and women warriorhood is inherent in several important ancient goddesses in addition to Athena, such as the Egyptian Neith. She was credited with the creation of the universe by weaving it like a spider. Neith became a goddess of hunting and warfare as well as a protector of women.

Neith was frequently depicted armed with a bow and arrow, and she was known for her wisdom and forethought, which ties in with her great skill as a celestial weaver. Later, some Greeks equated Athena with Neith, for obvious reasons. Both are prolific weavers and involved in strategy and war. Both are goddesses of wisdom, and like Neith, Athena was often shown armed, usually with a helmet, shield, and spear, the panoply of the hoplite. We find other goddesses associated with war in its most violent form as a counterpart to eroticism such as Inanna/Ishtar in the Sumerian/Babylonian tradition and Aphrodite in Greece. Both of these deities were often depicted as armed and very dangerous, and Aphrodite was regarded as a war goddess by the Spartans and their neighbors, the Argives.

There is one more Greek goddess we should mention: Artemis. This deity was perhaps the most dangerous. She represented what was most feared in Greek society—a woman not controlled by a man.

The reality was that in most of classical Greece the status of a woman was as daughter, woman of marriageable age, wife, and mother. It was inconceivable for a woman to live without the legal protection of a man, be that a father, a husband, or if they were widowed, the next male relative. Of course there were exceptions, such as the highly educated and cultured Hetaerae, companions of wealthy and prominent men, many of whom became very rich and influential themselves. But it was still because of their relationship with men, even though these were outside social norms. This is what is so remarkable about Clytemnestra: after killing Agamemnon, she holds power without a husband for seventeen years. (She takes a paramour, Aegisthus, but I don't think he counts. She was the boss.)

Clytemnestra's cousin, Penelope, the wife of Odysseus, staves off marriage when everyone thinks her husband is dead, and lives without a man for twenty years. The goddess Artemis encapsulates this power. She is of marriageable age but refuses it. In fact she wants nothing to with sex or eroticism and slays anybody who even comes close to her in this respect. She is the ancient embodiment of the contemporary 4B movement, which started in South Korea and means "four noes"—no dating, no sex, no marriage, and no children. The difference is that Artemis will kill to protect her independence. She is "untamed" and so is goddess of all wild things and the hunt. She is depicted armed with a bow and arrows, like her brother, Apollo, and she does not hesitate to use them to devastating effect.

Many of these mythological tropes have been absorbed into the character of Black Widow. Natasha is educated in a secret "Black

Widow" program at the so-called Red Room in Soviet Russia. The graduation of these highly trained female assassins required mandatory sterilization so they would never be distracted from their duties as killers, a modern version of the Artemis myth.

We need to place modern stories of women warriors within this existing culture of very powerful female warrior goddesses and other mythological characters like Clytemnestra and Arachne who use their intellects and strategic skills to both attack and defend. But what was the reality of female warriors in the ancient world, and does Black Window belong to a real ancient tradition of women in combat?

When considering this question most people will immediately think of the Amazons, legendary women warriors, who were said to live without men and were famed for their fighting prowess. Many will now know the Amazons from DC's *Wonder Woman,* but Marvel also sometimes depicts Amazons, and these are far fiercer and more threatening, closer to what we know of them from ancient sources. However, it is Black Widow who develops from her earliest incarnation as a glamorous 1950s femme fatale into Marvel's most Amazonian character.

There are three places we can seek out the Amazons: in ancient texts, artistic representations, and archaeological remains. None of these have conclusively proved that they ever existed, but I think there is enough evidence to strongly suggest that Amazon-like warrior women did. We first hear about Amazons in Homer's *Iliad,* where the Trojan King Priam remembers a great battle in his youth in Anatolia where "the Amazon women more than equaled the men."[2] Later, in the fifth century BCE, the historian Herodotus describes the region northeast of Greece called Scythia, which is now southern Ukraine and Russia, and he mentions a battle between Greeks and Amazons.[3] He says that the Scythians called them *Oiorpata,* which meant "man killers." The Greeks were able to capture many Amazons and put them aboard their ships as prisoners, but these fierce women overwhelmed them and took over the ships. Unable to sail, they drifted until they reached the Sea of Azov. Once ashore they found horses and lived off raiding and battle in Scythia.

Herodotus's Amazons live apart from men—that is, until they begin to meet young Scythian boys. Relationships are formed, but the Amazons refuse to return to the Scythians' homes, stating they want nothing of what they call "women's work," only hunting, riding, and fighting. Some of the Scythian men, so enamored with their Amazon partners, agree to leave with them, and they decide to head farther east across the Russian steppes. This is where Herodotus says the Amazons now live, although we never learn where they originally came from. They keep their martial ways, sometimes their husbands hunt and fight alongside them, and both men and women dress the same. The Amazons are permitted to marry but only after they have killed a man. As a result, some remain unmarried.

Herodotus's account is detailed, but like many of his writings, it is based on what he has heard rather than observed. This does not mean he is incorrect, and clearly people at that time believed that the Amazons in some form existed. Herodotus's account is also supported by recent archeological evidence. Several excavations carried out in Azerbaijan, Russia, and Georgia, all areas near the region Herodotus describes, have turned up burials of armed women with arrowheads and other weaponry dating from the Bronze Age. There can now be no doubt that at the very least many Scythian women fought alongside men in battle. Judging by the goods discovered in their graves, these women achieved positions of high status in their society.

This may be the origins of the myths about the Amazons. The warrior women of Scythia seem to have been well known to the fifth-century BCE writer Ctesias, who wrote how the Scythian queen, Sparethra, assembled a massive, mounted force of 300,000 men and

200,000 women against the invading forces of Cyrus of Persia.[4] I am sure the numbers were exaggerated, but it shows that women warriors were real in that part of the world. Cyrus went on to be defeated and killed by another Scythian warrior woman, Tomyris, who is still regarded as a national hero in modern-day Kazakhstan.

Not all the ancient sources place the Amazons in Scythia or Anatolia. The Athenian playwright Aeschylus mentions them in a play called *Suppliant Women*, which was produced in the 460s BCE. The play is about a group of young Black women from Egypt who arrive in Greece seeking sanctuary. Their ethnicity is important because it is noted by the chorus of Greeks and marks them out as different, even though they claim to be descended from a local princess named Io. We will come back to this compelling story later in the book, but for our purposes here it is important to know that the chorus say that these girls look like they come from a land near Ethiopia and that if they were carrying bows, the chorus would think they were "the unmarried, flesh-eating Amazons."[5]

There is evidence for African Amazons. We know of several warrior queens called *kandakes* from the Nubian regions of Kush and Meroe, bordering Egypt, who defied both Alexander the Great and Julius Caesar. The Naga Temple in Sudan has a great carving of Queen Amantiore of Meroe, fully armed and smiting her enemies, dated to 50 CE. Later in the eighteenth and nineteenth centuries, the Amazon myth was applied to the regiment of women warriors from the West African region of Benin; they were known as the Dahomey Amazons to European visitors. These fearsome women warriors, along with the ancient Amazons, were the inspiration for the Dora Milaje of *Black Panther*; the latter were introduced in *Black Panther Vol. 2 #1* in 1998 and described as "Deadly Amazonian high school karate chicks."

The myth of the Amazons became so widespread that a word that may derive from the ancient Iranian *ha-mazan* ("warrior") became the name of the great river system in South America in 1541. This was because the Spaniard Francisco de Orellana named it after the bands of indigenous women warriors he saw on its banks.

Black Widow encompasses both the danger and the fantasy of the Amazon warrior. Just as they were said to come from the edges of the known world, Natasha is trained deep inside the Soviet Union. Like the forced hysterectomy inflicted on the Black Widow graduates, so some myths about the Amazons say that they had their right breasts removed at birth to help them become better archers.

The myth most people know now most equates to the Black Widow trope—that men were seemingly welcomed to the Amazonian homeland, offered exquisite hospitality and sex, and then slaughtered afterward. Any male child who resulted from these unions was aborted, whereas girls were raised collectively in the Amazon martial traditions. The truth is that most of these stories were wholly fictitious and invented to exoticize what was known about distant warrior women who lived equally with men. This was so foreign to the Greeks that the Amazons were remade into a form of ruthless, man-devouring black widows. Then, as now, sex sells, and the weirder the stories the more interest is generated. Here we are, after all, still talking about the Amazons.

The less salacious accounts of the Amazons tell us that they made a deal with their neighbors that if married they would keep their customs and continue to hunt and fight alongside the men. We also hear stories of the Amazons having sex with their neighbors once a year, keeping the female babies, and giving away the males. The Amazons get more gnarly in accounts found in the Hippocratic corpus, which are the foundational texts of today's Western medical profession. These tell how the Amazons deliberately disabled male babies so when grown, the men would have to do sedentary domestic tasks. The historian, philosopher, and soldier Xenophon, writing in the fourth century BCE, goes further and reports that the Amazons were said to enslave their men.[6] In any event, in all these ancient accounts the Amazons are envisioned dominating men, and Marvel's Black Widow inherits this Amazonian tradition.

There are other myths about specific Amazon women that are very similar to what we see in the Black Widow story. These are usually about an Amazon queen who has been taken from her homeland. Black Widow was said to have been born during the WWII Battle of Stalingrad, adopted by a Soviet soldier, and then recruited into the KGB's Red Room program. Natasha is a former enemy, who in the Marvel comics defects from the Soviet Union after falling in love with Hawkeye. We see the same kind of story in two myths about the ancient Amazon queen Hippolyta. In the first, she is one of the labors of Herakles. He must retrieve her girdle, which has been taken to be the symbol of her sexuality. However, the term *zoster* really means "war belt." It was given to Hippolyta by her father, Ares, and it bestowed superhuman power. Think boxing championship belt, and you get the idea of what it looked like.

Hippolyta falls hard for the big man, and the couple try to slip away at night, but the sentries are alerted, and Herakles must fight his way out of the city. He barely manages to escape with the belt, but Hippolyta snaps out of her lovesickness and decides to stay. This is a narrow escape for Herakles and one of the most difficult fights of his life.

Hippolyta appears again in the myths of the Athenian hero-king Theseus. The stories of Herakles and Theseus are linked as the Athenians loved to replace the older Peloponnesian Herakles with their homegrown hero Theseus. In some versions of the myth, Theseus accompanies Herakles to retrieve the war belt and leaves with Hippolyta's sister, Antiope. In others Herakles gives Hippolyta to Theseus as his "spear-bride" after the task is complete. One of the oldest versions, from the philosopher Isocrates, has Hippolyta falling for Theseus.[7] He says the Amazons ride on Athens to get her back. This is appropriate for Hippolyta, whose name means "releaser of the horses." Nobody would want the Amazonian cavalry coming for them.

There are several different versions of the myth of the Amazon attack on the Athenians, but they all agree that it was a brutal campaign that lasted up to three months.

Finally Hippolyta (or her sister Antiope, in some accounts) made peace and agreed to become queen of Athens. Other writers claim she was killed fighting her own people alongside Theseus. Today the large rocky outcrop that sits before the Acropolis, where people gather to watch the sun set behind the Parthenon, is called the Areopagus, or "Hill of Ares," as this was the place where the Amazons were said to have made their camp. In one play by the Athenian playwright Aeschylus, Athena says that the Amazons built a citadel on the Areopagus and established a woman-run city to rival Athens.[8] Athena then says that it stands as a reminder against extreme forms of government and that "neither anarchy nor despotism" should ever rule in Athens.

The marriage of Theseus with Hippolyta and the treaty between Athens and the Amazons becomes a mythic metaphor for balance in Athenian society, between aristocrats and democrats, men and women, the old ways and the new. In welcoming the power of the Amazons into their city and memorializing them so prominently, the Athenians revered these warrior women as they did the warrior goddess Athena. Hippolyta continues to seize the imagination of poets long after classical Greece. For example, Shakespeare places her as a character in *A Midsummer Night's Dream*, which is set just before the wedding of Theseus and Hippolyta in Athens.

We don't know what happened to Hippolyta, but she disappears from the stories about Theseus's later life, except in that they had a son together, the suitably named Hippolytus. The boy grows up like a male version of an Amazon: he worships Artemis and spurns Aphrodite, and he loves to hunt, use his bow and arrows, and ride horses. Hippolytus is his mother's son. But Aphrodite is angry that this boy is coming to manhood and has no interest in eroticism and love, so she forces Theseus's new wife, Phaedra, to fall in love with her stepson. He pushes her away, and she ends her life accusing Hippolytus of rape. When Theseus finds out he banishes his only son and calls on Poseidon to curse him. Hippolytus flees on his chariot down the winding coast road, but a great sea monster rises up from the depths and startles his horses. Hippolytus loses control, and he dies. Like his mother, his name means "the one who releases the horses" and so Hippolytus, the only known son of the Amazons, perishes before he can become a man.

The Amazon heroine's representation in male-dominated societies acts as a cultural barometer on attitudes towards gender and women's sexuality. We see this in the ancient world where stories about the Amazons become more and more disturbing when told by Roman and early Christian writers—they cut off their breast to fight, they kill any man they have sex with, they even eat human flesh!

We can even see this in the relatively short time that the MCU has been active: The first appearance of Scarlett Johansson's Black Widow in the MCU, in 2010's *Iron Man 2*, is hard to watch now. She is introduced as a staff member from Legal, and Tony Stark invites her into his boxing ring to receive a lesson from Happy. She gets Happy in her signature leg lock and throws him, and Stark is immediately mesmerized by her physical beauty and martial abilities. After googling photos of her in her underwear, he says, "I want one" to Pepper Potts as if he is a modern-day Theseus taking his new trophy-wife Hippolyta back to Athens. By the time Marvel released *Black Widow* in 2021, Natasha had developed into a character with a good deal more personal agency and integrity, actually more like the personifications of Amazons we find in the classical period rather than the schlocky, sensationalized, and sexualized versions that came later.

There is an enormous difference between the version of Black Widow that first appeared in the early '60s comics—the demure, fur-coat-wearing, high-heeled Russian seducer with a veiled green fascinator atop her highly coiffured hair—and the arctic-white jumpsuit–clad, highly trained assassin from the 2021 movie *Black Widow.* Although both personifications exoticize the character, Black Widow's more recent sexuality is now closer to the way the male heroes have been presented in the MCU. Chris Hemsworth's Thor outfit and the formfitting costume worn by Chris Evans as Captain America remind us of the heightened musculature of ancient armor and sometimes even the state of male heroic nudity found in Greek art. Peggy Carter's reaction to Steve Rogers's brand-new supersoldier pecs in *Captain America: The First Avenger* puts the objectification back on the men.

Additionally, those myths about spiderlike women weavers indicate that their intellects are as much a weapon as their martial abilities. Their eroticism is often combined with advanced cerebral facilities that can manifest in the spinning of a complex web or tapestry. Agamemnon knows he should not step on those elaborate, woven crimson fabrics, and yet he does so, urged on by a persuasive Clytemnestra who offers him the appearance of both benevolence and glory. Natasha says it all in in *Iron Man 2* when she utters the Latin phrase "*Fallaces sunt rerum species*"—"appearances can be deceiving."

In myth, what makes the Amazons übererotic is that they don't need men. They fight for themselves, each other, and their women-only culture, and although occasionally thwarted in battle, they are never completely defeated and conquered. This trope is encapsulated by the myth of Penthesilea, the Amazon queen who fought at Troy. This story is detailed in the *Aethiopis,* another epic story of the Trojan War, now mostly lost.[9] In it the Amazons come to fight for Troy with King Memnon of Ethiopia and another nod to the possibility of African Amazons, although Penthesilea is said to have come from Thrace (modern Bulgaria). She was such a fearsome warrior that the poet Stesichorus, in a work now lost, claimed *she*, not Achilles, killed the Trojan hero Hector. Either way, she eventually meets Achilles on the battlefield, and the two clash in a mighty duel. Achilles finally delivers the death blow, and at that moment, as her life is ebbing away, her helmet drops, and he falls instantly in love with the woman he has just killed. Appropriately her name means "bringer of pain to men."[10] In yet another version of the Penthesilea story told by Smyrneaus in the fourth century CE, she inspires the women of Troy to take up arms. One of them cries out, "We are not inferior to men, we look on the same light, have the same number of limbs, breathe the same air, eat the same food . . . let us then join this fight!" This myth suggests that all women can be Amazonian.[11]

Despite the development of patriarchal systems in the ancient world, the archetype of the fierce woman warrior hero can be found in most mythological traditions. The Yoruba of West Africa have Oya, the woman warrior orisha, goddess of lightning, storm winds, fire, and fertility. The Aztecs told of Ītzpāpalōtl, a skeletal female warrior who guarded paradise. The Ancient Britons had Andraste, the woman war goddess who inspired Queen Boudicca to revolt against the Roman occupation, and the Vikings had their warrior goddess Frejya, who like the Greek Aphrodite and Mesopotamian Ishtar, was also a goddess of love. In the Hindu tradition there is Durga, a mother goddess associated with warfare and protection, and Chinese mythology tells of Jiutian Xuannü, the goddess of war, sexuality, and longevity.

In the MCU Black Widow becomes the tenacious leader who holds the Avengers together after the Infinity War and the devastation caused by Thanos, just as the Amazon Hippolyta is envisioned as bringing balance and peace to a warring Athens.

The ancient version of Natasha rebuilding the Avengers to defeat Thanos was Telesilla, a poet from the city of Argos in Southern Greece. We hear from several ancient sources that at some time in the late sixth century BCE the Spartans invaded their neighboring state, Argos, and at the Battle of Sepeia killed all their men. They then marched on the city, determined to sack it. However, Telesilla, who was already famous as a poet and performer, led the women of Argos to arm for war and take up positions on the walls. The Spartans attacked and were beaten back by Telesilla and her warrior women. When the Spartans withdrew, the Argive women had to rebuild their society without men. So, they enfranchised their enslaved people, encouraged the country folk to move to the city, and might well have created Greece's first democratic system of government twenty years before Athens.

Some seven hundred years after these events, the writer Pausanias visited Argos. He reported that over the theatre stood a large carving of Telesilla wearing a helmet and armor with scrolls at her feet.[12] A testimony to the bravery and industriousness of this woman warrior poet and her band of widows who defeated the strongest army in the entire Greek world.

In *Endgame*, Natasha is our version of Telesilla, keeping it all together through the trauma of the Snap to be able to mount a successful defense against Thanos, a cause she gives her life for. The Amazon hero has been a complex figure, mainly because she is nearly always framed in relation to a male world, and yet we find myths of warrior women time and time again being used in stories about the creation of democracy. This is also true of Black Widow, one woman among five men. Things are changing in the MCU as more women heroes are gaining prominence: the Scarlet Witch (much more on her in chapter 6), Captain Marvel, Echo, Spider-Woman, She-Hulk, Valkyrie, Mantis, Gamora, Shuri, Mighty Thor (Jane Foster), among many more. Yet the male characters still outnumber them three to one. Just as the ancient Greek Olympian pantheon was made up of six male, five female (or six if we include Hestia), and one figure who reflects both (Dionysus), we may someday soon be looking at a Marvel universe that projects the same kind of gender balance in its own mythology. That might well be as good for our democracy as the myths of the Amazon warrior women were for the ancient Greeks. Their stories warn us against the kind of extremism displayed by a Thanos or an Agamemnon. As the goddess Athena pronounced to the Athenians standing at the mythical camp of the Amazons, "From this rock shall come the respect to inspire my citizens and the fear to ever restrain justice . . . there will be no anarchy, nor the rule of tyranny, Citizens embrace the middle way!"[13]

CHAPTER 4

THE MADNESS OF THE MULTIVERSE

Helen of Troy is among the most well-known mythical figures to come down to us from antiquity. We know her as the famously beautiful woman, with the "face that launched a thousand ships," who absconded with Paris, the prince of Troy, leaving her husband Menelaus and igniting the ten-year-long Trojan War. But what if I told you that Helen was never in Troy, she never left her husband, Menelaus, and the entire conflict that cost so many lives on both sides and led to the complete destruction of the great city of Troy was based on a completely different yet parallel reality? Instead, Helen existed in two places simultaneously, or as the Greeks put it, "hurtling here, there and everywhere all at once and once again, across the unexpected and into unpredictability."[I] They called this state where simultaneous realities can exist at the same time the *antilogos*, or "paradox." We know it now as the multiverse.

The classical Athenian playwright Euripides tells this story in his play entitled *Helen*. He reminds his audience of the judgment of Paris, when the young man had to choose between the goddesses Hera, Aphrodite, and Athena. We are going to delve deeper into this story later, but for now Euripides tells us that he chose Aphrodite, the goddess of love, and was promised the most beautiful woman in the world in return. This was undoubtedly Helen, who was a princess of Sparta. Helen was semidivine, having been born from a liaison between her mother, Leda, and Zeus, who came to her in the guise of a swan. Every young warrior prince in Greece wanted to marry Helen. Eventually she was betrothed to Menelaus, a prince of neighboring Argos, and together they became the king and queen of Sparta.

All this the Greeks knew, but then came the twist: it was not Helen who left her husband and ran off to Troy with the dashing, reckless Paris, but a simulacrum created by Hera, who was still furious about being rejected in the judgment. For this the Greeks mounted a massive war against Troy. The "other" Helen was spirited off to Egypt to be protected there until such time as she would be reunited with her husband. In Euripides's play, Helen tells us that Zeus consented to this to "lighten the earth mother of the burden and the mass of humanity."[2] Sounds a lot like the ecological designs of Marvel's Thanos, who used the Infinity Gauntlet to exterminate half of all life in the universe.

Meanwhile across the sea in the parallel "universe" of the Trojan War, Helen is behind the walls, married to Paris and helping old King Priam identify the Greek heroes streaming across the wide Trojan plain, intent on destroying his city. Neither the Greeks nor the Trojans have any idea that the "real" Helen is languishing far away in Egypt. This story that there were two Helens existing at the same time goes all the way back to the Greek poet Hesiod, who was performing in the eighth to the seventh century BCE. In the Euripides version things end happily, at least, a rarity for tragedy: Menelaus and Helen are reunited after he discovers that she did not leave him after all. They manage to escape from Egypt and sail off into the sunset together again at last—who says there's no such thing as second chances in love?

Actually, Homer does. In his version of the post–Trojan War Helen and Menelaus story, they are both back in Sparta living together in a very strained relationship. Things are very emotional in this postwar palace as husband and wife exchange differing stories about the conflict, contradicting each other and generally getting on each other's nerves. Helen mixes their wine with an ancient version of Xanax and passes it around as if this political marriage that so many died to preserve can be maintained only by drugs. Interestingly enough she obtains these magical herbs from Egypt. What these two stories about Helen tell us is that the concept of multiversal realities is found in ancient mythology and that mythology itself with its multifaceted possibilities and constantly changing narratives is a multiversal concept.

People look to mythical multiverses when their own worlds are expanding and encountering new peoples, places, and cultures. We see this happening in ancient Greece, where stories of heroes and epic battles begin to change. During the eighth and seventh centuries BCE, when the *Odyssey* was performed, the Greek world was recovering from the Bronze Age collapse. People were traveling once again, trading with new peoples, and exploring far-off places with vastly different customs and languages. Homer's *Iliad* introduces us to two peoples, the Greeks and the Trojans, yet they seem culturally almost the exact same, with the same gods and the same language. By the time we get to the *Odyssey*, which is a newer story, we see the hero encountering a vast array of places, some of them seemingly otherworldly, like the isle of the divinity Calypso, the home of the sorcerer Circe, the rocks of the Sirens, and even the realms of the underworld. These kinds of "multiversal" myths tell us that things are changing in people's perception of the world they live in, and these stories are reflecting those tensions.

We see this in the early 1970s when current events and scientific advances were rapidly and often disconcertingly challenging long held beliefs. Prior binary cultural associations of "good" and "bad" wars, "civilized and primitive," East and West, religion and spirituality, even "heaven and earth" were being challenged as the post–World War II world began to change. People traveled far more, they had much greater access to media through television, and the news was full of both scientific revelations about the universe, fueled by the Space Race, and reports of the destabilization of the old colonial world, wars, revolutions, coups, protests, all being transmitted right into your living room every day. In 1971, Cygnus X-1, the first black hole, was discovered and soon found its way into the popular imagination along with the concept of "wormholes" that seemed to offer gateways to unknown dimensions.

This preoccupation with the expanding world found its way into popular culture too. In a 1973 episode of *Doctor Who,* a black hole–type phenomenon harbors the creator of the Time Lords and is able to propel them through time; and in 1977 the Canadian progressive rock band Rush, in a song named "Cygnus X-1," asked, "Is there something more? / Atomized—at the core / Or through the Astral Door / —To soar." For Marvel, there was Morton Kribbee, or "Black Hole," a minor character who first appeared in a Howard the Duck story in 1976. After he absorbed a particle of a black hole into his chest, he could pull matter toward him and destroy it. The world and the cosmos suddenly seemed like a very unknown, uncertain place, and if Earth has so many radically different cultures within it, what about the universe itself? It was no coincidence, then, that in 1977 Marvel had Uatu, the Watcher, introduce a new Marvel comic book series called *What If* by claiming, "I have windows into the strange parallel worlds of what might have been." This allowed for the cross-pollination of characters and existing story lines, with the first issue asking, "What if Spider-Man had joined the Fantastic Four?" The multiverse was already in the air.

In the years following the launch of the Russian satellite Sputnik 1 in 1957, multiversal change was already fermenting, yet this brave new world was rooted in the mythological past. The American space program evoked the mythic world of the Greeks by naming its rockets Mercury, after the Roman messenger God, and Apollo after the Greek god of music, medicine, and prophecy. NASA's first human-piloted space flights were named Gemini after the Greek mythological twins, and the command module of the ill-fated Apollo 13 mission in 1970 was called *Odyssey*. Even the name for the space pilots, "astronaut" and "cosmonaut," were derived from the ancient Greek words meaning "star sailor" and "universe sailor."

Along with the new frontiers of the Space Age came popular interest in ancient mysticism, alternative forms of spirituality and mind-altering substances. Even the name for this, "the counterculture," reflected a multiversal attitude as many people wanted to explore alternate worlds any ways they could. As Russia's Yuri Gagarin became the first man in space in April 1961 followed by the USA's Alan Shepard that May, Timothy Leary and Richard Alpert were experimenting with hallucinogenics at Harvard, and in New York at Marvel Comics, Steve Ditko was developing a new kind of character—Dr. Strange.

Stephen Strange is a genius neurosurgeon who damages his hands in a car accident and becomes psychologically unmoored. He finds hope in a secret Eastern center of spiritual training called Kamar-Taj. There he meets the Ancient One, becomes a master of the mystic arts, and learns how to move through the infinite dimensions of the multiverse. Ditko and Stan Lee locate Strange's home at the Sanctum Sanctorum in Greenwich Village, said to have stood on a powerful intersecting point for ancient energy lines once used by Native American traditional healers. This was not just an aesthetic choice. "The Village" was already associated with the Beatniks, the alternate folk scene, altered state experimentation, and increasing interest in Eastern mysticism and spirituality. The more the scientific wonders of NASA propelled America into the infinite and unknown reality of space, the more a counterculture developed looking for alternative meanings. Dr. Strange is a man of his times.

The training Strange receives at Kamar-Taj is an amalgamation of Hindu, Buddhist, and Daoist traditions filtered through a Western eye. Like many of us who have engaged with any aspect of these spiritual systems from meditating, practicing Yoga, or contemplating enlightenment, Dr. Strange is a fictional representative of our own cross-cultural experimentation. But rather than viewing this as superficial or a form of cultural appropriation, Dr. Strange is able to access an unseen mystical realm that is both very ancient and infinitely powerful. His character combines the magic of a sorcerer with the analytical and scientific mind of a brilliant physician. Because of this he becomes the figure most associated with the multiverse in the MCU. Dr. Strange's relationship to the unseen realm of mystical power reflects the ideas of the inventor of the term "multiverse," the nineteenth-century father of American psychology, William James.

William James was born in 1842 in an affluent New York family. His brother was the novelist Henry James, his sister was the diarist Alice James, and he was the godson of Ralph Waldo Emerson. Although he suffered from a number of debilitating ailments as a child and young man, he traveled extensively before studying medicine at Harvard. He went on to publish hugely influential works on human emotions, psychological experimentation, and philosophy and held the chairs in both psychology and philosophy at Harvard until 1907. In many ways James is the academic embodiment of Dr. Strange, as for all his scholarly, medical, and scientific credentials and expertise, he was also a publicly practicing mystic and member of the Theosophical Society, which described itself as an "esoteric new religious movement" and united ancient Greek philosophy with occult practices, Eastern mysticism, and Jewish Kabbala.

The Theosophical Society that James joined in 1882 had been cofounded a few years earlier by a Russian mystic called Madame Blavatsky and Colonel Henry Steel Olcott, a Civil War veteran and lawyer who had served on the inquiry into Abraham Lincoln's assassination. Around the time James joined the society they were establishing a center in India where Madame Blavatsky claimed they were rediscovering ancient wisdom and uniting science, religion, and philosophy. She declared that she was able to communicate telepathically with a sect of Tibetan monks who had trained her in their secret monastery in the Himalayas. The parallels with Marvel's mythical "Ancient One," the spiritual leader of Kamar-Taj, are quite compelling. James was fascinated by the occult and spiritualism, and was known to participate in seances and study people who claimed to be psychics.

It was at a public lecture at Harvard in 1895 entitled "Is Life Worth Living" that James first coined the term "multiverse," and we need to take his spiritualist beliefs into consideration alongside his academic and clinical expertise. In his speech, James said, "Visible nature is all plasticity and indifference, a multiverse, as one might call it, and not a universe." What he meant is that the natural world, of which we are part, is chaotic, multifaceted, and complicated. By "plasticity" he indicated that all things are constantly changing, including us. James's use of "multiverse" is usually dismissed as not relevant to the astrophysical use of the term, as he was seemingly lecturing on psychology, but if we "Dr. Strange" William James and delve briefly into his deeply held beliefs in ancient magic, we can see that he was actually spot-on.

James's multiversal concept highlighted what he saw as a fundamental problem with our spiritual belief systems. He said that for many people faith in the essential goodness of our deities or in an intelligent design of everything is challenged by the savage realities of life. To counter this, he suggested that many parallel possibilities can all exist simultaneously. This theosophically influenced theory found its way into his influential view of psychology, and the idea of a cosmic multiverse was placed within the mind. James's theories—on schizophrenia, multiple personality disorder, and the notion that people's personalities naturally change and develop as they age and gain experience—are a clinical manifestation of the multiverse in psychological terms. His views on both the cosmic and personal multiverse and how they were connected were a highly sophisticated analysis of human consciousness and natural phenomena. This was decades before physicist Hugh Everett's Many Worlds Theory of quantum mechanics in 1955, which is usually taken to be the first theory on the multiverse. On this one, I'm with American psychiatry's own version of Dr. Strange.

As for Hugh Everett, in his PhD thesis he dared to dispute the prevailing views on quantum mechanics, which is the study of subatomic particles and their physical behaviors. The perceptual truth of quantum reality—that there is only one reality at the point of viewing a particle—had been advanced by Nobel-winning giants such as Werner Heisenberg, Niels Bohr, and Max Born. But Everett himself was inspired by a famous thought experiment involving a cat in a box.

In 1935 the Austrian physicist Erwin Schrödinger, another dabbler in Eastern mysticism, asked us to imagine that there is a cat in a box with a vial of poison and a decaying radioactive source that at a certain point will smash the vial and kill the cat. Schrödinger concocted this concept to criticize quantum mechanics, which proposed that the cat could be both alive and dead at the same time, until the point of observation. He showed that at the point of human perception when the lid is lifted there can be only one reality. The cat is either dead or alive, regardless of when we chose to observe it. The act of observation is not then the action that affects matter. However, Everett saw something different: Schrödinger's cat proves that multiple realities can exist simultaneously, but we can see only one of them at a time and the two realities can never intersect. The observer is not aware of these "other worlds." Everett's example is the fact that we cannot perceive the Earth moving around the sun, even though we know it does. So, we can accept other worlds exist while also accepting that we can never see them. Most realities are therefore hidden from us and multiversal.

Both Schrödinger's cat and Hugh Everett were cited by Tony Stark in a 2002 Iron Man story written and drawn by Mike Grell.[3] Tony is contacted by an archaeologist, Dr. Ellen Mallory, with a truly remarkable find from a grave in a field of megaliths in Wales, buried since the turn of the eleventh century. It is Iron Man's helmet. She has tested it, and it's genuine, so how did Iron Man's helmet from the early 2000s find its way into a Celtic grave one thousand years prior? Tony resolves to use a new device he has been developing that allows him to travel through a wormhole to go back in time and find out the truth. He reassures Pepper Potts by saying that Hugh Everett developed "a multiverse theory" and that "infinite universes were created by moment-to-moment decisions we made as we went along." Pepper is seriously concerned as Tony suits up and enters his new time machine, dialing its temporal setting to 1002 CE. He tells her, "Within Schrödinger's box all possibilities exist," and as he activates the sequence he adds, "We're never going to know for sure until we open the box and have a look." Pepper responds, "That's what Pandora said."

Tony is propelled through a wormhole back in time to medieval Wales. On arrival his suit has reversed its polarity, rendering it useless, and he is taken prisoner by Aislinn, a woman with the blood of the Earth Mother who wants to know how his lightweight and incredibly strong armor is made. Meanwhile, back in 2002 New York, Dr. Mallory rushes to Stark's lab and shows Pepper what's inside the helmet she recovered—a human skull. Is it Tony's? Pepper wants to find him, but Dr. Mallory begs to go instead: it would be an archaeologist's dream, she says. She knows the landscape, and besides, Pepper needs to stay to operate the machine.

When Dr. Mallory arrives in the castle courtyard where Tony is being held, she meets Aislinn face-to-face. Then there is a huge surge of energy, and the two women merge together. Now it becomes clear: Mallory is Aislinn in 2002. She has been waiting one thousand years for this moment to double her powers by merging with her ancient self. Why? To protect the world from the devastation brought upon it by men like Stark who are rapidly depleting the Earth of its resources. (She kind of has a point, no?) This was her plan all long. She takes Iron Man's suit and positions herself in the stone circle at the time and place where Pepper has arranged to pull Tony back to 2002. What she does not know is that although Tony had repaired his suit, he decided to save power and not reverse the polarity back on the helmet. Aislinn is decapitated, and her plan fails. It was her skull in the long-buried helmet, not Tony's.

Now, there are a lot of plot holes in this comic book story, such as: how come Aislinn–Dr. Mallory doesn't run a test on the skull and realize it's her own? More important, the story itself defies Everett's cardinal rule that it is impossible for two realities to ever coexist in the same place and time. Everett thought about this question in biological terms, asking, Do a pair of cells that split from one original cell remember their prior existence as that progenitor cell? Or to put it another way, can parallel worlds communicate with each other? He thought not.

The Iron Man and Aislinn tale asks us to consider two realities from different times (1002 and 2002) that momentarily exist simultaneously. This pushes us far beyond Everett's theory but is well within the realm of mythology. Perhaps a cell can't remember its origins, but mythology can. Ancient stories encode and pass down cultural memories in the form of narratives from one generation to another. Like Everett's progenitor cell, the first creator of the myth is not aware of the different versions of the story that might be told later. However, the "receiver" of the story often is, and we know we are being connected to something deeper and older when we experience such a powerful myth. This can create deeply memorable narrative moments. The psychiatrist Carl Jung, who met William James in 1909, shared many of his spiritual and scholarly views, and exchanged research with him, developed his own theory of human memory encoding called the collective unconscious.

Jung thought humans shared an ancestral mythology that was passed down through the generations and had been encoded in our cells, even though we may not be at all aware of them. The collective unconscious acts on us as these common mythic archetypes are innate, and Jung believed that by becoming aware of them we can better understand our own mental states. For example, one Jungian archetype is the Magician, a person who is capable of innovation and creativity but also malevolent harm. A Jungian perspective on some of the multiversal characters we have met in this chapter, be it William James, Dr. Strange, Tony Stark, or even Jung himself, might characterize them as the Magician type. This would mean that the stories we tell about them tend to follow a certain mythic pattern. For Jung, archetypes were a person's unconscious response to the things they had experienced in their lives, a kind of psychological personal mythmaking and even another way to consider the multiverse on a psychological basis.

The MCU tries to thread this mythic memory needle by offering "Easter eggs" to the fans of the Marvel universe, while also (sometimes) serving audience members who know nothing of the former myths. Before my Marvel journey, when I first saw *Black Panther*, I had absolutely no clue what the white guy with one arm and a mullet was doing in Wakanda in the end credits scene of *Black Panther*. That is, until I went back and watched *Captain America: The Winter*

Soldier and made the connection. T'Challa, the Black Panther, believes that Bucky Barnes, the Winter Soldier, killed his father until it is revealed that this was a false flag operation. Brilliant! This scene was about forgiveness, redemption, and understanding, and it looked forward to Bucky's defense of Wakanda in *Infinity War* and *Endgame*.

As we have seen, myths are multiversal in themselves. Several different versions can exist at the same time and place. In Homer, Odysseus goes down to the edge of Hades where he meets the ghost of Agamemnon, the commander of the Greek army at Troy. Odysseus is surprised to see him there, believing he had survived the war. But Agamemnon tells him that when he got home his wife, Clytemnestra, tricked him. She welcomed him kindly, even though he had sacrificed their daughter to appease the gods and sail on Troy. Then, once inside, he was ambushed and killed by her lover, Aegisthus. Now the Athenians were all still reciting the *Odyssey* when the playwright Aeschylus told a different version of the same story in his play called *Agamemnon*. He understands his theatre audience knows that myth well, so he uses it to deliver a shocking plot twist, or *peripeteia*, as Aristotle called such a device. This time Clytemnestra slaughters Agamemnon herself. When she appears from their house covered in his blood the audience must have been stunned. (Fun Marvel fact: Mike Coulter, who plays the MCU's Luke Cage, played Agamemnon for me as a drama student at University of South Carolina. He was excellent in the role and "died" brilliantly at the hands of his axe-wielding stage wife.)

The countless versions of ancient myths can confound and frustrate people trying to get to know them. Looking for "canon"—an authoritative version of a story that all others divert from—is the mythic equivalent of opening Schrödinger's box. Finding canon can seem like an obsession to some Marvel fans on the Quora and Reddit boards. The multiversality of myth defies this "fidelity discourse"—

the quest for the "original" version. We should instead ask *why* the myth has adapted and changed. In *Agamemnon* Aeschylus wanted to make a point about the imbalance between male and female forces in his culture by swapping out the killer. With that adaptation he was asking the increasingly male democracy of Athens if it was on the right track by lessening the power and influence of women in Athenian society.

As for Hugh Everett, after being frustrated that his pioneering work did not gain any traction in his field, he left the world of academic physics for the Pentagon, where he found a practical application of the Many Worlds Theory. He analyzed the numerous different scenarios presented by a nuclear war with Soviet Russia and concluded that every time there was only one result: mutually assured thermonuclear destruction. This real-world use of the multiverse has certainly helped keep a delicate peace between nuclear powers since World War II.

Then there is Marvel's own Jungian Magician, Dr. Strange. We saw him run his version of Everett's Many Worlds Theory in the MCU's *Avengers: Infinity War.* There, he uses the Time Stone to see more than fourteen million outcomes to conclude that there was only one scenario where Thanos could be defeated. This is the one presented in *Endgame*. Here screenwriters McFeely and Markus did something very similar to Aeschylus in *Agamemnon*. They surprised the hell out of their huge opening weekend audience with the death of Tony Stark.

Since Everett, many astrophysicists have embraced the concept of the multiverse. Today, if one visits the "Cosmic History" page on NASA's website there is a description of what is termed "Cosmic Inflation." This is the theory that immediately after the Big Bang the universe expanded faster than the speed of light for less than a second. This led to a kind of rippling of the fabric of the universe and small pockets of dark matter like bubbles developing. These expanded to form different universes, hence a multiverse. As Cosmic Inflation is thought to be continuous and infinite, so are the multiple universes created during the process. Cosmologist Laura Mersini-Houghton has now proposed that the recent discovery of pockets of dark energy in our universe is verifiable evidence for the existence of a multiverse. She writes, "Even our universe is just one tiny grain of dust in a much more intricate and beautiful cosmos."[4]

For all the contemporary excitement, the multiverse is not a new concept. Vedic mythology has Lord Shiva showing his mortal disciple Arjun his infinite form of "hundreds and thousands of incredible forms of infinite shapes, sizes, and colors." He says that all of these other universes reside in his semblance, which in itself is infinite. Arjun can only see Krishna this way because the god has given him temporary divine sight. "He revealed Himself as the wonderful and infinite Lord whose face is everywhere."[5] Arjun feels that if he could see a thousand suns blazing in the sky it would not come close to the glorious infinity of Lord Krishna. He does not see "any beginning, middle, or end" to his god. The chorus of Euripides's *Helen* say much the same thing when they are trying to figure out that multiversal story: "What is a god, what is not a god, what is between mortals and the gods, who can even say they have searched the farthest and found the limit?"[6]

In Buddhism the Avatamaska (Flower Wreath) Sutra tells how the universe is made up of infinite universes that are all nestled within one another and existing at the same time. In a drop of water is an entire ocean, in a speck of dust a whole world, and so on. In these limitless multiverses there are countless Buddhas. One can enter the "realm of reality" by accepting the interconnectedness of everything and becoming at one with this infinite "emptiness." Compassion, ethics, deep meditation, mindfulness, and becoming a bodhisattva (enlightened one) are the requirements to enter the Avatamaska multiverse.

Now while I like a bit of Yoga and have even been known to meditate from time to time, I don't think I'm getting into the Buddhist multiverse anytime soon. Perhaps my ancestors from Schleswig Holstein (Denmark/Germany) and Saxon and Danelaw Britain might have been more familiar with the Norse myth of nine cosmic realms arranged up and down the world tree, Yggdrasil. Humans live in Midgard, while the gods are up in Asgard. Niflheim is the misty realm beneath, and Helheim is the land of the dead. Marvel has made good use of these mythological Norse multirealms in both the comics and the MCU, naming Thor, his divine family, and the people he lives with Asgardians, after the heavenly realm.

In ancient Greece, philosophers such as Leucippus and Democritus proposed a version of the multiverse based on the concept of atomism, a theory that the universe is made up of an infinite number of minuscule particles that constantly collide to create material forms. They thought that as our universe is made up of these infinitesimal particles all interacting everywhere, all the time and all at once, and creating potentially limitless forms, there must therefore be other universes.

Anticipating Marvel's *Loki* and *Deadpool & Wolverine* by about 2,500 years, Leucippus wrote that chaos was a real celestial element known as the Void, an element in opposition to the self-organization of the atoms. In their intrinsic nature as moving objects, Leucippus's atoms constantly form patterns that often repeat. This means that the universal laws of this atomist multiverse are deterministic, and all things have causality without the need for any kind of intelligent design to be at work. Even the formless Void exists in opposition to the organization of the atoms.

The multiversal ideas of the Greek atomists influenced Islamic philosophers including the twelfth-century polymath Fakhr al-Din al-Razi, who wrote that there was a universal void in an infinite cosmos but only God could fill the void at will with countless other universes. This view was echoed in eighteenth-century Germany by Gottfried Leibniz, who proposed that of all the many worlds created by God, ours is the most perfect.

Marvel has always been a many-worlds universe. Right from the start characters were teamed up and cross-pollinated from one comic book to another. This explodes with the development of the Marvel Cinematic Universe as stories and characters were tied together across different media platforms. Within this multiversal concept characters can even meet themselves. In the superb 2012 Thor comic book story line "Godbomb" written by Jason Aaron, Thor teams up with his younger and older selves to defeat the resentful supervillain Gorr the God Butcher.

Gorr is intent on destroying all the gods of the multiverse in a hate-fueled attempt to free his peoples from dependence on divinities. He wants to punish the gods for not answering his prayers when his family died during a famine. In attempting to rid the multiverse of all its gods, Gorr is seeking a kind of self-sanctified end to the multiverse itself.

In the MCU's version of the story of Gorr the God Butcher, *Thor: Love and Thunder,* we are taken to Omnipotence City. This is a kind of United Nations of divinities, presided over by Russell Crowe's comic version of Zeus. In both Jason Aaron's graphic story and director Taika Waititi's filmic one, we find a fictive manifestation of one of the most prevalent multiversal concepts in ancient religion and mythology: polytheism.

"Polytheism" simply means "many gods" and was the norm for most peoples until the rise of the big three monotheistic Abrahamic religions: Judaism, Christianity, and Islam. While there were some monotheistic religions in antiquity, such as Zoroastrianism from Iran and Judaism in the Levant, polytheistic systems developed from older animist religious structures. These regarded all natural objects as having spirituality. We see the remains of an animist system in Greek and Roman mythology where alongside the Olympian pantheon, there are river gods, nymphs, sea-spirits, furies, and all manner of *daemones*. This is a word meaning "divinities," which was turned to "demons" by later Christians.

In surviving animist traditions, such as many Native American rites, we see the concept of multiple realms operating beside the one in which humans live. The Lenape, on whose ancestral lands I live in New York, believed in the realm of *Manitou*, a cosmic force that inhabited everything around them. Accessing the realm of the Manitowak, or life spirits, involved being guided by a shaman into trance states. Sometimes this involved taking natural psychotropics and completing a vision quest to access the alternate spirit world. This is another multiversal concept of reality.

Many animist religions incorporate some form of ancestor worship, and during their festivals and rites, the dead would cross over from their realm into ours. Marvel dramatized this in the 2023 TV show *Echo*, where Maya Lopez, originally a Native American character from the *Daredevil* comics, is depicted drawing power and protection from her Choctaw ancestors. They cross over from another realm to stand with her. So, for most adherents of animist practice the concept of a multiverse as reality made up of many dimensions would seem quite normal.

The animist concept of multirealm "slippage" sat uncomfortably alongside monotheism. For example, many Vikings were attracted to Christianity, but much to the confusion of early missionaries, they just placed Jesus within their own pantheon. Most polytheistic traditions tended to be quite flexible in accommodating change and incorporating new deities. This is illustrated by a magnificent stone Viking cross from the tenth century CE that can be seen in the churchyard of St. Mary's Church in Gosforth in northern England. On this Christian symbol are depictions from Norse mythology including a wonderful horned Loki and scenes from Ragnarök. On a slab from the same period, now embedded in the church wall, Thor is depicted battling Jörmungandr, the great serpent of Midgard.

Thor, both the Marvel character and the Norse god, offers us a good example of how the spread of mythical stories through multiple cultures creates multiversal story worlds. Thor is best known as the hammer-wielding deity from Norse mythology, and this was the model for the Marvel character created in 1962 by Jack Kirby, Stan Lee, and Larry Lieber. Of course, Thor has a much older and varied legacy, including the stories found in the Icelandic texts known as the Eddas, which date from the early thirteenth century CE. Even there Thor (Þórr in Old Norse) has many different names and personalities. These include Ásabragr (God-Lord), ÁsaÞórr (God-Thor), Björn (Bear), Einridi (Lone Rider), Hardhugadr (Hard Heart), Hlóridi (Loud Weather), Rymr (Clamor), and my personal favorite, VingÞórr (Uproar-Thor).

Thor is a Norse version of a common, much older, Indo-European sky-weather god found throughout other myths and rituals. The Saxons in England knew him as Thunor. In northern Germany he was called Thunar, from the Old German word *Donar*, meaning "thunder." When Thor meets Zeus in Omnipotence City, he is in effect meeting another version of himself. The way in which this Indo-European sky god fragmented into different localized versions shows how divinities also become multiversal.

Thor is also much older than his first attested mention. This is on a woman's brooch found at Nordendorf in Bavaria from the sixth or seventh century CE, which has the word *wigiþonar*, meaning "Battle Thor." But we can also trace a connection between Thor and the Celtic god of thunder Taranis, who was known to be worshipped widely in pre-Roman Europe. When the Romans encountered the Celtic and Germanic peoples through trade and then colonization, they equated this thunder god with Mercury, the Roman messenger god, or Hercules, because they saw Thor's hammer as being like Hercules's club.

There's an enormous naked representation of what may be ancient Thor, etched out of the chalk hillside near the tiny village of Cerne Abbas in southern England. With his prominent erect penis, this Thor has been named "the Rude Man" for obvious reasons. That this naked and aroused pagan figure stands over an important Christian abbey, on a site with ancient wells that have been sacred for thousands of years, reveals how different traditions can be incorporated into the same location. The mythical multiverse can exist in one place at one time, although I wonder what the pious monks and pilgrims at the abbey made of Thor's massive appendage, and I don't mean his hammer or club.

Eventually European Christianity eradicated Thor and his fellow Norse deities, although his stories remained entwined in the folktale tradition and his name is enshrined in what we now call the fifth day of the week, counting from Sunday to Thursday.

Monotheism did not destroy the multiverse. The twentieth-century American philosopher David Lewis suggested that if we can conceive of an alternate reality, like heaven or hell, then it must exist in a real alternate world to be conceptually possible. He called this the Possible Worlds Theory. This means that if I imagine myself in an alternate life as a champion Formula One driver, then there is a version of me in another world driving a McLaren at 250 miles per hour. *The Stanford Encyclopedia of Philosophy* states that one of the biggest challenges to the Possible Worlds Theory is what it calls the "incredulous stare"—the look you may be giving to these pages right now because, let's face it, Lewis's theory seems very hard to believe.

Lewis had an answer: Yes, the theory may seem ridiculous, but it's worth the cost of potential ridicule. It is an exceptionally efficient device to think with, and humans use this so-called counterfactual mindset all the time to think creatively and problem-solve. Lewis figured that based on this alone, the theory ought to be accepted as fact. According to him our minds are in themselves multiversal.

David Lewis's Possible Worlds Theory could be viewed in action on our screens in season 1, episode 5 of Marvel's *Loki*, in which Loki finds himself in the Void. In this incarnation the Void is the place where all the variant versions that appeared in other worlds are dispatched after being "pruned" by the Time Variance Authority cops. In the Void Loki meets several possible variants of himself including Boastful Loki, Kid Loki, Loki as an alligator, and—my favorite—Classic Loki, played by Richard E. Grant.

Lewis adamantly believed that a possible world cannot interact with the real world as it then simply becomes a concrete part of our real world. In *Loki*, writer Tom Kauffman and director Kate Herron gleefully blow that logical rule right out of the philosophical water. This is the essence of myths, which are stories about *possibilities*.

What allows the tales of Marvel, and others, to be effective is our ability to enter a mythical story world and get emotionally and attentionally caught up in the events that take place there. When we get absorbed by a movie, play, book, or comic, we know we are not in that world ourselves, yet we can imagine it happening. We too can travel in time, albeit mentally—to the past through memory and to the future based on projection. In fact, many cognitive theorists, myself included, would maintain that we don't ever think in the present, but are always ever so slightly projecting ourselves into the very near future. Eye-tracking studies have indicated that our eyes make a saccade a nanosecond before they have the accompanying conscious perceptual thought.

This makes sense of Lewis's Possible Worlds Theory, so maybe that incredulous stare is starting to morph into a knowing nod. We need to inhabit a cognitive multiverse of possibilities to survive as tool-using, fire-making, society-living, and mutually communicating humans. We are wired to plan ahead, and the billions of complex neural connections that are available in our minds give us the mimetic ability to create those possible worlds. This ability to think in the future, to "what if," allows us to perform cognitive tasks as simple as putting on a coat because it is raining outside or as complex as using quantum physics to hypothesize the existence of the multiverse.

Living in a perpetual state of cognitive prediction means that sometimes we simply get it wrong. Our perception can lead us astray, as professional magicians (not the Jungian kind) know full well. A world of endless possibilities can be exhausting and scary, so humans seek out patterns, consistencies, and regularity to temper this. Myths help by providing us with narrative explanations for things we may not be able to understand, or what the mathematician Charles Coulson termed "God of the gaps." A lightning bolt can be explained as a weapon of an angry sky god, or as the Greeks demonstrated, extreme human behaviors can be thought to have been sent by the gods.

Lewis's Possible Worlds Theory was onto something. It can account for why so many cultures adopted polytheism in that their many gods and animist beliefs were projections of their counterfactual minds. As societies became larger, more anonymous, and more highly structured, their spiritualities started to reflect a smaller and smaller number of deities. This is the so-called "big gods" theory, which also leads to monotheism. If this is the case, why are multiversal ideas increasing and so prominent in Marvel?

First, there is the rise and now almost total prominence of computer technologies in our lives, to the point where most of us are completely dependent on them. Independently, computers are reliant on binary-code-driven processing networks, but when coupled with another computer, then another, and so on, their computational power grows exponentially. Add the global interconnectivity of the internet, and we have a truly multiversal generating machine right at our fingertips.

My phone can manage about five thousand times the processing power of my first 1980s home computer, and our multiversal access is carried around all day in our pockets. With the rapidly increasing developments of artificial intelligence where our computers gain processing power by learning from us, we can see that the future of multiversal computer science is almost infinite. Yet, despite this massive diversity of information, we tend to retreat into an echo chamber of opinion, looking to inoculate ourselves from too many possibilities.

This increasingly globalized and often confusing world has led many to draw mythic analogies with multiversal concepts. The contemporary astrophysical explorations of the cosmos are cloaked in science but exist in a kind of mythological nexus. We are still seeking the story of creation and the unseen powers that govern our universe. Marvel's mythic content mirrors this rise in multiversal cognition. Many godlike, omnipotent figures have appeared in Marvel, such as the One Above All, the Beyonder, or the First Firmament. Yet, the Marvel myths themselves quickly usurp their supreme powers, and we are thrust once again into a world of multiversal uncertainty. In this way Marvel myths are not quite science fiction, but rather, scientific mythology.

Marvel is aware of the power of its myths and how the multiverse operates as both a scientific concept and a spiritual idea. In 2004 Mark Waid introduced the "House of Ideas," a term previously used by Marvel to describe itself, as a story element depicting the Fantastic Four busting into a small room occupied by Marvel founding creator Jack Kirby sketching at a table. The mythic heroes think they have found the almighty, but Kirby replies, "What you see is what I am to you . . . that's what my creations do, they find the humanity in god."[7] He goes on to describe the creative process that makes Marvel's myths a blend of "the ordinary and the cosmic." As James wrote of the multiverse, "Parallel possibilities can all exist simultaneously."

The use of multiverse stories in Marvel has proven to be extremely profitable. In the MCU, *Avengers: Endgame* was a metatheatrical multiversal vehicle. In effect, it replayed the same basic plot as the movie that preceded it, *Avengers: Infinity War*. This plot device proved an incredible success with *Endgame*, which grossed $2.797 billion dollars, making it the second-highest-grossing film of all time, just behind another mythologically inspired movie, *Avatar*.

Today, Marvel's multiverse is a vast complex of parallel realities that has become so intertwined and multifaceted that it risks the very existence of *everything*, as some fans bemoan the endless and therefore nonprobabilistic narratives that have been presented. Some might even say that the full-scale adoption of the multiverse in the MCU has shattered the carefully wrought narrative through line that began with *Iron Man* in 2008 and culminated gloriously with *Avengers: Endgame* in 2019.

The MCU's wholehearted adoption of the multiverse in what is described as "Phase 4" (2021–22) has sent the studio into a kind of multiversal retconning hyperdrive.[8] Now heroes can return from the dead, time can be traversed, and old story lines can be effortlessly rebooted. This has been de rigueur in the comic universe since the Watcher introduced the concept in the late '70s. Often this kind of storytelling works brilliantly, such as in *X-Men: Days of Future Past*. Both the 1981 graphic incarnation and the 2014 movie depict a character going back in time to change the outcome of a very bleak future. Though not strictly multiversal, this fantastic story opened up ways in which Marvel narratives could sidestep linear, temporal, or one-dimensional narratives.

The MCU Phase 4 movie multiverse was reflective of our world at that time. We were locked down under Covid-19 restrictions and interacting with each other via screens in our homes. We were even denied the ability to physically travel and explore other real places. Dr. Strange's interdimensional hopping became something of a mimetic wish fulfillment fantasy during those isolating times. While Marvel has now fully opened the nonlinear lid on the multiverse, what they have found is not the singular stable reality of Schrödinger's cat but instead a Pandora's box of endless story possibilities that run the risk of seeming *impossible*. A *Multiverse of Madness* indeed.

What happens then when Marvel's myths are intermixed with the concept of an infinite number of possible worlds? Could this be a problem? Professor of ancient religion Jennifer Larson has shown that for the stories of mythological superheroes and gods to be remembered effectively they need to be minimally counterintuitive concepts. What she means is that they should have one or two very memorable things about them attached to something we understand well. So, a man who is a genius at tech creates a special suit and we have Iron Man, or a boy from Brooklyn gets superpowers and has a strong, iconic shield—Captain America. A hero with many, many different superpowers can become too difficult to comprehend. We start to get overwhelmed by all the possible counterintuitive concepts. Back in the late nineteenth century William James wrote that despite the multiversal qualities of our existence, "there is included in human nature an ingrained naturalism and materialism of mind that can only admit facts that are tangible." Is the multiverse tangible?

At first sight the multiverse would seem to be a storyteller's dream—an infinite number of possibilities where the normal limitations of plot lines can be overturned, reconfigured, or retconned at any time for any reason whatsoever. But in mythological terms is this a good thing? Is the multiverse, which has become so prevalent in the MCU, the polar opposite of what makes myths memorable and is instead an overwhelming, maximally counterintuitive concept? Does the multiverse offer a gateway into wondrous, countless, new, interconnected, mythic worlds, or has it become a narrative millstone for Marvel? Like the great boulder the Titan Sisyphus must repeatedly push up that hill in Hades, could the multiverse roll down and crush the life out of Marvel itself?

Aristotle warned against this kind of mythic implausibility in his famous treatise on performance, *Poetics*. He wrote, "Even chance events are found most astonishing only when they appear to have happened for a purpose."[9] This is because our minds are complex, probability-generating machines. We rely on the active inferences we make of what we perceive around us, which are constantly compared to what we already know. If what we perceive seems completely implausible our cognitive process gets stuck, like Odysseus marooned for seven years on Calypso's island.

Cognitive scientists have named this predictive processing, or what the philosopher Andy Clark calls "surfing uncertainty." This is the theory that as we don't have the cognitive resources, or "free energy," to fully take in everything we see, hear, feel, touch, and taste, we must guess. When I look out my window and see a tree, it resembles other trees I have seen. I don't worry that the part of the tree I can't see is somehow not treelike. I don't walk up to every tree and check. Instead, I quickly scan the scene, see the tree, compare it with the image of a tree stored in my memory, and pay it no more attention.

Our minds work in the same way when we experience stories. Anything surprising or out of place grabs our attention and makes the story memorable and worth telling again. However, if the storyteller goes too far beyond our expectations, we may reject it out of hand as simply unbelievable. The best myths need to fit within our sense of the world we already live in, even if it takes us to another legendary one. Perhaps the concept of a multiverse we might adopt is more like the Vedic version of an infinite Krishna or the Buddhist notion of endless, nestling worlds. And the possibilities *are* endless.

Even the nihilistic antihero Deadpool gets this. In the 2012 comic *Deadpool Kills the Marvel Universe,* he goes on a massive killing spree. He slays the Watcher, all the Marvel heroes, and even his own real-life Marvel creators. Yet the multiverse prevails when he comprehends that his perceptual reality is but one reality of thousands upon thousands. Deadpool's realization is "You can hack away forever and never find the beginning . . . or the end."[10] The chorus of Euripides's *Helen* would agree with him (though a little less psychotically).

Marvel does seem aware of this multiversal dichotomy with their creation of the Time Variance Authority (TVA), a mythical bureaucratic organization that controls the proliferation of the multiverse. This is a meta device for what has happened to Marvel itself. The TVA was first featured in the *Thor* comic in 1986 and then on TV in *Loki* in 2021. In a homage to longtime Marvel writer and editor Mark Gruenwald, and a bit of a Marvel in-joke, the employees of the TVA in the comic were all drawn to look like Gruenwald. Owen Wilson's Moebius character in *Loki* also resembles him. A fitting tribute to the person who originally categorized the different realms of the ever-increasing Marvel multiverse.

In the early 1980s in the *Captain Britain* comic, British creators David Thorpe and Alan Moore decided to call the part of the multiverse we all live in "Earth-616." Since then, the Marvel universe has spun almost out of control, and in the 2015 comic *Avengers World #21* there is now an Earth-28744923048932! No wonder in the movie *Iron Man 3* Tony Stark suffers sporadic panic attacks after his first brush with another dimension in the Battle of New York in *The Avengers.* For all its creativity the Marvel multiverse can seem overwhelming—either a brilliant means of expanding narrative horizons, or a descent into bewildering chaos. Perhaps it was Aristotle who said it best, "The playwright is ether a genius or insane."[11]

CHAPTER 5

PLATO'S BLACK PANTHER

The story of Atlantis is one of the most famous yet misunderstood and misused ancient myths we think we know. Atlantis, the lost city, seems to be everywhere. It appears as the home of Aquaman in DC, a 2001 Disney movie, a BBC fantasy TV series, and in episodes of *Transformers, Doctor Who, Teenage Mutant Ninja Turtles, Phineas and Ferb, SpongeBob SquarePants,* and *Rick and Morty,* to name just a few. Even MacGyver looked for the mythical lost city. In Marvel it is the home of Namor, one of its earliest characters, who first appeared in 1939. The story has seized our imaginations for generations, and there are always new books and internet articles from people who tell us they have found Atlantis. Yet nobody has.

Why are we so fascinated with this particular myth? There are many tales of lost cities, be it Xanadu, El Dorado, or Camelot, but there's something particularly compelling about Atlantis. The myth itself has been used for hundreds of years, not only to entertain us but also to promote highly dangerous and even destructive ideas. Myths can be incredible, time-traveling connectors to the wisdom of our ancestors, but they can also be used to justify and even launch the most horrifying human activities.

The main reason that the Atlantis myth has become so pervasive is that the story originates within the works of one of the ancient world's most influential thinkers, Plato. While all myths contain essential truths about the culture where they are found, Plato used his story of a lost, sunken city as a single allegory in a much bigger project about defining the ideal state. The problem was that Plato was regarded as such a proponent of rational thought in Europe during the Renaissance and Enlightenment that his made-up story was taken literally. The truth is that Plato used mythology and mystic religious themes in all of his works.

Then there is the story itself, which tells of an advanced superstate that occupied a continent somewhere off the coast of Africa beyond the Mediterranean in the Atlantic Ocean. This body of water was named after Atlas, the titan who lived at the edge of the world and supported it on his massive shoulders. Atlas is also the namesake of the Atlas Mountains, the great mountain range that runs through northern Africa, where Atlas was said to be found. So even Plato's choice of the name "Atlantis" gives us a clue that this place was always meant to be mythical.

It is a compelling idea that there was once a lost continent somewhere in the Atlantic Ocean. When Europeans first became aware of the Americas in the fifteenth century, many thought that this was Plato's Atlantis. When they began to find the remains of highly advanced cultures there, rather than credit them to the ancestors of the indigenous people they encountered, many assumed that these must have been made by refugees from Atlantis. You can see where this is going: the new application of the myth falls in lockstep with the new colonial enterprises and the ideas of cultural and racial superiority that came along with them.

By the twentieth century the myth of Atlantis was very well known and mostly completely misunderstood. Most people were receiving it not from Plato but rather in works such as Jules Verne's *20,000 Leagues Under the Sea*, in which Captain Nemo visits the sunken city in his incredible underwater ship, or in Edgar Rice Burroughs's *The Return of Tarzan* from 1913, in which the lost city of Opar, a colony of Atlantis, appears. There were countless novels based on the myth, and serious and nefarious attempts to find it.

In 2022 when Marvel's *Black Panther: Wakanda Forever* opened, a movie that also mined the Atlantis myth, the second most watched Netflix show that November was entitled *Ancient Apocalypse*. Its premise was that an advanced age old civilization was destroyed by flooding around twelve thousand years ago and that this event inspired the story of Atlantis. Then, according to this show, the refugees from this cataclysmic event spread throughout the world, taking the knowledge of their advanced culture to places such as Bolivia, Mexico, Egypt, and Indonesia. They taught the peoples of these places how to build pyramids, live in cities, and develop great civilizations. This entire theory, which has no basis in any archaeological, ancient DNA, or textual evidence at all, maintains that the people who lived there could not have done it for themselves. Basically, it was the same old wrongheaded mythical chestnut recycled for a new audience.

What Marvel did with *Black Panther*, especially in its MCU incarnations, was take the Atlantean allegory of the advanced lost city and place it in Africa. While this could be seen as a reappropriation of a myth—taking a European story and reframing it as an African one—I think it is the other way around. As we shall see, Atlantis was always an African story, albeit once told by a Greek. In telling the story, *Black Panther* brings us closer to what Plato intended than most of the many thousands of books, articles, and websites about Atlantis.

Our fascination with Atlantis has a long history. In the sixteenth century when the Americas were first becoming known to Europeans, eminent thinkers such as Sir Frances Bacon in England, Francisco López de Gómara in Spain, and Alexander von Humboldt in Prussia all believed that the so-called new world was the lost continent of Atlantis. Then, when the impressive remains of the ancient Maya culture were found by Europeans, they assumed they must have been built by a more advanced culture. But who?

One theory was put forward by Ignatius Donnelly in 1882. He was the son of Irish immigrants, an American congressperson, and the cofounder of a failed utopian community in Minnesota called Nininger City. It was described by the *Minneapolis Post* as "Donnelly's lost Atlantis on the Mississippi" because he was the author of a book entitled *Atlantis: The Antediluvian World.* In it, he claimed that Atlantis was destroyed by a great flood and its people dispersed to establish all the major ancient civilizations of the world. He believed these were the Aryans, fair-haired blue-eyed people whose descendants, according to Donnelly, can be found today in Ireland! The theory sounds totally wacky, right? Except Graham Hancock, the author and presenter of Netflix's *Ancient Apocalypse,* cites Donnelly eight times in his 1995 book *Fingerprints of the Gods.*

Stories of Atlantis abounded in Europe, both as fiction and history. However, in Germany in 1930s the myth started to be used to promote ideas of northern European racial superiority, antisemitic views, and other Nazi propaganda. Albert Herrmann, a professor at Berlin University, wrote that Atlantis was a lost Germanic continent, and Alfred Rosenberg, who went on to be a prominent Nazi, argued in his book *The Myth of the Twentieth Century* that Jesus Christ was a descendent of Aryan refugees from Atlantis. Hitler awarded the book a prize in 1937 and said it "laid the firm foundation for an understanding of the ideological basis of National Socialism." Such views were championed by Edmund Kiss, a German architect who went on to become an officer in the Waffen-SS.

Kiss was credited by the Nazis with locating Atlantis. He believed that the ancient site of Tiwanaku in Bolivia was created by refugees from the sunken city fleeing a global ice age created by a moon strike on Earth. For Kiss and other proponents of these theories, the Atlanteans were Nordic people and members of the Aryan "race," the supposed ancestors of all "pure blooded Germans." He even published a book called *The Last Queen of Atlantis*, which surmised that the northern land known to the Greeks as Thule was Atlantis. In reality Thule was most likely Iceland. Kiss's book also told of a mythical Nordic Atlantean leader with the implausibly modern northern European name of Baldur Weiborg.

If this all seems like a plot from an Indiana Jones movie, Spielberg was not far off. Kiss's elaborate theories made their way into Hitler Youth magazines and other Nazi publications. His 1937 book *The Sun Gate of Tihuanaku and Hörbiger's Theory of World Ice* so impressed Heinrich Himmler that he ordered the research division of his SS to investigate where the Atlanteans migrated to. He then presented a leather-bound copy of Kiss's book to Hitler on his fiftieth birthday in 1939.

What has been missed among all those Nordic giants, Irish culture heroes, white-skinned, auburn-haired visitors, and ancient cataclysms is who told the original story of Atlantis and why.

We know about Atlantis from two texts by the Athenian philosopher Plato, called *Timaeus* and *Critias*, both written in the fourth century BCE.[1] All other mentions of the place in antiquity derive from these first references to Atlantis. There is to date no physical evidence at all of Atlantis despite the hundreds, even thousands, of attempts to find the ancient sunken city.

In these dialogues, Critias, a young Athenian student of Socrates, tells his teacher how his grandfather heard the story of Atlantis from Solon, the famous Athenian lawgiver. Solon said that he had been in Egypt where a priest told him about Atlantis. What he learned there was that nine thousand years before, the sea god Poseidon had built a fortified city in a land somewhere past the Pillars of Herakles (probably Gibraltar). Poseidon initially built Atlantis as a prison for a mortal princess named Cleito so he could rape her. Cleito bore ten children to Poseidon, and they became the leaders of the city as it expanded. They increased the fortifications, and the original citadel of Cleito was surrounded by concentric circles of waterways. The Atlanteans went on to develop many advanced technologies and a powerful navy. But Atlantis was a repressive place, ruled by a confederation of monarchs, with no citizen participation. The city waged war on Europe and Africa, and enslaved the peoples of the Mediterranean. The priest tells Solon that only egalitarian Athens, with its just society, was able to stand up to Atlantis. When Poseidon's city was defeated and shamed by the plucky Athenians, the furious god shook the Earth, flooded its causeways, and sank it beneath the seas.

Plato tells the Atlantis story for a reason: it is a response to a philosophical discussion about the ideal city-state put forward in his work *The Republic*. This is an exploration of a utopian *kallipolis*, or "beautiful city," where justice, virtue, and ethics reside in harmony with each other ruled over by a benevolent philosopher-king. Plato even travelled to Sicily to try to influence the real Dionysius II of Syracuse to lead with these principles. Unfortunately, Dionysius ended up showing his true nature as a petty tyrant, and Plato had to leave Syracuse after a spell in prison!

Critias and *Timaeus* were written when Plato returned to Athens and can be viewed as a metaphor for the corruption he found in Syracuse, which, like the fictional Atlantis, was a western Mediterranean naval power. Atlantis is a corrupt city, built to facilitate rape and imprisonment, and obsessed with material objects, status, and wealth. On the other hand, the Egyptian priest told how the Athenians at that time lived in an agricultural collective society where land and property were evenly distributed. This is a story of the smaller, humbler, and more just state defeating the far more powerful and wealthier despotic one.

In creating the myth of Atlantis, Plato was using an allegory to prove a point about what kind of city Athens should be. At that time in the mid-fourth century BCE, Athens was no longer the strong naval power it had been a century earlier, but it was regarded as an important site of art, culture, learning, and trade. Athens was also a democracy, which Plato was not that happy about. He felt that when he was a young man the city had devolved into a kind of mob rule that he called a *theatrocracy*, a "spectacle state" where the people were swayed by flashy presentations and emotions, rather than reason.[2] His own teacher, Socrates, who is the main character in his dialogues, was executed by a democratic court in 399 BCE after Athens lost the long war with Sparta and had suffered several coups and a good deal of civil strife. Plato never forgave the Athenian democracy and so was passionate about finding a political system that he felt was truly just. However, the kind of repressive aristocracy that ruled the mythic Atlantis was not what he had in mind.

It is clear why Plato centers the story around Solon. He was a historical figure who has also been shrouded in myth. Solon probably lived from around 630 to 560 BCE and was credited with introducing reforms that curtailed the power of the landowning aristocrats and stopped people being thrown into servitude because of debt. This was all the more remarkable because Solon was an aristocrat himself and hailed from a very old Athenian family with roots back to an ancient king. Because of his reforms Aristotle called Solon "the champion of the people." Solon was then said to have left Athens for ten years to travel the known world, and the first place he was said to have visited was Egypt.

We hear in Plato that the story of Atlantis was told to Solon by a priest of the goddess Neith at her temple at Sais, now called Sa El-Hagar, in Egypt. Little survives today, but in antiquity there was a large temple complex on the northern Nile Delta and a spectacular ceremonial lake. The Greek historian Herodotus visited in the fifth century BCE and reported that Sais was one of the resting places of the god Osiris, who he said was Dionysus.[3] He wrote about secret mystery rites that were held there and connected them to the mysteries of Demeter at Eleusis near Athens. The mysteries were incredibly important to the Greeks, many of whom underwent the long imitation process to be a *mytsai*—a person who had undergone the secret rites of Demeter, a term derived from the Greek verb "I close," meaning that they could never reveal what they underwent on pain of death. Plato was a *mystai*, and there are veiled references to the mysteries all over his work. Herodotus thought that the mysteries originated in Egypt before coming to Greece, so it is significant that the story of Atlantis is told to Solon, a quasi-mythical Athenian founding father figure, at the place where the mysteries were said to have begun. Perhaps an unintended result of this connection is that for time immemorial the story of Atlantis would itself be shrouded in mystery.

The temple of Neith, the African goddess of war and strategy who Herodotus compared to Athena, stands on the Nile Delta, where the people who worshipped, traded, and worked there absorbed and transmitted the cultural influences of Africa up and down the great river from Nubia and Ethiopia, along Africa's Mediterranean coastline, and southwest across the extensive connections crisscrossing the Sahara. The temple looked southeast via the Arabian Peninsula, due east through the Middle and Near Eastern worlds, and directly north to Greece. If ever there was a place of extensive ancient cultural exchange it was Sais. Little wonder the priests there had all the best stories.

That Egypt was viewed by many Greeks as a place of ancient wisdom and culture is incontestable. This also applied to other parts of the African continent, such as Nubia and Ethiopia, as well. In the mid-eighth to mid-seventh centuries BCE, a time of intensive cultural exchange between Greece and Africa, Egypt was ruled by Pharaohs from the Nubian Kingdom of Kush (modern-day Sudan). We see this fascination with all things African in Homer's *Iliad* and *Odyssey*, where the Ethiopians regularly dine with the gods. The Greeks had been crisscrossing the Mediterranean Sea since before the Bronze Age, exchanging influences with the peoples who lived there, and founding cities, including Naukratis in Egypt. Aristotle said that there were so many Greeks scattered along the Mediterranean coast that he described them as "frogs living around a pond."[4] Most people still tend to think of Mediterranean countries as Greece, Turkey, the Levant, Italy, Spain, and France, but just a quick look at a map reminds us that about half of the Mediterranean coast is the northern shore of Africa.

The problem is that this interconnected cultural relationship between Africa and Greece in antiquity has been viewed through the lens of Europe and its imperial and colonial enterprises. It was either ignored or deemed incomprehensible based on the view most people held at the time of Africa as an "uncivilized" place. However, the 1970s and '80s began to see sophisticated approaches to ancient Africa by scholars such as Frank Snowden Jr. Today things are perhaps even more fraught, with ancient Greek and Roman culture being hijacked by groups looking to promote those same old misguided ideas about ethnic and racial superiority. Stepping away from our own contemporary culture wars, we know that the situation in antiquity was far more fluid and dynamic. While ideas about racial superiority are not found in antiquity, the Greeks still saw the world as Greek or non-Greek, based on language and culture. They called anyone who did not speak Greek a barbarian, which means people who say "ba ba ba ba." With that being said, they knew that the Persians and other peoples in the East had highly sophisticated, wealthy, and developed cultures as did the many peoples they encountered in Africa.

Although the Greeks certainly recognized the political boundaries of the kingdom of Egypt, they also regarded it as a part of Africa or Libya, as the continent was also known. As for the ancient Egyptians themselves, we don't even find them using a specific name for their region until the Middle Kingdom, around 2000 BCE. What's more, their communities were connected to all points of the compass on the African continent via extensive trade, military, diplomatic, and festival routes. In pre-dynastic Egypt, the people who lived along the banks of the Nile practiced cow-herding and horticulture in the same way as people had done for thousands of years stretching from what is now Kenya to the Mediterranean coast of Egypt.

The Egyptians themselves, like many people of the Mediterranean basin, reflected the genetic makeup of the people who lived around them, those who migrated there, and those who conquered them. This included people from North Africa, the Middle East, and later, Greece, as well as Nubians and others from the south who we would now identify as Black.

When the scale and sophistication of ancient Egyptian culture became clear to Europeans in the eighteenth and nineteenth centuries, Egypt was conceptually broken away from Africa and regarded as a separate and distinctive place. Today when we visit the Metropolitan Museum in New York, for example, the Egyptian galleries are in a completely different section from the African ones. This creates an artistic and cultural division that did not exist in antiquity. Additionally, many Egyptians today balk at being described as African, preferring to identify as being of Egyptian nationality. However, we should not project modern ideas about the nation-state, religion, and ethnicity back on antiquity.

Another idea about ancient Egyptian identity is that they migrated there from the Near East. This one has shades of the Atlantis myth about it, in that it claims that the cultural advances of Egypt were not African but by people from the Levant. There are a lot of problems with this view, one being that the ancient Egyptians did not speak a Levantine language, which they surely would have done had they come from that region, and the second being that the ancient DNA evidence gathered so far does not support this.

I will let prominent Egyptologist Shomarka Keita have the final word on the subject of ancient Egyptian identity:

> *Who were the ancient Egyptians? What was their "identity"? What was ancient Egypt? They were a people and society that emerged in the Saharo-Nilotic [Sahara Desert and the Nile from Egypt to Tanzania] region of Northeast Africa. They created a culture that was flexible in its ability to assimilate foreigners and borrow and transform things of interest from many places. Their groundings in the Saharo-Nilotic African world were never lost.*[5]

When Stan Lee and Jack Kirby introduced Black Panther in 1966, they were well aware that they were addressing the lack of Black characters in their comics. In that first *Fantastic Four* story we are introduced to Wakanda as an African nation that had never been colonized, a secret place with advanced technologies unknown to most people. It was an African Atlantis. This attempt at a positive Afrocentric portrayal was surely a product of its times and can seem a bit clumsy now, but *Black Panther* was at least trying to speak to Marvel readers during the height of the Civil Rights era. A glimpse into Marvel's motivations behind the creation of characters like Black Panther can be found in one of Stan Lee's Stan's Soapbox commentaries that appeared in the Marvel comics dated November 1968, where he wrote passionately about the destructiveness of bigotry and racism and that "unlike a team of costumed super-villains, they can't be halted with a punch in the snoot, or a zap from a ray gun," rather they needed to be exposed to be destroyed.[6]

When Marvel's new character Black Panther hit the comic racks, the modern nation-state of Egypt was building the massive Aswan Dam, which at that time, was among the largest in the world. The huge structure cost more than $1 billion and was intended to create hydroelectric power, be a plentiful water source, and control the annual flooding of the Nile. The dam would create the more-than-two-thousand-square-mile Lake Nasser, but it would also submerge an area of rich archaeological interest, including the great temples at Abu Simbel built by Ramses II. Archaeologists and engineers rushed in to save these ancient structures before they would be lost forever in a modern version of the submerging of Atlantis. Once they started to dig, what they found proved astounding.

Scholars had known about the cities of Kush, Meroe, and Napata to the south of Egypt dating from about 3000 BCE to 300 CE. They had already excavated some temples and pyramids and assumed these were built by the Egyptians who had invaded and conquered them. What they discovered in their frenetic rush of activity before Lake Nasser was created was that these were not isolated Egyptian structures but parts of an entire, powerful, and very wealthy Nubian kingdom. It was as if they had uncovered a lost civilization.

Archaeologists had now recovered irrefutable material proof of a powerful Nubian culture, and monumental cities such as Meroe and Napata. The old model of Egyptian colonization crumbled. Now it is clear that there was a constant back-and-forth of influence, culture, and power up and down the Nile in antiquity, not some false divide between "Black" or "Sub Saharan Africa" and Egypt. Yes, there were certainly times that Egyptian armies came south and dominated the region, but there was also at least a century when Nubian Pharaohs ruled over Egypt, the so-called Twenty-Fifth Dynasty. Despite attempts by the Assyrians, who eventually defeated the Kushites to erase them from history, we know the names of these ancient Nubian rulers: Piye, Shabaka, Shebitku, Taharqa, and Tantamani.

In 1972 Marvel briefly changed the name of Black Panther to

Black Leopard and were quite overt about the reason why, having T'Challa say, "The latter term [Black Panther] has *political* connotations. I neither condemn nor condone those who have taken up the name, but *T'Challa* is a law unto *himself.* Hence, the *new* name—a *minor* point, at best, since the panther *is* a leopard."[7] T'Challa was quite correct—"panther" is a Greek word that indicates a big cat with a speckled coat, what we would call a "leopard," another Greek word that means "spotted lion." Panther skins were symbols of Kushite royalty, a black panther skin is worn in the *Egyptian Book of the Dead* by King Pepi as he enters heaven, and the Nubian goddess Bastet, who was also worshipped in Egypt, was often depicted as a black panther. Those real Kushite Pharaohs of the Twenty-Fifth Dynasty were in many ways the progenitors of Marvel's mythical Black Panther. The uncovering of Kush in the late 1960s and the discovery of a vibrant, powerful, ancient African kingdom is like the fictitious revelation of Wakanda, or the mythic story of Atlantis in reverse—Kush being saved from the deluge.

The director of both *Black Panther* movies, Ryan Coogler, has spoken about the Eurocentric domination of Atlantis.

> *Historically, a lot of myth internationally about this idea of a hidden place in the water—lost continents and things like that—you could go into a Google wormhole looking at this. I think that because we live in a society that's very much permeated by Western thinking and Western ideas, that Greco-Roman concept of Atlantis, Plato's Concept, [has] permeation of our consciousness. But there are other concepts . . . I wanted to make something that could stand in a cinematic pantheon beside those films and be different, but still truthful.*[8]

Coogler is talking about the creation of the lost underwater kingdom of Talokan in the MCU's *Black Panther* 2022 sequel, *Wakanda*

Forever. This version of Atlantis was ruled over by his reboot of Namor as the serpent god from Maya mythology called K'uk'ulkan. This is based on an Aztec myth about the realm of Tlālōcān, a hidden paradise associated with the afterlife. Yet the fictional African kingdom of Wakanda itself is in many ways another version of the lost city of Atlantis, albeit a more positive one. From the time of its first appearance in Marvel's *Fantastic Four* comic in 1966, this mythical African nation was conceived as having advanced technologies based on deposits of the rare meteoric metal Vibranium. Likewise, there is a mythical precious metal detailed in Plato's account of Atlantis called Orichalcum, a brass or bronze-like alloy that was said to have been used to build the mighty Atlantean walls.

The MCU's *Black Panther* movies helped open hearts and minds of a new audience to a positive and confident depiction of Africa that challenged prevailing stereotypes. Of course, it could not be all things for everybody. Some saw the role of the villain Killmonger as problematic—the African American cousin fighting against the African king. Was this a comment on the effects of racial oppression or the propagation of a racist stereotype? But the world of *Black Panther* was embedded with historical Egyptian and Yoruba gods, and African languages, customs, textiles, and designs to present a flourishing and formidable Wakanda.

When I saw *Avengers: Endgame* at my local movie theatre, there was a huge cheer from the audience towards the end. T'Challa, his sister, Shuri, and Okoye, the commander of the Wakandan women warriors the Dora Milaje, appear, backlit by the glow of an interdimensional portal to join the fight against Thanos and his forces. Captain America is exhausted, and all seems lost, and yet it is the Wakandans who come first to save the Earth, just as they did at the culmination of *Infinity War.* With Wakanda, Marvel reverses Plato's story that makes Atlantis a despotic regime. Here, the African lost city more closely resembles the mythical Athens that saved the ancient Mediterranean world. Though not an egalitarian society as Plato describes, Wakanda is certainly an equalitarian one, where men and women are equal in power, and Plato himself might have recognized in T'Challa something of his philosopher-king.

There is another important African connection to the Atlantis myth that is a little more obscure to us but would have resonated with the Athenians. It indicates that the ancient Greeks had their own version of a mythical Black Panther. In Plato, Critias says that the story of Atlantis was told to him by his father at a festival called the Apaturia. This was held in the fall when new citizens were presented to and accepted into their demes (districts), the local communities of the Athenians and the origin of the word "democracy" from *demos kratos,* meaning "power of the people from the demes." Athens for most of the classical period was a democracy, and the Apaturia was an important event.

The myth of the founding of the Apaturia festival is that a king from Boeotia, the region to the north of Athens, challenged the Athenian king to single combat. The elderly Athenian monarch sought a champion to fight in his stead. No Athenian stepped forward. Then a mysterious man from Pylos, an ancient city far west of Greece, responded to the call. His name was Melanthus or "the Black One," and the name of the Boeotian king he was to fight was Xanthus, "the Red or Yellow One."

Perhaps these names developed to highlight the contrast between the two warriors. The name Xanthus, or Xanthius, was often given to people from Scythia in the north who typically had red hair and were considered barbarians, what we would call a "ginger" (I am one, so I would know). As for Melanthus, he came from Pylos, a city associated with another compelling mythological figure known as Melampous, or "Black Foot." There's certainly a connection.

Now before I go any further, there is a lot of debate about names that contain the word *melan,* meaning "dark" or "black" in Greek literature. When these terms are analyzed along with the words for white (*leukra*) or fair (*xanthus*) they don't always line up into binary opposites. Sometimes, black is negative, as in the blackness of Hades, and sometimes positive and powerful, as in the black ships the Greeks sailed to Troy. Sometimes death itself was expressed by darkness and sometimes by paleness.

So, does the way the Greeks framed color mean every time we meet a mythological character with *melan* in their name we should assume they are Black? Probably not. The name may have been inherited, but when we do find a mythological character named "the Black One" or "Black Foot," then it's probably safe to say that this shows some essential feature about them.

Melanthus, "the Black One," comes from Pylos, and this geographic connection adds another important element to the story. Pylos was a thriving Bronze Age harbor city on the western coast of the Peloponnese. There is still an impressive half-moon beach there today, and one can easily imagine ancient ships from Africa, Phoenicia, Asia Minor, Italy, and other Greek cities docked there and trading their goods.

Melanthus and Melampous may be one and the same figure with slightly different names. *Melampodes* was also an ancient name for Egypt, according to an important Greek text on mythology known as the *Bibliotheca*.[9] Melampous (and by extension Melanthus) may be mythical names for an Egyptian, a Black man, or both.

The historian and mythographer Herodotus tells us that Melampous introduced the cult of Dionysus to Greece, was a famous seer, and learned much of his healing arts in Egypt. So here is a myth that a mystical Black hero came from Africa to Pylos bringing knowledge to achieve incredible things and new ways to worship certain gods. When Athens needs a hero, he shows up to fight in the city's name. It reminds me of T'Challa's entrance at the end of *Endgame*.

Pylos is also important to this story. We now have amazing new archaeological evidence of the African-Greek exchange found in a Bronze Age grave shaft in Pylos from around 1500 BCE. The recent excavations headed by Jack Davis and Sharon Stocker were already proving close connections to Africa when a gold cup with distinctive embossed spirals was discovered, which looked remarkably like one depicted on a wall painting in Thebes in Egypt from the same time.

Then in 2019, another remarkable find: several graves lined in gold leaf, an incredibly expensive undertaking in Bronze Age Greece. In one of those graves, a stunning gold pendant was uncovered and on it was something extraordinary—the face of Hathor, the ancient African goddess of fertility with deep roots in the cattle-herding culture of Nubia and Egypt. Why was this Greek noble from Pylos buried with such a distinctive symbol of African religion? Did he worship this African deity, or was it an important gift and sign of his wealth and status? We are starting to uncover tangible evidence that those stories of Black heroes and healers coming to the aid of the Greeks are rooted in a real connection between Africa and Greece.

There are more myths of this ancient "Black Panther." He was a shaman figure who became the king of Argos. Pausanias the second-century CE writer said that the region was settled by African refugees, including the beautiful city of Nafplio.[10] In the myth of the Danaids fifty young Black women fled Egypt and claimed descent from Io, the princess of Argos who had been transformed into a cow. According to this myth Io ended up on the coast of Africa, where she was touched by Zeus and founded the line of Egypt.[11] Io the cow is related to "Cow Faced" Hera, who looks back to the African goddess Hathor, depicted as a cow or with a cow face. It is the striking face of Hathor on that incredible Egyptian golden pendant found at Pylos.

The myth of the Danaids has one more amazing twist to reveal. The Argives lost a war with Egypt over the fleeing girls, and they were forced to marry their Egyptian cousins. Instead of consummating their forced marriages, the Egyptian girls all killed their new husbands on their wedding night. All except Hypermnestra, who fell in love with her cousin, Lynceus. This couple from Egypt then become the king and queen of Argos, founding the family of none other than Perseus and Herakles. Two of the most famous of all Greek heroes trace their lineage back to Africa. Today the ancient Greek hero Perseus, whose grandparents were African, would probably be described as mixed-race.

When Solon visited the Temple of Sais and heard the story of Atlantis, he would have stood under great columns capped with the beautiful cow face of the African goddess Hathor, the same face that was found on that magnificent gold necklace in Pylos. In that ancient visage he would have recognized the Greek goddess Hera and been well aware of the close ties between Africa and Greece. *Black Panther* offers us a new way to engage with the myth of Atlantis while also looking back at the myth's roots in the close reciprocal relationship between the early Greek world and ancient Africa.

The point of the Atlantis myth is that an opulent, materialist, arrogant, and oppressive imperial power was soundly defeated by a much smaller egalitarian democracy. Then Poseidon sank it beneath the sea. We will never find Atlantis because the gods were ashamed of it. Perhaps it is time we stopped looking.

CHAPTER 6

MEDEA MAXIMOFF

A young woman with incredible magical powers leaves her homeland in Eastern Europe. She helps a band of heroes who are intent on retrieving a golden talismanic object, which can change the destiny of realms. Because of her magical abilities the young woman is considered a sorceress and feared in her community. She sees this foreign band of heroes as an opportunity to escape with her brother and start a new life. But there is a price for this choice, and her dear brother is sacrificed to save the heroes as they flee her homeland.

This young woman continues to help the heroes in their quests, but her abilities are too powerful and seem out of control. She decides to try to live a settled life with one of the heroes and raise their two sons. But this is an illusion. Her powers are misunderstood and feared by others, and she is regarded as a mysterious outsider. Her partner cannot live in the world she created for herself, and she sinks into despair. Dark forces appear within her. Finally in an act of tragic proportions, she destroys her children and removes them from the world she made.

Other people now see her as a witch and angrily condemn her. She fully embraces this identity and soars above them in the sky, resplendent in her new unearthly powers.

Some may recognize this as the story of Marvel's Wanda Maximoff or the Scarlet Witch, and others will see the myth of Medea, the sorcerer of Greek mythology. Their stories are remarkably similar. What is it about witches that both compels and repulses us? Has it always been this way, or are they a mythological product of deeper forces operating in our culture? In this chapter we are going to look at three powerful women who were labeled as witches: the Greek story of Medea, Marvel's Wanda, and a woman who dared to challenge the origin story of Europe, Marija Gimbutas.

Most people came to know Wanda Maximoff from the 2015 movie *Avengers: Age of Ultron*. She left her home in the fictitious Eastern European nation of Sokovia after her brother, Pietro, sacrificed himself to save Hawkeye. Wanda then joins the Avengers, but after her powers are considered too unpredictable, she is removed from service and placed under the guardianship of the "living" android Vision. They fall in love, but Vision dies fighting Thanos. Then in the 2021 TV series *WandaVision* she is living in sitcom-like domestic bliss with Vision and their two sons. But it is all an illusion to ease Wanda's grief. Ultimately, she faces a stark choice, relinquish her powers to a witch called Agatha, or embrace her sorcery and destroy her imaginary family. At the culmination of the series, she ascends above Westview in her new guise as the Scarlet Witch and leaves to embrace her supernatural identity.

WandaVision, created by Jac Schaeffer, was a brilliant piece of serialized television, witty, metatheatrical, absorbing, and ultimately heartbreaking. This is the essence of an effective myth: the fictional story world reflects the real tensions, concerns, and questions of those it is told to. In parodying decades of American sitcoms, this show asked us to look at women's roles in our society and rethink the concept of the witch. Have we always marginalized and feared women with exceptional abilities? Can such a woman find love, acceptance, a home, and a family? *WandaVision* humanized the witch figure, even as we watched her become increasingly drawn to the dark side of her powers.

Medea is most well-known to us from the myth of Jason and the Golden Fleece. Jason was the son of King Aeson of Thessaly in northern Greece and the kingdom's rightful heir, but his father was overthrown by Pelias, Aeson's half brother. Pelias, determined to hold on to power, ordered all the male family members of Aeson to be killed. Jason was just a baby and was saved by the quick thinking of his mother, Alcimede. She had women surround Jason and scream, cry, and wail as if he had been stillborn. Alcimede then smuggled the child out of Thessaly to be raised by Chiron the centaur. (Yes, that's the same Chiron who schools Percy Jackson in the Rick Riordan books.)

Jason reaches adulthood and returns to Thessaly to confront Pelias. Rather than fight, Pelias seems to accept that the rightful heir has returned and says he will give up the throne once Jason brings him the golden fleece. This was the coat of a magical flying ram that was kept in a cave guarded by a serpent in the far-off land of Colchis on the eastern side of the Black Sea (modern-day Georgia).

Jason assembles a band of fifty heroes to help him in his quest, including Herakles and the famed shipwright Argus, who builds a new ship for them named the *Argo*. Jason is guided by Hera, because as the guardian of mothers and newborns she wants to see him succeed and claim his rightful place. Pelias had also killed an elderly woman as she sought sanctuary in Hera's temple, so she really wants him gone.

After a long journey with many adventures—and if you haven't, do watch the exceptional 1963 movie *Jason and the Argonauts* with those brilliant stop-motion capture special effects by Ray Harryhausen that still put a lot of today's CGI to shame—Jason arrives in Colchis. There, the king Aeëtes, not wanting to do battle with the Argonauts, sets Jason three tasks to win the fleece. First, he has to yoke two massive, bronze, fire-breathing bulls that Hephaestus made, then plow the earth with them, and finally sew that ground with serpent's teeth.

These are near-impossible tasks. Not only do the bulls instantly incinerate anyone who comes near them, the dragon's teeth produce fully armed warriors ready to fight. Ray Harryhausen's rendition of them as skeletons armed with swords and shields was particularly effective. Jason is only able to complete these heroic tasks because of the help given to him by Aeëtes's daughter, Medea. She has deep knowledge of the arts of the *pharmakos*, ancient shamanistic healing practices using herbal remedies, poisons, and antidotes. She is supremely intelligent and connected to the divine as the granddaughter of Helios, the sun. Medea rubs a secret ointment on Jason to protect him from the fiery breath of the bulls, and she confuses the warriors by throwing a rock between them, causing them to fight each other and sparing Jason.

Aeëtes is not worried yet. The golden fleece is guarded by a fearsome serpent that will devour anyone who goes near it. In some versions of the myth, the serpent does ingest Jason; there is an Athenian vase from the fifth century BCE that shows a limp Jason hanging out of the great snake's open mouth.[1] Here Medea has put Jason to sleep and again protected him with an ointment. In other versions the serpent is lulled to sleep by Medea. Either way, Jason would never have completed any of these tasks without her.

Why does Medea help this foreigner steal from her father? We are told that Hera, Jason's guardian, has Aphrodite make Medea fall in love with him, but this also has dire consequences. The couple flee with their prize, and Medea brings her younger brother with them. As they are pursued by the king, Medea kills her brother, cuts him into pieces, and scatters them so her father will be compelled to stop to retrieve his body, allowing Jason and Medea to escape with the fleece.

When they arrive in Thessaly, King Pelias refuses to cede the throne to Jason as he had agreed, so Medea tricks his daughters into killing him. She shows them how to revive an old ram by chopping it up, putting the parts in boiling water, adding her herbs, and presto! A lamb jumps out. The daughters try to copy Medea's healing magic by chopping up their father, but it doesn't work. However, the plan backfires when the people find out what Medea has done, and so Medea and Jason are forced to flee yet again and eventually settle in the city of Corinth as exiles.

For the Greeks, Medea was not only the daughter of a strange foreign king, but what Sarah Iles Johnston has described as a powerful "reproductive demon." She shared a sanctuary near Corinth at Akraia next to the temple of Hera, who presided over childbirth. Women there prayed to both goddesses for help during pregnancy and birth. Childbirth could be precarious in antiquity, with high infant mortality rates. At Corinth, it was Medea in her guise as a local goddess who helped with birth as a kind of divine midwife. But just as Medea could bring forth a baby and seem to revive it when in peril, she also had the power to take the child's life.

Medea is a priestess and a healer too. Her home of Colchis was renowned as a place of ancient healing arts, especially by women, so much so that Hippocrates, the "father of medicine," went there to study and learn from the local "mothers of medicine." It is not a coincidence that Medea's name sounds like "medicine," as the Greek root *médos* means "to think deeply, to have knowledge, and to plan." Hence our words "meditate," "mediation," and, of course, "medical." We should view Medea and her knowledge of herbal pharmacology, toxins, and her medical abilities with this in mind. When we read about her chopping up people, is this a mythical reference to ancient surgical practices? Or a ritual *sparagmos*, a sacrificial act of tearing the flesh?

Once we know Medea as a goddess of childbirth and death, the story of the golden fleece reads quite a bit differently. The fleece was in Colchis to begin with because two children were under threat of death. It was sent by the cloud goddess Nephele, to fly her two offspring, Phrixus and Helle, away from their homicidal stepmother. Helle didn't make it and fell into the sea at the Dardanelles on the northwestern coast of Turkey, which is why it was called the Hellespont. Phrixus was taken in by King Aeëtes, and so he gifted the king the golden fleece.

And remember, Jason was also supposed to be killed as a child. His mother saved him by pretending that he was stillborn. Jason was figuratively brought back from the dead. In this way he was *regenerated.*

Medea is connected to the Scarlet Witch in a direct line of wise women, priestesses, and female healers also found in Greek myth. Medea's aunt is Circe, the sorcerer on whose island Odysseus spends a year after she magically turns his crew into pigs and then regenerates them as men again. Her other aunt was Pasiphaë, the mother of the half man–half bull Minotaur who was imprisoned in the labyrinth in Crete. As the daughter of Helios, Pasiphaë may have been a version of a Minoan sun goddess. These powerful, knowledgeable women were frequently associated with Hecate, a goddess of magic, the moon, the night, and the crossing points from one realm to the next. Hesiod, the archaic Greek poet, wrote than Zeus honored Hecate "above all others," respectful of her great powers. Hecate is the deity that Medea places above all, and in some myths Medea is even her priestess.

Wanda Maximoff's backstory has many parallels to Medea's, although humbler. In the MCU she is the daughter of Iryna and Olek and was raised in Novi Grad, Sokovia. A Stark Industries missile hits her apartment building and kills her parents. In the comics, she and Pietro are adopted and raised by Romani parents Marya and Django. Her real mother is later revealed as Natalya Maximoff, an earlier incarnation of the Scarlet Witch. Like all myths, the comics have different versions of her parentage, including the superheroes Whizzer and Miss America.

Sokovia is a fictional place. It is presented as being in central Europe next to Slovakia and the Czech Republic, modern countries that are located close to Ukraine. Myths are often unconsciously coincidental as they can imbed long forgotten memories in the stories we tell. This region is currently the epicenter of cutting-edge work being carried out on ancient DNA that is changing what we thought we knew about the ancient peoples of Europe, Northern and Central Africa, and much of East Asia. What is now showing up in the DNA has long been transmitted by our myths: prior to a massive migration/invasion around 3300–2500 BCE of a people who were the first to domesticate horses and herd cattle from the Eurasian Steppes (Ukraine to Manchuria), men and women may well have held equal power.

Medea and Wanda are both part of a long tradition of mythical memorialization of cultures that once existed where it was normal for women to exercise knowledge and authority alongside men. Hence, we have found evidence of women warriors, like the Amazonian myths we have already looked at, as well as women leaders, priests, and medical practitioners. Medea and the Scarlet Witch are mythic memories of these medicine women and fertility goddesses. Whereas now we have come to see them as witches and marginalized, even detested, figures, in antiquity they would have been perceived as the Killer Regeneratrix, the ancient goddess of the cycles of life. This term was initially applied in the 1970s by another gifted woman who was among the first to publish evidence for a mass invasion into Europe from the Steppes and propose that this migration supplanted an existing "equalitarian" society. Many at that time regarded this as a fringe view, radical feminism, or Earth Mother–movement nonsense. Others even believed that the author considered herself as some sort of Witch.[2] This was the archaeologist and anthropologist, Marija Gimbutas.

Gimbutas was a noted scholar of archaeology and anthropology at UCLA. In the 1950s she advanced a bold theory known as the Kurgan Hypothesis. It proposed that there was a mass migration of the Kurgans, a male-dominated culture from the Eurasian Steppes. The Kurgans, now more widely known as the Yamnaya (both terms mean "people of the burial mounds"), moved west from what is now Ukraine, through Europe, east to India and toward China, and south into Anatolia. They were the first to domesticate horses, develop wheeled transport that could travel large distances, and use pastoral agriculture. This was the mobile tending of large herds of livestock. Their diet was rich in meat and dairy, and they were semi-nomadic, constantly moving their herds to new pastures.

Gimbutas set out that prior to the Kurgan/Yamnaya migrations, European religion was more matrifocal, and social structures were more equal between men and women. She cited the plethora of female "Venus-figures" found throughout Europe as evidence of a kind of common Earth Mother worship. Until, that is, the Indo-European Yamnaya moved in with their father figure–sky god, and patriarchal top-down social system.

In addition to her extensive scholarship, Gimbutas published several popular books such as *The Goddesses and Gods of Old Europe* (1974), *The Language of the Goddess* (1989), and *The Civilization of the Goddess* (1991). Her theory of a matrilineal past attracted much attention from people looking for alternate spiritual and cultural models from the prevailing patriarchal systems. As a result, Gimbutas's work was often disparaged, avoided, or even demonized by many in the scholarly community. To some, with her adoption into the New Age movement, she had become the equivalent of an academic witch, the scholarly version of Medea and the Scarlet Witch.

Gimbutas's theories about Old European goddess worship were

derided as feminist fantasy or just serving a spiritual movement intent on venerating a female Earth deity. One misogynistic professor even wrote that her work was the product of a woman going through menopause and that she was seeking a theory of female fertility because she had lost hers![3] Others saw her insistence on a mass Indo-European migration as a reflection of the Russian invasion of her native Lithuania in World War II. Her evidence of Indo-European migrations was suspected as too essentialist. It even reminded scholars of the kind of historical profiling carried out by the Nazis in the 1930s to claim Aryan "racial purity." Gimbutas's Kurgan Hypothesis was broadly rejected along with any idea that there might have once been any cultures that were matrilineal or what she called "equalitarian," with men and women sharing power.

But in the latter part of the twentieth century archaeological evidence started to mount that offered support for Gimbutas. Ancient Colchis, Medea's homeland, was protected from the Yamnaya invasions because of the Caucasus Mountains to the north. Of forty-four Bronze Age burial mounds found in the area, three-quarters of them have women interred in the place of honor at their centers. Excavations have also unearthed many women buried with weapons and horses. It seems that the women of Colchis not only served alongside the men, but they also held positions of power. Here power might have been shared between the genders and not concentrated solely by one to the detriment of the other.

Like Medea and Wanda, Gimbutas hailed from "elsewhere" in the east, in her case Lithuania, which had become part of Soviet Russia. She had written about the repression of Goddess worship in Europe by the church and the denigration of wise medicine women as evil witches. These women were often persecuted and killed. She wrote that historians should have the skills of a seer: they needed both scientific methodologies and insight to envision the ancient world. Gimbutas used the term *Ragana,* which is taken from the name of a

Lithuanian wise woman, a mythical figure she knew from her own culture, and one that is now mistakenly associated with witchcraft.

Today, to call someone a witch is an insult usually intended to malign a woman who has skills and knowledge that seem challenging to the status quo. Between 1563 and 1736, four thousand women were accused of witchcraft in Scotland alone, and many were healers and midwives.[4] Midwives were believed to be witches due to their advanced knowledge and traditional female information networks that were seen to stand outside "scientific" clinical medical practice. Although things are finally changing, there is still institutional tension between some doctors and midwives in many parts of the world. This problem has not gone away. A 2021 report from the International Confederation of Midwives said, "The continued under-resourcing of the midwifery workforce is a symptom of health systems not prioritizing the sexual and reproductive health needs of women and girls and not recognizing the role of midwives—most of whom are women—to meet these needs."[5] The central importance of women's reproductive health in ancient spiritual life endures today, encapsulated by the bitter political and religious division over access to abortion, contraception, and women's health care.

Both Medea's and Wanda's preoccupations with their children should be viewed in the context of this continuing fixation with controlling women and procreation. Plato thought that no new ideas could be brought to life without an intellectual midwife. In Plato's dialogues, Socrates says that he is the son of a midwife and that he practices the same art. He explains that through their extensive knowledge midwives can, "using incantations and potions, give or take away pain, induce a birth or a miscarriage." Socrates says he does the same thing, but with men, not women, and not on their bodies, but their souls. He calls his philosophy "practicing his mother's art."[6]

If Socrates, the founder of modern academia, can describe himself as a midwife, why could Gimbutas not perceive herself as a *Ragana*? Yet, many in the academy continued to view Gimbutas with suspicion up until and beyond her death in 1994. The *Los Angeles Times* wrote in 1989, "Gimbutas remains a black sheep within academia; even colleagues who admire her other work express skepticism about her description of ancient Europe." By the 2000s the Kurgan Hypothesis was pretty much dead, and in 2009 even Cambridge University classicist Mary Beard described Gimbutas's work as "frankly dotty." I have found that this is still the prevailing sentiment among many of my distinguished colleagues. But perhaps not for much longer.

In the 2000s there were rapid advancements in the ability to sequence DNA from ancient human remains. As a result, in 2015 astonishing new ancient DNA evidence about the origins of the Indo-European peoples was published. Marija Gimbutas was right.[7]

The new ability to sequence ancient DNA has been a revolution in archaeology. The center of this rapidly developing technology is the David Reich Lab at Harvard, which since 2015 has produced several studies on Yamnaya/Kurgan DNA distributed across Europe. These studies found male Yamnaya DNA (the R1b haplogroup) quickly mixing with the local female DNA of Europe. This was in line with migration patterns of the highly mobile Yamnaya supported by material evidence. It also agreed with the spread of their language, called Proto-Indo European. This is at the root of Ancient Greek and Latin and what is now spoken by more than 46 percent of the world's population, including the language you are reading now.

With DNA and isotope research we can find geographic origins, familial groups, genetic dispositions of physical characteristics, diets, diseases, and even neurological traits in certain populations. As DNA sequencing techniques develop and increasing amounts of ancient materials are analyzed, we are learning more and more about the Yamnaya people and their journey from the Eurasian Steppes.

What is remarkable is how rapidly and how far the patriarchal Yamnaya and their descendants spread. Their migrations brought major changes to Europe, North Africa, the Mediterranean, the Near and Middle East, and India. This happened around 3000 BCE, at the dawn of the Bronze Age.

Take the island of my birth as an example: Britain was inhabited by an indigenous population who had migrated by land before the English Channel was formed some 500,000 years ago. At the end of the Ice Age, around 12,000 years ago, a population of hunter-gatherers lived in the British Isles. Around 6,000 years ago people originally from Anatolia (Turkey) came bringing agricultural knowledge and mixed with the indigenous people. These were the ones who built Stonehenge around 3000 BCE. Then soon after, something drastic shows up in the DNA. Within just a few centuries there is a more than 90 percent turnover of the gene pool from these Britons to people with R1b DNA. These were the descendants of the Yamnaya, who had migrated to Britain from northern Europe. Now in the DNA of the British population after these migrations, we find hardly any trace of the earlier male line.

There are various theories about what happened. The new pastoral farming techniques, high mobility, metalworking skills, and material wealth brought by the Yamnaya quickly supplanted the existing British culture. Existing marriage-exchange bonds frayed, and new ones were set up favoring the Yamnaya and the resources they could provide. Gimbutas proposed other reasons for the incredible effectiveness of the Yamnaya spread—warfare, conquest, and genocide.

The DNA evidence does show the Yamnaya initially entering Europe at a rate of forty men to one woman. It is fair to surmise that these well-armed, mounted warriors and their sky father god might not have been the friendliest new additions to the neighborhood. Scholars are debating what happened, and perhaps the DNA will yield more answers. In the meantime, we need only to look at far more recent colonial expansions in places such as Puerto Rico to see a similar "disappearance" of male lines of indigenous populations though conquest, warfare, and deliberate genocidal policies by invading people. Gimbutas suggested that as the "Old European" cultures were subsumed, so were the existing matrifocal religions and equalitarian cultural practices.

As the Yamnaya moved, they left us no writing, nor do we know their mythology. Except, we do find common themes in the Indo-European texts of the cultures the Yamnaya rode into. These include the Hittite *Kingship of Heaven*, the Vedic *Mahabharata*, the Greek *Iliad* and *Odyssey*, the Saxon *Beowulf*, the Viking *Poetic Edda*, and the Irish *Ulster Cycle*. The archaeologist David Anthony has suggested that the common theme in these myths is the reputation of the great warrior, what the Greeks called *kleos*, or glory. This may have been vital to a mobile, pastoral, patriarchal system where the community is spread out over very large distances. This means the people would hardly ever interact directly with their leaders. Epic poetry might have developed to bolster the reputation of a far-off king and act as a social glue between distant members of the same ethnic group.

Gimbutas's technique was to combine the material evidence of archaeology with the content of myth, what she termed "archaeomythology." For her, the disappearance of so many pre–Bronze Age goddess idols at the same time as the Yamnaya migrations is evidence of spiritual erasure. The Indo-European epics all feature dominant male sky gods and patriarchal political and social structures, but rather than a complete erasure, I think they show us a transition. Left over in this process is a mythic memory of Gimbutas's old Killer Regeneratrix. We see this deliberately placed between the lines of the myth of Medea and in the collective unconscious of the creators of the new stories of the Scarlet Witch. The Regeneratrix has been unknowingly retconned, and now we view her very differently.

What is noticeable about Anatolian, Egyptian, Greek, and many other ancient mythologies is that they portray tensions between male and female forces at the cosmic level. In *The Epic of Gilgamesh*, which was adopted and developed under the Indo-European Hittites, a male ruler with almost unlimited power is brought to his senses through his interactions with Inanna, the Sumerian Killer Regeneratrix. The Egyptian creation myth places the female deity Nut as a sky goddess stretched out and dominating the male Earth entity Geb. Nut was known as the "Mistress over All" and the god that birthed all the other gods. The Greek myths reflect a constant negotiation between older female deities and the Zeus-led Olympians. However, Zeus still must balance his powers with Hera and the other four, sometimes five, Olympian goddesses.

It is the sacred marriage of Zeus (sky) and Hera (earth) that upholds the Olympian system. This is the mythic expression of the merging of two contrasting religious structures, one male dominated, the other female. Even the ways in which the Greeks received their myths were a vestige of this blending. Greek drama is a tangible manifestation of Indo-European poetry, performed at cult festivals by masked characters acting out pre–Bronze Age shamanistic traditions. Small wonder then that Greek tragedy has some of the most powerful women characters found in Western literature. This, despite being written by men and performed by men for an audience of men.

Euripides's play *Medea* is a blend of these different spiritual traditions. It is still communicating the age-old myth of the Killer Regeneratrix in this new Indo-European performance form. Tragedy had been around only for three generations when *Medea* was staged in Athens in the mid-fifth century BCE. In the play we meet Medea and Jason years after the quest for the golden fleece. They are living in Corinth; Jason is a middle-aged former hero, living off his old reputation. Medea is a mother of two children and lives as an outsider in a foreign land.

The king of Corinth, Creon, offers to bring Jason into his royal family by marriage to his daughter. Their laws do not recognize the union of Medea and Jason. Creon orders Medea to leave Corinth forever but grants her one day to prepare, declaring he will put her to death if she is still in Corinth the next day. Then to make things even worse, Jason tells Medea that their children can stay, only she must leave. He says that this is the best thing as they will be citizens of a Greek city and part of the royal family.

Medea resolves to kill her children. This is the act she is most well-known for today. When the play is restaged as it often is, the role of Medea is usually played as if she is suffering a form of mental illness, or overtaken by vengeance. Her foreignness and her sorcery make her dangerous and unpredictable. It's impossible to watch this story and feel anything but horror at what she does. But the Greeks would have viewed it completely differently.

Remember, Medea is the granddaughter of the sun god and was worshipped as a Killer Regeneratrix at Corinth, the very city where the play is set. She plans her escape to Athens by helping their king with his own reproductive problem. King Aegeus had gone to the oracle at Delphi to ask the gods how to conceive an heir, but he does not understand the prophecy he receives: "Do not unplug the wine skin until you return home." Medea knows exactly what it means, as I am sure you might, basically stop masturbating or having sex with anyone else until you lay with your wife. This advice ultimately produces the great Athenian hero Theseus.

Like many women in Greek mythology, Medea fights with fabric, a symbol of female intelligence. She poisons a wedding gown and headdress for Jason's new bride, and both she and her father, who tries in vain to stop his daughter's flesh burning, die. Jason rushes to his former house to confront Medea, and she appears soaring high in the air on a chariot drawn by serpents sent by Helios. She has killed their children and has their bodies with her. Jason will not even be able to bury them. Now he has nothing but his enormous grief. She does to him what he tried to do to her, only much, much worse.

As she soars in the air like a goddess, she makes one demand, that the people must found a shrine to her at Akraia near Corinth. There it is—the Killer Regeneratrix in all her glory, the mythical character connecting herself directly with real religious practice. I've been to her sanctuary at Akraia at Perachora, directly across the bay from Corinth, and it is still a place that feels very sacred, with a small harbor and a massive Temple of Hera above. The Greek geographer Strabo tells us that the Temple of Aphrodite at Corinth had more than ten thousand prostitutes, so one can only imagine the kind of women's health needs this large port city needed. You can envision women crossing the waters from Corinth propitiating this powerful deity, praying for a safe birth or seeking an abortion, and consulting with the priestesses there who must have been experts in midwifery.

Though Medea's children seem dead to Jason, the audience would wonder if they are now divine too. After all, the Regeneratrix has the power to give life as well as take it away. Whatever we now make of the end of this story, what is abundantly clear is that Jason has paid dearly for underestimating Medea's powers.

Perhaps Euripides was trying to get the Athenian men—there were no women in the theatre—to see that their culture was becoming too male and out of balance. Women's voices were effectively silenced by the increasingly male-dominated Athenian democracy. Women had no voting, property, or legal rights. It is ironic that the ancient Greek society we think of as the most male-centered is Sparta. This is certainly where Frank Miller's head was when he created the graphic novel *300*. Yet in Sparta the women held property, and they were able to pass it down to their daughters. If a Spartan man died, the property of his family was kept by his wife and not automatically transferred to his male heir. As a result, many Spartan women grew incredibly wealthy and used their fortunes to collectively influence Spartan policies and laws. Aristotle even went so far as to describe Sparta as a *gynocracy*—a society ruled by women.

Classical Greek society was not yet fully patriarchal, and a story such as *Medea* could remind the Athenians not to negate, underestimate, or suppress female power. Many Greek myths deal with this same theme, from the *Iliad* and *Odyssey* to the homecoming stories of the Trojan War, such as Clytemnestra's killing of Agamemnon and the terrifying female Furies' pursuit of his son Orestes when he dares to kill his mother.

Today in the American cultural landscape where Marvel operates, and in most of their overseas markets too, patriarchy has become dominant. Thank the Indo-Europeans, people in the Levant, and certainly the Romans for that one. Most people who identify as religious in America worship one male sky father, with no wife and no female offspring. Medea reminds us that it wasn't always that way, and Marija Gimbutas and the new DNA evidence have proved it. Yet the age-old reproductive demon is still with us rearing her beautiful and terrifying head again in the mass-market guise of Wanda Maximoff. It's just become a lot harder to see.

Wanda's central European birthplace is reminiscent of the Yamnaya homeland in Ukraine. Her name, derived from the Polish/German word for "wanderer," evokes this ever-migrating people. Her status as a powerful witch conjures the idea of an old matrifocal religion. The stories about how she creates then lets go of her children are classic Killer Regeneratrix. These associations are even more fascinating because they don't seem to have been conscious on the part of the Marvel creatives. In Wanda the myth of matriarchy and the reality of patriarchy are merged, more by a process of cultural osmosis than conscious narrative construction.

Marvel is a modern mythic mirror of our times, and the patriarchy is on full display. As Wanda tells Dr. Strange in *Multiverse of Madness* (or *MOM* as it has become known, funnily enough), "You break the rules and become a hero. I do it and I become the enemy. That doesn't seem fair." Today, we watch Euripides's *Medea* through our patriarchal eyes. It is impossible today to empathize with Medea—a mother who kills her children. Instead, we see the play either as a terrifying metaphor for the status of women, a portrayal of insanity, or a twisted revenge fantasy carried out on Jason.

Just like Medea, Wanda is considered a dangerous foreign witch. After a botched operation with the Avengers in Lagos, she is confined to quarters and suspended from service by Tony Stark for "her own protection." Steve Rogers objects, calling it internment. Stark points out that Wanda is not a citizen and that "they don't grant visas to weapons of mass destruction." This is very similar to what the Corinthians in Euripides's play think about the foreign witch, Medea. "I'm afraid of her, in case she has some new plan in mind. She is a deep thinker, you know, and she will not put up with this kind of abuse. I know her and I am terrified."[8] This is what the people of Corinth say about her.

Just as Medea fled her homeland and joined the Argonauts, Wanda left Sokovia and changed sides for the Avengers. Medea is expected to remove herself from Jason's life as he becomes "respectable" by legally marrying a Corinthian princess. Wanda is expected to hide away, out of sight, while the Avengers are being adjudicated by the United Nations. Medea manipulates the people of the city of Corinth in much the same way Wanda does in New Jersey's Westview. In both cases the domestic life they intended to live is completely and utterly exploded by the machinations of others.

In Corinth it is the local king; in Westview, the dark witch Agatha Harkness.

With all this in mind, might we view Medea and therefore Wanda differently? Like Wanda's conjured boys, is the death of Medea's children an illusion meant for Jason and the local townspeople, and a vivid reminder of how limited Jason's patriarchal powers really are? In *Multiverse of Madness* Dr. Strange tells Wanda that her children do not exist, and she created them with magic. "It's what every mother does," she replies, reminding us of the universality of the Killer Regeneratrix and how this mythic entity is still in lots of ways an extreme representation of many women today.

In Athens, the Killer Regeneratrix supreme was Demeter ("the mother"). Her daughter Persephone was snatched by Hades and dragged to the underworld to become his wife. When Demeter found her, she refused to let anything on Earth regenerate until her daughter was returned. Zeus brokered a compromise, which was another one of those Olympian male-female balancing acts. Persephone would spend half the year on Earth with her mother and half in Hades. The myth is an explanation of the seasons and how plant life grows, thrives, dies, and then grows again. Demeter knew that without the power of the Regeneratrix nothing could live.

In some versions of the Medea myth, she does not kill her children but flies off to seek refuge at Demeter's sanctuary at Eleusis, near Athens. Initiates seem to have been promised a blessed afterlife by embracing the contradictions of the Killer Regeneratrix, that life is death and death is life. What's amazing is that the Eleusinian Mysteries offered the Greeks an alternative religion to the Olympians, where the mother goddess reigned supreme. Demeter was also said to kill a child when she tried to make the baby of the local king immortal by burning off his living flesh. Demeter is really the vestige of one of Gimbutas's "great goddesses" and is equated with the Earth Mother, Gaia. There is an inscription on the healing shrine at Epidaurus in the Peloponnese, part of a hymn to Gaia that says it all: "To you it belongs to give means of life to mortal men and to take it away."

In the Marvel canon Wanda, the Scarlet Witch, is a modern version of Gimbutas's Killer Regeneratrix, but unlike Medea, Wanda finds that there is no place where she can fully embrace her powers. The patriarchal world she finds herself living in has no such mechanism to either recognize or honor her abilities. So, she embraces the Darkhold and tries to dominate the multiverse. Eventually, she sees the futility in what she is doing and seemingly sacrifices herself. It is as if our modern Medea has nowhere to go. The question is, will scholars in two thousand years interpret this as a triumph of patriarchy?

It's an unsatisfying end to Wanda's MCU journey but hopefully not the character's finale. We need stories of powerful mythic women like Medea and Wanda to remind us of the dangers of living without balance. So, let's give the last word here to another witch-figure, Agatha Harkness, from *WandaVision* season one, episode nine and hope that one day it might not be true.

"Same story, different century. There'll always be torches and pitchforks for ladies like us, Wanda."

CHAPTER 7

WOLVERINE'S WILD WEST

It is the symbol of Rome: two infants suckling at the teats of a she-wolf, the moment of the founding of the eternal city as Romulus and Remus are saved from certain death by the wolf, raised in the forest where they live as outcast "wolf boys." One of them will go on to found the great city and empire that bears his name; the other will die young.

In ancient Greece the earliest rites to Zeus were held at a place called Wolf Mountain and involved transforming young men into wolves, presided over by a legendary king called "Wolfman." The Olympian god Apollo, who Nietzsche thought of as the embodiment of rationality and harmony, carried the title *Lycian*, or "wolfish." Myths of people changing into wolves abound in ancient Greek and Roman mythology, so much so that it could be said that what we now call "Western culture" is based the concept of werewolfism. What does this mean, and, more important, what does it tell us about how we see ourselves and our mythic cultural origins?

I want to unpack this with the help of one of Marvel's most popular and enduring werewolf-like characters, Wolverine. Though not strictly a wolf, I know, as a real wolverine is actually a large type of weasel, Marvel created this character as their version of the werewolf myth. I am going to use a six-part graphic novel created by Paul Jenkins, Andy Kubert, and Richard Isanove, published by Marvel in 2001 called *Wolverine: Origin* as a mythic template. This narrative is set in late nineteenth-century Canada and billed itself as the "greatest story never told." Marvel braggadocio aside, from a mythic perspective they may be right. The story of Wolverine echoes what might be one of the oldest mythic themes we know, and perhaps it can help us understand the wild origins of the Western world.

To get to grips with the Wolverine myth, I am going to set the story of *Wolverine: Origin*, and other relevant Marvel story lines, directly alongside their ancient mythic precursors and new archaeological research currently coming to light. Some of these connections would have been known to the Marvel artists; others are communicated by our cultural mythic collective consciousness, which means the myths in question are still germane. These are deep, dark tales of destruction and death, anarchy and angst, violence and lawlessness. There are shattered families, animalistic urges, human disfigurement, berserk rampage, slaughter and sacrifice, sexual awakening, and diabolical rites of passage, and I think they tell us more about ourselves and the world we have made than most of us would care to admit.

The first image presented in *Wolverine: Origin* is a disheveled boy in coveralls with a ragged straw hat and unkempt hair. He is standing on a hill of long grass and holds a long scythe parallel to the ground. Beneath the curved blade, a little way down the hill, sit two more figures. One is a well-groomed young boy and the other a girl in a flowing dress with red hair. We will soon learn that the seated pair is James Howlett, the sickly son of ultrawealthy Canadian property owners, and his companion Rose, an orphan girl from the village who lives with the family. The standing boy with the menacing-looking scythe is known as "Dog," and he is the son of the brutal groundskeeper, Thomas Logan.

It's an evocative autumnal image, colored in orange shadowy hues. The scythe acts as a foreshadowing of the carnage that is to come. It is a well-known symbol of death and the instrument of the Grim Reaper. However, this first panel unconsciously taps into a far older motif of mythic performance and storytelling, one that stretches all the way back to the ancient wheat fields of Mesopotamia, Anatolia, Egypt, and Greece. Those ancient farmers at harvest time understood that when they used their scythes to reap the wheat, they were taking part in an act of destruction on the bounty provided by the Earth Mother. To counter this anxiety, they sang funeral songs and laments for the crops they were effectively killing. These told of mythical young men who died or disappeared, cut down in their prime before they came to manhood. In the Indo-European tradition these figures between boyhood and manhood were known as *koryos*. In ancient Greece they were the *ephebes*, in India the *Vratya*, to the Celts the followers of Cunomaglus, and in Scandinavia the *vargr* (outsiders/wolves). What makes them so similar is that in mythology they all live with or will transform into wolves.

As the *Wolverine: Origin* story unfolds, we see the enormous European-style stately home that the Howletts have built among the hills of Alberta in Western Canada. We are on the edge of the colonial world, and the introduction of Rose, in a horse-drawn carriage through the gates of the grand estate, shows us that the rigid British class system is also in place. A foreign culture has established itself in a new territory, just like the Yamnaya in Europe five thousand years ago.

James Howlett's perennial sickliness is placed in contrast to the robust callousness of Dog, who saves James from drowning but is then punished by his abusive father for associating with the upper class. Then at Christmas, James is given a new puppy, while Dog is punished for receiving a gift from the Howletts. A few years later, Rose rejects the advances of the adolescent Logan, and he becomes aggressive. James tells his father, and Dog is punished once more. In revenge Dog kills James's pet while forcing him to watch. This act of seemingly senseless violence and resentment leads to the expulsion of Dog and his father from the estate.

There's something deep inside Thomas and Dog Logan that won't let them accept what has happened to them. Fueled by anger and resentment, Thomas Logan returns with his son and murders James's father. At this, James goes into a reflexive wild state, slashing at Dog's face and then throwing himself on Thomas Logan, tearing at him with long claws that have suddenly extended from his hands. The beast within is revealed.

James's reclusive mother, who we see earlier with deep claw marks across her back, is distraught at the death of Thomas Logan. She cannot stand the sight of her disfigured son, calling him a "damned abortion!" She can take no more and ends her life with Logan's rifle. Dog is left whimpering on the floor as Rose runs out into the night after James. Later when interviewed by the constable and James's grandfather, Dog tells them that Rose killed both men. The next day, Rose and James go to his grandfather for help. He wants nothing more to do with James, hands them some cash, and tells them to leave now. Rose and James board a train and head out far west.

The implication is clear: James Howlett is the son of Thomas Logan, and both have some kind of mutation that manifests itself through a state of extreme anger and deadly claws. James Howlett is "now transformed into something more and something less than human" and goes berserk.

The word "berserk" is derived from Old Norse and means to wear a bearskin in battle. It is closely linked to another Norse term—*vargr*, or "wolf." In Book 6 of the eleventh-century Norse *Ynglinga Saga* of Snorri Sturluson, we hear how Odin, the All-Father and god of war, martialed his armies and instilled abject fear into his enemies.

Odin's warriors fought with no armor: they were mad dogs and wolves; they gnawed at their shields and were as powerful as bulls or bears. They slaughtered men, and neither fire nor iron could harm them. These were called the berserkers.

Odin was said to ride with a wild pack of wolves at midwinter and was known to be a shapeshifter. His status as the lord of war was supported by his association with the aggressiveness of the wolf. In this guise, Odin is the god of the berserkers and leader of the wolf pack. Generations of Viking warriors emulated their god by charging into battle wearing next to nothing except the pelt of a wolf or the skin of a bear.

Going "berserk" has been defined by psychologists as a form of excited delirium syndrome "characterized by bizarre, violent, and agitated behavior, combativeness, altered mental states, and delirium, shouting, hyperactivity, extreme endurance and unusual strength."[1] According to the last three editions of the *Diagnostic and Statistical Manual of Mental Disorders* (DSM), it is a category of intermittent explosive disorder and connected to the Malaysian concept of "running amok." Malaysians believed that when a person was in this state a divine tiger spirit entered their body, and they went into a trancelike, überaggressive condition. Psychologist Jenny Wade has described berserking and running amok as "war magic" and linked it to therianthropic (human-to-animal transformation) shamanistic practices. This act of transformation from man to wild animal might have been a ritual to negate the psychological, moral, and even biological prohibitions on killing another human.

Veterans Administration psychologist Jonathan Shay in his influential 1994 book *Achilles in Vietnam* viewed Homer's *Iliad* through the lens of US combat veterans dealing with posttraumatic stress disorder. He concluded that if a warrior survived such a berserk state it led to lifelong psychological and physiological injury. He wrote "once a person has entered the berserk state, he or she is changed forever."[2]

This is James Howlett's plight. He responds to the trauma of his father's murder by entering his own berserk state. He transforms into Wolverine and exerts incredible aggressiveness. James has unleashed a primal animalistic persona. Shay's list of characteristics of the berserk state can be directly applied to Wolverine.

Beast-like—Wolverine's claws come out.

Godlike—He heals from injury and cannot be harmed.

Socially disconnected—He is the quintessential loner.

Crazy, mad, insane—He often loses all restraint.

Insatiable—He is never satisfied or at peace.

Devoid of fear—One of the bravest Marvel characters.

Inattentive to own safety—He is often reckless.

Distractable—His memories are buried deep within.

Indiscriminate—He often causes a great deal of collateral damage.

Invulnerable—He has an adamantium skeleton and he self-heals.

Exalted, intoxicated, frenzied—His power is compelling.

Cold, indifferent—His basic mode, although Wolverine does fall in love.

Insensible to pain—He feels it momentarily, but it never stops him.

Suspicious of friends—Wolverine all over.

One of the first definitions of PTSD in the DSM is that "the person has experienced an event that is outside the range of human experience." This traumatic event is then persistently reexperienced by recurrent and intrusive distressing recollections, dreams, hallucinations, and flashback episodes. PTSD is baked into the character of Wolverine. He is first introduced as an experimental Canadian supersoldier whose body and mind have been manipulated into a deadly weapon of war, and in *Wolverine: Origin* the story goes back further and tells how the boy's genetic mutation is revealed by the horrific murder of his father.

As Wolverine's story lines unfold, we learn about his associations with the military, then about his life as a loner struggling with past traumatic memories. The character reflected the growing recognition of the effects of combat trauma and PTSD in some returning military veterans. It could be said that Wolverine propagates the superficial trope of the damaged veteran who goes berserk and runs amok. While it was a major benefit for many veterans and others to have PTSD recognized, the symptoms are far more complicated and nuanced than the Hollywood version of the "Vietnam flashback" or "going postal" trope that became familiar in the 1980s. Yet there is a complexity to Wolverine and his loyalties and relationships that makes him one of the most compelling characters Marvel has ever created.

With Wolverine the PTSD explanation can only go so far. What about those claws? While there is certainly a connection between seeing the effects of rabies on humans or animals and stories about werewolves, there is a mythical basis for these kinds of transformations. It is very deep and extremely old, and it lurks at the foundation of Western culture.

First, I should define what I mean by Western culture. The term has become slippery since the end of the Cold War when the idea of the West was held up in contrast to the Eastern bloc of Soviet Russia. But "the West" is an older concept that some have traced as far back as the ancient Greeks who saw the Hellespont (the Dardanelles in northwestern Turkey) as the divide between East and West. This is overly simplistic, of course, as there were many Greeks living on the western coast of what is now Turkey and around the Black Sea. Then the Roman Empire divided itself along Eastern and Western geographic lines, and the Christian churches that followed kept this division.

The concept of "the West" still survives, whether viewed as a cultural movement with roots in ancient Greece and Rome, an ethnic one based on European ancestry, a geographic area covering North America and Europe, or as a misbegotten racial idea of "whiteness." Even though I think it is justifiable to question the use of the term, we must also admit that the idea of "the West" is still a powerful modern myth.

What does this all have to do with Wolverine? Quite a lot, I think. In many ways Wolverine is the most "Western" of all Marvel characters, not only because he spends his formative years in the far western provinces of Alberta and British Columbia, but also because as a legendary character he represents a fundamental and disturbing characteristic of Western culture that can be traced back through the werewolf and vampire myths of medieval Europe, the founding of Rome, the oldest legendary inhabitants of Greece, and the Bronze Age Yamnaya warriors. Whatever we call it, Western culture stands on myths of werewolfism that are at least five thousand years old.

We need to return to the Yamnaya to excavate this mythic tradition. In 2016 the archaeologists David Anthony and Dorcas Brown published their research into a bizarre archaeological find unearthed in Yamnaya tombs near the village of Krasnosamarskoe in the Russian steppes, which they dated between 1900 and 1700 BCE. They discovered the bones of fifty-one dogs, seven wolves, and six unidentified canines. This was strange as dogs had never been found buried in this quantity before. What's more, the dogs and wolves were butchered in very specific ways. The skulls were expertly quartered through the center of the eye sockets and the remaining bones cut into small one- to two-inch pieces. Anthony and Brown concluded that they had been used as part of an important winter solstice festival when adolescent boys on the cusp of adulthood were initiated into the *koryos*. This was a band of wolf boys who would leave their society for several years and live in the wilds, hunting, killing, thieving, and generally existing outside the confines of their culture. To become men, these boys slaughtered dogs, covered themselves in canine pelts, left their homes, and "ran with the wolves."

The canine remains from those Yamnaya tombs seemed to have been used to consecrate the initiation of young men into an Indo-European wolf pack. They would then leave their families to become the vanguard as the pastoral Yamnaya horde migrated. Think of the young Dothraki warriors from *Game of Thrones*. The Yamnaya were far more cultured, but the effect of a band of ruthless marauding horsemen on the communities they came across was probably quite similar.

The DNA evidence shows the Yamnaya increasingly migrating both east and west through the broad grasslands of the Steppes, and then into Europe, Anatolia, India, and Mongolia. We may see a remnant of this practice preserved in the Vedic *Atharvaveda* from 1200 BCE India. In it we hear of the *Vratya*, a secret band of young wolf warriors who are sent out to all points of the known world. Members of the *Vratya* were considered social outcasts and impure members of a mystical roving band. Their patron god was Rudra, the "roarer" or "frightening one," and the "one who is untamed." The *Rigveda* describes Rudra "as fierce as a terrifying wild beast"[3] and in the *Atharvaveda* we hear this:

This humble veneration I have given to Rudra's dogs with mighty jaws
Terrifying hounds who bark and howl, who gorge on raw flesh
I praise you loud-shouting hosts and your long-haired acolytes![4]

The effects of James Howlett's first berserk state mirror the initiation rites of Indo-European wolf warriors. He is separated from his family by acts of violence and then forced into exile as his wolfish nature appears. James also suffers a loss of his old identity. He hardly remembers who Rose is or how close they were. James's grandfather wants to rid himself of "the creature," shunning "the revolting thing as I would shun a rabid animal." James and Rose travel together to the quarries of the Northern Frontier of Canada, a desolate spot Rose describes as on "the edge of humanity." On the way she notices something remarkable—James's wounds are healing rapidly on their own. This is one of Wolverine's distinctive features: he can be harmed and almost instantly heal as if he were invulnerable.

Invulnerability is one of the attributes given to the Indo-European wolf warriors. It is said fire and iron cannot harm the Norse berserkers, and David Anthony imagines the wolfskins worn by the Yamnaya also offered a sense of magical protection. In ancient Greek myths we find this trope of the berserk wolf warrior in famous heroes like Achilles and Herakles. Achilles is also invulnerable (except for his heel) and the stories about him involve the consequences of his terrifying rage. Achilles's war band at Troy, the Myrmidons, are described by Homer as "hungry as wolves, that tear and gnaw on raw flesh, their hearts filled with war-frenzy that never dies."[5] Even the Greek word for "raging madness," *lússa*, is related to *lúkos*, which means "wolf." This is where we get the term "lycanthropy" meaning "werewolfism."

In *Wolverine: Origin* at the ramshackle Canadian quarry camp where James and Rose end up, she describes the people as "a pack of wolves." After two summers James is shown hunting deer in the wild. He seems like a Stone Age hunter-gatherer stalking the forest looking for prey. As he skins the deer Rose exclaims that she never thought James would become "some man of the forest." James, now adopting the name Logan, replies, "It's the way I am now, Rose. This is maybe who I am supposed to be." The boy is undergoing his rite of passage into manhood that closely follows the ceremonies of the Indo-European *koryos* wolf bands.

Logan is still deathly afraid of his own berserk state after the havoc he caused at the Howlett estate. One night, seeking refuge in the forest, he finds himself surrounded by wolves. Rather than fleeing, he stands and stares them down. His claws materialize. He becomes entranced by the eyes of the alpha wolf and collapses to the ground, only to be howled over and accepted into their pack. Now every night Logan runs with the wolves. By day he still works his heart out at the quarry, so much so that his older workmates name him after a wild animal known for its aggression and persistence. "That's what that kid is," says one of them. "He's a wolverine."

The name "Wolverine" means "little wolf." The species is not a canine but a large member of the weasel family that includes badgers and otters. It is a solitary animal, preferring to hunt on its own, and is quite small, standing at around one and a half feet tall and around thirty-five to forty inches long. Wolverines are native to northern North America and Canada, and are known for their ferocity in being able to bring down much larger animals.

Marvel's Wolverine clearly stands in the long mythical tradition of transformative wolf warriors, yet his therianthropic association is also quite apt. When Len Wein was asked to create a Canadian superhero in 1974, he thought of quintessential Canadian animals. A badger was obviously rejected for being too sedate, but the ferocious diminutive wolverine that hunts alone with its long sharp claws seemed right on the mark. So, in a 1974 edition of *The Incredible Hulk* Wolverine, as a mutant experiment created by the Canadian army, is sent to confront the Hulk when he crosses into Canadian territory. This was Wolverine's first-ever appearance.

In Canadian First People's mythology the wolverine holds a special place as a surly and aggressive trickster. The Innu called the man who transformed into the wolverine Kuekuatsheu. Like the wolf, the Innu see wolverines as a bridge between the world of humans and the wild, as they tend to forage in camps. Kuekuatsheu has a powerful roar that belies his size, long, strong claws, and a wily nature. The Innu tell a story that Kuekuatsheu created the world by building a raft during a great flood. He made an island from soil and rocks, and this grew to become the Earth.

In another Innu tale, Kuekuatsheu is a man who can change into a wolverine whenever he needs to defend himself. A terrifying giant skunk called Wâniyûyâu, who can also change into human form, goes on a killing spree, massacring all those he meets. Kuekuatsheu has the skunk-man follow his trail to divert him from harming any more people. After a long pursuit, they finally meet on a frozen lake, and Kuekuatsheu tells Wâniyûyâu he is disturbing everyone with his disgusting smell. Enraged, Wâniyûyâu transforms into the giant skunk and moves to attack. Kuekuatsheu changes into the wolverine, leaps on the skunk, and clamps his powerful jaws around Wâniyûyâu's anus so he can't release his deadly smell. Kuekuatsheu then calls on his family to spear the great skunk until Wâniyûyâu is dead. He runs to the sea to wash off the scent of the skunk, releases the part of him that is wolverine, and returns to human form.

Now that's an act of heroism!

Marvel's Wolverine has many of the same characteristics as the Innu version. He too is ferocious and brave but is also surly and prone to insulting his enemies. Although the wolverine hunts alone, he seeks out a family. For Logan it is the X-Men, or married life in Japan; for Kuekuatsheu it is the family members who help him defeat the giant skunk. Yet it is the qualities of the wolf that are most imbued in Logan.

Logan first runs with the wolves in the wilds of British Columbia. Just off its far western coast lies Vancouver Island, inhabited by the indigenous people called the Nootka. They have long practiced a wolf-transformation ritual that is remarkably like what we find in the Indo-European traditions. This strange ceremony was first reported on in 1803 by an English armorer, John Jewitt, who spent three years enslaved to the chief of the Muchalat Nootka after his ship was overrun by Nootka warriors and the crew killed.

Jewitt wrote that during the midwinter festival there was initially much revelry, until things seemed to take a darker turn. First the Nootka performed mock executions on a group of young men. Then a band of older warriors dressed in wolf skins and masks burst into the village from the forest and carried these boys off while howling and baying. The villagers mourned the loss of the boys before resuming the midwinter festivities that continued for another three days. Every so often the wolf men would appear at the tree line, scampering on all fours. On the fourth day, the villagers approached the forest and called the wolves repeatedly to the point that they entered a trancelike state. The wolf men finally approached with the captured boys, left them, and disappeared into the woods. The boys were taken by the older men into lodges where their wolf spirits were exorcised, and now purified, they were ready to rejoin the community.[6]

Myths of human-wolf transformation abound not only in European folklore but in indigenous American mythologies and African traditions. Brown and Anthony have suggested that this may be one of the "oldest mythemes [fundamental narrative item] recoverable through comparative mythology," dating back as far as the Paleolithic period.[7] The question is, did these very similar rituals and myths spread with people as they migrated, or did they develop independently as different peoples interacted with dogs and wolves? Barry Lopez, in his beguiling 1978 book *Of Wolves and Men*, writes how the wolf has "exerted a powerful influence on the human imagination" and tells of a myth from the Bella Coola people of British Columbia that somebody once tried to turn all the animals into people but only succeeded in making the eyes of the wolf seem human.

Andy Kubert, the artist of *Wolverine: Origin*, dramatically captures the essence of the wolf when Logan falls into a trance state. The alpha wolf is reflected in Logan's blue eye, and Logan is mirrored in the yellow eye of the wolf. On the opposite half-page panel, those compelling yellow eyes of the alpha stare out at us over the entranced Logan, who lies semiconscious with his raised claws. The Nootka ritual comes to mind.

Transformative wolf-boy rituals are particularly prevalent in myths emanating from European peoples and the cultures that influenced them. One of the most famous is of the wolf-boys who founded Rome. Romulus and Remus were the sons of Rhea Silvia, the daughter of King Numitor of the Latin city of Alba Longa. Numitor was overthrown by his brother Amulius, and Rhea was forced to become a vestal virgin so there would be no sons of his brother to challenge the throne. However, Mars, the Roman god of war, impregnates Rhea, and she bears Romulus and Remus. The twins are to be killed by Numitor, but instead they are placed in a basket on the River Tiber and carried away.

The boys wash up on a riverbank about twelve miles north of Alba Longa and have no way to survive. That is, until they are found by a she-wolf. She carries them to a cave at the foot of the Palatine Hill, which the Romans will later call the Lupercal, as *lupus* is Latin for "wolf." The boys are then found by a woodsman named Faustulus who takes them to his wife, Acca Laurentia, and they raise them in their cabin in the forest. When the boys come of age, they gather a gang of similar lost boys and become a group of wolf-boy brigands in the forest stealing from travelers. Eventually they help their grandfather overthrow Amulius and reclaim the throne. They return to the place where the she-wolf suckled them and decide to establish their own city. In a dispute over the walls of the new town, Romulus kills Remus, and the settlement is named for the surviving brother—Rome.

The basic story is well-known, but there is a lot going on just beneath the surface. Romulus and Remus's mother is called Rhea, the title of the Latin Earth Mother, their equivalent of Gaia. Their next "mother" is the she-wolf, signifying their transformation into wolf-boys, and their third mother, Acca Laurentia, was also known as a fertility goddess and in some stories carried the name "Lupa," which was a slang term for a sex worker in Rome. Another famous myth tells how Acca Laurentia became a wealthy woman after spending the night satisfying the insatiable Hercules and then marrying a rich Etruscan. On her death she bequeathed her wealth to Rome. This is a woman with agency and in control of her own wealth.

It's notable that the wolf-boys are nurtured by powerful female deities, and even Acca Laurentia's connection to sex work is presented as a powerful asset and a boon for Rome. Here we see a connection between the older equalitarian cultures of the peoples of Italy identified by Gimbutas and the newer patriarchal order brought by the Indo-European migration in the guise of the wolf-boys Romulus and Remus. In this way, wolf-boy myths are prevalent in the West because they reflect the cultural shift from matrifocal or equalitarian to patriarchal society. It is notable that we are not reading stories of "were-women," although Acca Laurentia in her guise as a she-wolf comes close. However, she is not the protagonist in the story of the founding of Rome.

The myth of Romulus and Remus as wolf-boys stayed current in the minds of the Romans until at least the fourth century CE. Images of the she-wolf suckling Romulus and Remus were struck onto coins and set in bronze and stone, and annual rites that celebrated the wolfish origins of Rome were practiced in the streets.

This was one of the most popular festivals in the Roman calendar, and vestiges of it still echo in the way we celebrate Valentine's Day. Let me explain.

Each spring on the ides of February (the 14th or 15th of the month) the Romans took part in the Lupercalia, named for the place where the she-wolf nurtured Romulus and Remus. Representing the brothers, two groups of young men met at the site of the she-wolf's lair, where they would sacrifice dogs and goats. The animals would be flayed, and strips of their hides given to each youth. The boys would undress, line up, and on the command of an officiant sprint off on a tumultuous footrace around the Palatine Hill to the roars of a huge crowd lining the route. On the way young women, keen to receive a fertile blessing, and maybe even a future sexual partner, would encourage the lads to give them a quick lash on the bum as they went by. This slightly kinky ritual forms the opening scene of Shakespeare's *Julius Caesar*, which was inspired by the ancient writer Plutarch's account of the Lupercalia. In the play, Caesar is hoping to appear as the inheritor of the crown of Romulus and has his loyal and younger lieutenant Mark Antony run the race in his place, saying, "Forget not, in your speed, Antonius / To touch Calpurnia; for our elders say / The barren touched in the holy chase / Shake off their sterile curse."[8] Calpurnia is Caesar's wife, and he longs for an heir.

Mark Antony won the Lupercalia that year (I'm sure it was fixed). He tries to crown Caesar with the winner's laurels, but the crowd is not having it. Caesar will not be king today. What Shakespeare captures is the importance of the Lupercalia and its wolf-boy runners to the Roman sense of identity.

After the Roman Lupercalia race, the party really got going and culminated in a naughty night of drinking, reveling, and almost anonymous hookups. It was the dawn of spring after all. No wonder the early Christian church fathers hated this pagan festival that the

Romans refused to give up. Pope Gelasius I in 494 CE tried to curtail it, but the incredibly popular celebration survived.

Today we hold Valentine's Day on the ides of February. The day is named for an early Christian bishop who was martyred in the third century CE for trying to convert the people of Rome. It has always been a bit of a stretch to link this pious saint with the romantic overtones of the day we now name after him. It may be that certain elements of the Lupercalia have survived in our modern "Hallmark" ritual, including the sense of anonymity that underlies Valentine's Day. We send or receive cards from secret admirers, whereas the young Romans got together after a quick whiplash during the run with new lovers. The Romans connected several randy local gods to the Lupercalia including Faunus, a kind of rambunctious Roman Pan figure, who we see in human guise in the Romulus and Remus myth as the herdsman who finds them with the she-wolf; Inuus, the spirit of sexual penetration; and Silvanus, a deity associated with the forest and wild animals, commonly depicted accompanied by a wolf.

Where did this crazy day of werewolfism come from, and what was its purpose? The bands of young men stripping naked and wearing animal skins and the dog sacrifice remind us of the Yamnaya evidence and the accounts of boy wolf packs in the *Vedas*. Perhaps this staged rampage through the streets of Rome where transformed young men act out assaults on women holds a dark memory. The Romans told myths about the sexual assault and abduction of women, including the so-called Rape of the Sabine Women. This was when, after founding Rome, Romulus and his wolf-boys realized they needed wives and decided to carry off the neighboring Sabine women.

The Romans are often presented as rational, organized engineers, but their overtly patriarchal society was also capable of astounding acts of violence and repression. Imagine a festival today where hundreds of young men dressed as angry wolves and ran through our towns and cities lashing any women they came across with a whip! It must have been an incredibly heady, complicated, erotically charged, and borderline dangerous day.

There is another important clue to what the Lupercalia was all about. The Roman sources tell us that a Greek refugee named Evander from Arcadia first consecrated the Lupercal as a religious shrine. He came from a place in the central and mountainous Peloponnese called Pallantion, for which Rome's Palatine Hill was said to have been named. Evander was believed to have been the first leader of the community that will become Rome, but it is his close links to Greek werewolfism that are most interesting.

Evander was a Pelasgian, meaning an original Greek, and his homeland, Arcadia, was regarded as the place where these early Greeks lived after they were invaded or faced migrations. In any event the myths about the Arcadians famously teem with werewolves.

The most well-known of these is the tale of Lykaios ("wolf man") who lived on Mount Lykaion (Wolf Mountain) and was said to sacrifice and eat humans. As punishment, Zeus turned him into a wolf. There was another story that Arcadian boys were transformed into wolves and if they managed to not taste any human flesh for seven years they would be returned to human form and allowed to rejoin society. Again, this myth sounds a lot like the Yamnaya ritual.

It also is notable that Apollo, a god usually associated with prophecy, music, and healing, is often known as Lycian ("Wolf") Apollo. This may be because as a god he is the eternal young man, always depicted around eighteen years old, and in this guise, he stands for the liminal existence of the wolfish ephebe. The wolf association drifts into academia too as Aristotle's school in Athens, close to a temple of Apollo, was called the Lyceum—"the place of wolves."

So, the Roman fascination with wolves may be a common Indo-European trait and the Medieval European demonizing of the wild wolf-boys into possessed evil werewolves a Christian reaction to what they viewed as pagan and shamanistic. Just as the mask was reviled as an instrument of transformation away from the image of God in humans, so animal transformation was placed in the same category. Whereas the Greeks regularized the spirit of the wolf through the personification of Lycian Apollo, the Romans went so far as to institutionalize the berserk qualities of the wolf warrior within their military hierarchy in the role of the Aquilifer. This was the finest soldier in the legion who was entrusted with the guardianship of the divine symbol of that legion, a golden eagle mounted on a pole, and he wore a wolf pelt or bearskin.

When Julius Caesar first landed in Britain in 55 BCE with two legions comprised of ten thousand men on eighty ships, he was met at the shore and cliffs above with a large and imposing British force. His troops were unable to come ashore without having to wade in deep water where they would be ambushed by spears and arrows. For a moment it looked as though his battle-hardened troops would refuse to disembark and Caesar's imperial ambitions were thwarted. Then a lone warrior clad in a wolf's pelt draped over his head leapt off the ship and into the frigid water and forged toward the horde of Briton. He held high above him a long spear shaft topped with a golden eagle. This wolf warrior was the standard bearer of the Tenth Legion, and its most experienced and trusted soldier. He knew that if he fell the eagle of the legion would be lost.[9] This was the worst thing that could happen to a Roman soldier, as it meant that even if they defeated the enemy and survived the battle, their legion would be disgraced and "decimated"—one man in ten randomly executed. And so, the legionaries of the Tenth followed their Aquilifer, jumping off their ships, chest deep in the cold gray waters of the English Channel, weighed down by their armor, large shields, and weapons. They forced themselves upon the pebble beach, but many of them never made it ashore. Those who did rallied to the wolf-skinned Aquilifer, where centurions barked orders and pulled them into battle formation. After a day of intense, fierce fighting the Britons finally retreated in disarray and Caesar was victorious. Every Roman conquest was led by their sacred eagles entrusted to warriors dressed as wolves.

Marvel has tapped into something of this lupine tradition, knowingly or unknowingly, with the character of Romulus, who first appeared in print in the Wolverine story in 2006. Romulus claims to be from a divergent form of humanity descended from wolves called the Lupine. In a later story line, Romulus's sister, the aptly named Remus, confesses that it was all a myth. Romulus is eventually captured by Wolverine and imprisoned by SHIELD, but I am sure we have not heard the last of this transhistorical wolfish supervillain.

Marvel's Romulus reminds us that if we want to look for a place where the concept of "the West" began, it is probably Rome. Their empire was permanently divided in 395 CE into the Eastern and Western dominions at the western edge of Greek and Egyptian provincial territories. The cultures and languages of modern Europe and the Roman Catholic Church are descended from this time, as is the later Ottoman Empire in the East, which eventually captured Constantinople, the capital of the Roman Eastern empire in 1453. Both empires shared mythic founders who were nurtured at the teat of a she-wolf, and their vast imperial territories were won by their armies led by men dressed as wolves. All of which we can trace back to the invading/migrating Yamnaya and their advance parties of mounted wolf-boys.

The story of Romulus and Remus contains something else: the idea that Rome was a city of migrants, which looked to a band of wolf warriors from the East for its origins. This was the mythic Trojan warrior Aeneas, who fled the burning city after the Greeks sacked it, carrying his father Anchises on his shoulders and holding his son Ascanius in his arms. Here was the symbol of the future of Rome and its male lineage.

When Rome's first emperor, Augustus Caesar, seized power after the assassination of his adoptive father, Julius, he knew he needed to consolidate his reign by attaching his family to a national myth. Caeser claimed that the name Julius came from a Trojan ancestor called Iulus, the son of Aeneas, who was also known as Ascanius. Augustus had the poet Virgil compose a great Latin epic poem about their mythic Trojan ancestor Aeneas, called *The Aeneid*. In that epic work we hear how Aeneas flees the burning city, leaving his Trojan wife, Creusa, to die in the flames. When Aeneas realizes she is not with him, Creusa's ghost appears and instructs him to leave and make his destiny founding a new, far greater city. Virgil describes Aeneas and his small band of followers fighting their way out of Troy, "like ravaging wolves, in the dark mist, driven blindly by the cruel rage in their bellies."[10]

Aeneas's mission is nearly thwarted in North Africa by his affections for Dido, the queen of Carthage. However, he abandons her in the night and sails off to Sicily where he buries his father. After landing in Italy, he marries Lavinia, the daughter of King Latinus, and forges an alliance with the Latin people, founding the line that will produce Romulus and Remus. It is notable that Virgil includes the Greek king Evander from Arcadia in this story, another migrant who has come from the region dominated by the peak of Mt. Lykaion. The mythical creation of the West that began with Rome is predicated on the legendary wolf warriors of Greece and Asia Minor.

So, if the mythological underpinnings of Western culture are based in large part on what we now view as a form of werewolfism, what does that say about us? Therianthropy does seem to be a very old way that humans coped with survival as far back as the Paleolithic period, with many peoples practicing forms of human-animal transformation. What we may have inherited from the marauding Yamnaya is the use of wolf therianthropy to advance their particular brand of patriarchy involving organized violence, territorial control, and the development of mass pastoralism. In many ways the American mythos of the mounted cowboy heading out west driving cattle or the teams of covered wagons establishing homesteads is the same story as the Yamnaya. For some it is an epic myth of migration, a "manifest destiny," for others, usually those already inhabiting those lands, a story of violent invasion. Both are myths of "the West."

The Greeks were certainly influenced by the Indo-European migrations, but in the classical period their culture had not fully embraced patriarchy as the Romans did. Their sky father, Zeus, was shown as a force to be reckoned with but one still tempered and often outdone by Hera, one manifestation of an older Greek Earth Mother.

We find a different ending to a story of berserking wolf-boys and ravening lion-men in the *Odyssey*. Odysseus and his crew land on a mysterious unknown island and see smoke rising from the interior. Odysseus sends out an advance party, and they come upon the home of the sorcerer Circe, which is surrounded by wolves and lions. Here, these terrifying creatures behave like docile puppies, wagging their tails and seeking treats. Circe has tamed them. Odysseus's men are beguiled by this sight and the alluring Circe, but before they can do her any harm, she transforms them all into pigs. Circe releases them from her spell only when she and Odysseus reach an accord. For a year, as the seasons turn, Odysseus stays with Circe, learning to respect the cycle of the Earth. Only then can he leave on his long journey home. The myth of Circe tells us that there is a natural cycle of death and renewal inherent in the seasons that can calm the savage spirit and restore a sense of balance. This is what the Greeks called *omonia*, from which we derive our term "harmony," and they regarded it as an essential element for a peaceful society.

Marvel's wolf man, Wolverine, is well aware of the dominant culture that is always seeking to exploit his powers, and so he is frequently depicted seeking solace in nature and away from the company of men. *Wolverine: Origin* concludes with a clash of two such wild warriors. Dog Logan has grown into a huge young man and is sent by the ailing elder Howlett, who on his deathbed is now full of regret, to find James. When we see Dog in the quarry camp in British Columbia, he is wearing a bearskin draped over his head and shoulders, the quintessential therianthropic berserker. Dog confronts James, now also known as Logan. The berserker fights the *vargr,* but it is Rose, the force of harmony in this story, who ends up dead as she is accidently killed trying to get between them. A distraught and confused Logan, detesting human society, recedes to the wilds where he rejoins his wolf pack and withdraws from the world of men.

The Marvel comic book story ends with a despicable scene. The final few frames show the quarry's contemptable cook ransacking through Rose's few possessions. He picks up her journal where she has recorded her and James's story and nonchalantly tosses it into the fire as worthless junk. Like the wolf rituals of the Yamnaya, the sacrifices on Mt. Lykaion, or the origins of the Lupercalia, the written record is lost forever and only the myth remains.

CHAPTER 8

THE HERO WITH A THOUSAND (OTHER) FACES

Why are so many modern superheroes and villains masked? What is it about masks that makes us not want to take our eyes off them? Why are they a ubiquitous element in all human cultures? Marvel's first recognized publication, 1939's *Marvel Comics #1*, had a character created by Al Anders called the Masked Raider. This was a western hero who dons a dark face covering and swears to "forever fight the lawless." Then, in 1940, Captain America was introduced wearing his signature winged blue half mask emblazoned with a red "A." When his friend Bucky joins him, he also dons a small mask to become his loyal sidekick. Other early Marvel masked heroes include the Fiery Mask, a New York vigilante (1940); two disguised assistant district attorneys known as the Falcon (1940) and Purple Mask (1940); and the Phantom Reporter (1940). Right from the start masks were an integral part of the Marvel universe.

Of course, not all Marvel heroes wear masks. Thor goes unmasked, as do the Fantastic Four. But consider how many highly popular comic heroes are depicted in masks: Spider-Man, Spider-Woman, Iron Man, Black Panther, Deadpool, Ant-Man, Daredevil,

Iron Fist, Cyclops, Moon Knight, Magneto, and Wolverine (well, sometimes). We must consider why so many beloved characters are disguised by masks and what this has to do with mythology.

In antiquity we don't find masked heroes; the closest is Herakles, who wears his famous lion skin. Herakles never tries to disguise himself—his lion skin is a sign of his hero status and identity. It also offers him protection as it was impenetrable, predicting the shielding nanotechnologies of Marvel outfits by some three thousand years. Many Greek warriors did wear a masklike helmet known as the Corinthian, after the city in the Peloponnese where it was said to have originated. They tended to personalize their shields and armor. So much so just the sight of Patroclus wearing the armor of Achilles causes the Trojan army to turn and flee, fearing that Achilles has returned to the fight. The Corinthian helmet covered the entire head, neck, ears, cheeks, and nose of the warrior, and it has become a distinctive emblem of ancient warriorhood. It is now most often associated with the Spartans, the Greek city-state that fielded an army famous for its fighting abilities and for never surrendering in battle (both myths promoted by the Spartans, by the way).

The mythos of the Spartans and their enigmatic masklike helmet was magnified by Frank Miller's 1998 comic *300*, and then the 2006 movie directed by Zack Snyder. In both renderings, the Corinthian helmet is iconic. We see the Spartan hoplite phalanx arrayed against the massive Persian force with those masklike helmets staring menacingly out from above the row of round shields and spears. Here we get some sense of the psychological impact of these "masks" to intimidate the enemy. It is as if the Persians faced warriors made of bronze and not men at all.

The Corinthian helmet has become a ubiquitous symbol for warriorhood; it is the logo for the challenging Spartan Race event and is found on modern military insignia, including the crest of the US Military Academy at West Point and the Special Reconnaissance

Regiment of the British Army. A similar type of helmet is found atop the Mandalorian in the Star Wars universe, as well as the helmet of X-Men's supervillain Magneto, who wears it to prevent Professor X from manipulating his mind.

Magneto's use of this masklike helmet recalls the effect of wearing the ancient version in warfare. The classical scholar Sebastian De Vivo has shown how it created a sensory barrier to the chaos of battle, muffling sound and seriously compromising peripheral vision. This forced the soldier to look forward as if wearing a bronze version of horse blinders. Using this type of headgear in battle would have been advantageous to Greek warfare. Infantry formed up in long lines behind a shield wall, where the man at your side would have been dependent on you for protection. Moving in unison as a unit and advancing forward would have been essential for success in battle. The Corinthian helmet not only instilled fear into the enemy gazing on it, but it also helped the psychological state of the warrior who wore it. De Vivo surmises that these helmeted warriors "become, in a sense, inhuman; their individuality as human beings (rooted . . . in the recognition of the face) is effaced by the Corinthian helmet."[1]

The Corinthian helmet was less an instrument of disguise and more of transformation. This was well understood by Marvel's Phantom Reporter, who captures something of the psychological effects of wearing a mask, as written by David Liss in the 70th anniversary edition of *Daring Mystery Comics* in 2009:

I needed an edge, and maybe
the mask . . . was the answer.
Those costumed heroes
cover their faces to
keep their names a secret,
but I thought maybe it was
for other reasons too.

Maybe fighting a man in
a mask is distracting . . .
frightening even.
Maybe the mask was the
only chance I had to get
out of there alive.

For the ancient Greeks the god of transformation, particularly via the altered states brought on by wine, dance, drama, and trance, was Dionysus, and his symbol was the mask. The myth of Dionysus is also one of transformation; he is the son of Zeus and the mortal woman Semele. In some versions of the myth, Semele was alone with Zeus after a night of lovemaking. She made him promise to appear to her in his divine form, the way Hera viewed him. The result was catastrophic—Semele burst into flames at the sight of her lover in his unmasked form. Semele was pregnant with Dionysus, and Zeus sent Hermes to snatch the unborn baby from the flames and bring him to Olympus. There he was sewn into Zeus's thigh, where he would come to term and be born again transformed into a god.

Nurtured by a mortal woman and then a god, Dionysus reflected this transformative state. He was a male god who dressed in women's clothing; he was Greek and yet from abroad; he was now divine but once was mortal. In the version of Dionysian transformation told by the secret Greek mystery cult known as the Orphics, the infant Dionysus was cleaved in two by a thunderbolt stolen by the Titans as he gazed at his own masklike face in a mirror. Then, like Osiris in the Egyptian myth, his dismembered body had to be reassembled, and he was worshipped as the "twice born." This essential dual nature of Dionysus was reflected by his mask, and when the Greeks wore it, they encapsulated the quality of the transformative god. That meant that the presence of Dionysus was often denoted simply by a mask hung on a pole. In artistic representations he is the only god depicted facing out at the viewer, staring at us with his wild hypnotic eyes and mesmerizing, masklike face. As Dionysus was the god of altered state, the mask was seen as an implement of possession in that the wearer was inspired ("breathed into") by the character they were wearing.

The Greeks regarded the mask of Dionysus as the point of origin for acting, a concept still with us today. *The New York Times* described Tom Hiddleston as "a British thespian with serious chops."[2] The *Loki* actor, who studied classics at Cambridge, would know that the term "thespian" is derived from a mythical Athenian performer called Thespis, who was said to have been the first actor. Thespis performed a revolutionary act when he stepped out of a chorus to answer them and covered his face with a mask.

Of course, Thespis was not the first person to ever wear a mask. In Yorkshire in England, eleven thousand years ago, thirty-three people took part in a ritual wearing mask headdresses made from the skulls of deer. These had large antlers, and two sizable eyeholes cut through the bone. Compelling Neolithic masks more than nine thousand years old with disturbing grins and glaring eye sockets have been found in the Judean desert. So have masklike stone heads in ritual spaces at Göbekli Tepe in Turkey. We also see representations of masks on figures painted in Paleolithic caves and rocks. The six-thousand-year-old haunting Dahongyan shaman wears a mask and stares out as us from a rock wall in Guizhou in Southwestern China.

Multiple masked shaman figures from around four thousand years ago have been found on rocks in the Lower Pecos Canyonlands in western Texas. Even older is the strange mask staring out of the rock walls in the Cave of the Trois-Frères in southwestern France dated as far back as 13,000 BCE. This figure, known as "the Sorcerer," is a human-animal hybrid and suggestive of the kind of altered-state visions participants in shamanistic rituals might have experienced. Oldest yet from forty thousand years ago is the so-called Lion Man of Hohlenstein-Stadel in Germany. This small figurine is the earliest depiction of a humanlike form yet found, and it may well be of a Stone Age shaman wearing a lion mask. From the earliest times masks were essential elements in the performances of our myths.

This ancient aspect of mask practice is captured superbly in the MCU's 2018 movie *Black Panther.* In it the former US Army special operator Erik Killmonger asks a museum curator about the African artifacts in a glass display case. She points out two masks. One is Ashanti from the nineteenth century, and the other from Benin that she dates to the sixteenth century. Killmonger points to an axe in another case. When the curator begins describing it, he rejects her description, telling her it was stolen by the British Army and is made of Vibranium. This is the metallic ore that can change matter and is the power behind the technologies of the secret kingdom of Wakanda. Killmonger is there to steal the axe, which he and his accomplices do, after they kill the curator and the museum's security guards. But as he turns to leave Killmonger pauses to gaze on one more African mask. It is a version of the fearsome Igbo Mgbedike, or "Moment of the Brave" mask designed by the movie's costume designer, Ruth Carter, after African originals. It has striking long horns, and an impressive mane. The supervillain Klaue asks Killmonger, "You're not telling me that's Vibranium too, eh?" As Killmonger lifts it from its stand and carries it away, he responds, "Nah, I'm just feeling it."

Something very much like this scene played out in 2020, but without any violence. An activist in France, Emery Mwazulu Diyabanza, removed a nineteenth-century Chadian funeral post from its mounting at the Musée du Quai Branly in Paris, saying that he was claiming the stolen property of Africa. With most African cultural artifacts in the museums of its former colonial powers and their allies, he might have a point, even if some disagree with his methods (he was fined by a French court). A disembodied mask, placed on a plinth in a glass case in a museum gallery does not begin to signify the enactive power of the object when worn in ritualized performative ceremonies. Worse, that mask may have deep spiritual significance to the people who still live in the lands where it came from. Killmonger encapsulated how we are now often removed from the power of the mask and only see it as an instrument of disguise, not a conduit to the divine, our ancestors, and our myths.

In the Museum of Great Britain, Killmonger felt something calling him to the Igbo mask. This comes from the region that is now part of modern Nigeria. The Igbo used masks as both representations of their ancestors, and the living embodiments of the gods. Secret societies were formed, made up of the leading men of a community who joined a kind of council of elders. They acted as local judges, averters of evil, defenders of their people, and the living embodiment of the gods of Earth. These men would don the impressive masks and elaborate costumes of the *Mmanwu*, or "spirits of the dead." Although the people probably knew well the identity of the men who performed these rituals, while they were masked they were possessed by their ancestors and transcended their mortal identities. The masks gave them a special kind of authority, and when they wore them, they became *mythic*.

Europeans have similar cultural practices, including the tradition of mumming, where masked characters ran through towns and villages causing havoc and warding off evil spirits. This practice continues on a grand scale every year with a great street parade in Philadelphia first developed by immigrants from Britain, Ireland, and other parts of Europe. The term "mummer" is derived from the Old French word *momer*, or "to mask," and it may even go back to the ancient Greek masked spirit of mischief called Mormo. She was a kind of goblin whose mask influenced the development of Greek comedy. Such masked festivities can still be seen today in the Austrian Tirol.

On Fasnacht participants wear grotesque and frightening masks at Shrovetide at the start of Lent in February or March. This mask tradition has the same seasonal roots as Mardi Gras in New Orleans, the Apokries festival in Greece, the Mamuthones carnival in Sardinia, and many other similar spring festivals.

It's ironic that one of the most important periods in the Christian calendar, Lent, involves the carnivalesque donning of masks and the embodiment of evil forces as part of the ritual. The early Christians despised the mask, which was a feature of Roman performance culture. They felt it defied the notion of the one true self and the visage that God had made for humanity. Wearing a mask created multiple false personas and brought pagan deities and heroes to life. Early Christian writers such as Augustine, Remigius, and Isidore viewed the theatrical mask as an article of false representation and harlotry. To them the theatre was a place where audiences were intoxicated by the deceptions of the Muses. Masks became associated with demons, devilry, and disguise. We see this attitude to the mask in the story of Marvel's *Daredevil*. Matt Murdock's satanic headgear is a psychological weapon, instilling fear in his enemies, but also contrasting his relationship to the Catholic Church.

If Daredevil thought that by wearing a mask he would maintain a disguise, modern face recognition studies would suggest otherwise. In cognitive studies participants recognized people they knew much more quickly when their faces were blurred. When they were shown moving images of the dots from electrodes attached to people's joints, they were able to name those people very quickly by recognizing just their movements. It seems that we visually process the movement of others rapidly, and when that person is masked, we notice it even more intently.[3] This is true when one experiences masked theatre practices such as Japanese Noh, Kabuki theatre, or Indian Kathakali, where gesture and movements are precise and practiced for years by the performers. But something else remarkable happens when watching masked theatre. The fixed expression of the mask seems able to change through a range of emotions—how can this be?

I had asked myself this same question after I returned to my alma mater, University College London, and saw the masks for the first production of a Greek play I was ever involved in. They were lined up on a shelf in the little Greek and Latin library, and they still looked exactly like the people who had worn them years earlier. It was uncanny and a little bit eerie. The ancient Greeks knew this, and when vase painters depicted actors holding their masks, their own faces looked a lot like the masks they had in their hands, as if they had somehow melded together. Using face recognition studies, neuroscience research, and cognitive theory, I viewed the ancient tragic mask differently and realized that it was an incredible mind tool that helped make ancient drama a truly compelling experience.[4] I think this research can also help us understand the masks of Marvel.

Humans have a propensity for faces, and when they are absent, we compensate by focusing on the movements of the body even more than we normally do. Kinesthetic empathy, the ability to "feel" the movement of others in our own bodies, also engages when we look at still images as well as other people moving. The dynamic graphic art of comic books capitalized on this perceptive quality right from the start. On the cover of *Marvel Comics #1*, released in 1939, we see the Human Torch bursting through a melted ship's bulkhead with arms outstretched and fingers extended toward a recoiling villain. This would make any youngster want to grab the comic from the rack and eagerly thumb through its pages. Likewise, on the cover of the first *Captain America* comic the sheer velocity of Steve Rogers's mighty right hook smack-dab in the face of Hitler, forcing the tyrant to the ground, must have felt cathartic. Jack Kirby meant us to feel the weight of that punch. The straining tendons in Rogers's neck and his determined grimace are heightened by his half-face mask.

This allows the viewer to project their own perceptions of Rogers's emotional state onto the striking image.

Masks are mind tools for the active projection of the viewer. They work by stimulating the facial processing systems in our brains that are situated within the left and right fusiform gyruses. These are found at the base of the brain and connect to other regions involved in perceiving, recognizing, and evaluating faces. We know this through the measurement by fMRI machines of blood oxygen levels that are active in those areas when people look at faces. Remarkably in 2012 at Stanford University Hospital, scientists were able to place electrodes directly onto the right fusiform gyrus of a patient who was about to have brain surgery.[5] When those electrodes were stimulated, they effectively lobotomized the area, shutting it down. The patient was conscious and alert when they activated the electrodes, and an incredible thing happened—he said that the faces of the medical staff and scientists gathered around him "melted away." When the electrodes were turned off, their faces returned!

Our fusiform face areas are very active, and this means that humans find faces everywhere, whether it's a face in the clouds or the visage of Jesus on a slightly burned tortilla. This is probably an evolutionary survival mechanism. We need to know if there is another human out there and if they mean us harm or not. Even when we don't want to, our minds force us to see faces and then perceive the emotions we find on them. This is the uncanny and slightly uncontrollable place where the mask exists within our complex perceptual mechanisms.

Because of our overactive facial recognition networks, we tend to respond powerfully to caricatures as well as the schematic lines of comic book characters. As we noted before, the word "character" is derived from the Greek word *charassein*, meaning "to carve or engrave." What exactly is being engraved? The features of a mask. The Greek noun for "mask," *prosopon*, means "before the gaze," a clue that the function of the ancient mask was not only what it did to the wearer, but how it was perceived by the spectator. In Greek drama, masks were so fundamental to the performance of myth that Aristotle wrote that if you wanted to understand the intrinsic power of theatrical visuality (*opsis*) you needed to consult the mask maker.[6] He knew the ancient, shamanistic, and uncanny properties of the mask and how they were an enormous part of what made Greek drama so compelling.

These strange qualities have been famously noted by the Japanese roboticist Masahiro Mori and his theory of the uncanny valley. Mori showed how humans love representations of faces, even from the most basic of elements, like a sock puppet or a ball of fluff with eyes. However, once the likeness of a face becomes too real, we are horrified and reject it as having dipped into the "uncanny valley." This is the cognitive realm of zombies, the near dead, and now freaky computer-generated assistants—they seem real, but we just know they are not.

In 2009 with the release of *Avatar*, the only movie to date that has outsold *Avengers: Endgame*, director James Cameron claimed that with his CGI Navi he had crossed the uncanny valley.[7] Really? The critic Lawrence Weschler called out Cameron on this claim, noting that the metallic blue skin tone of the alien Navi characters was a lot easier to produce than normal human skin. Because they were aliens their appearance did not trigger our uncanny valley response as happens with the 2004 movie *The Polar Express* (freaky!). The technology available was certainly a lot better for 2022's *Avatar: The Way of Water*, but the Navi are still blue and alien. With game and AI technologies advancing and computer animation becoming ever increasingly realistic, the uncanny valley seems to be getting far smaller. But have any of these fancy new applications crossed it? Those deepfakes, still look, well, fake.

The answer is yes, something has, and it is not a digital image created by a quantum computer system and a massive team of brilliant scientists in a multi-billion-dollar lab. Mori's original schematic of the uncanny valley shows it clearly if we care to look. About halfway along the upward slope across the valley Mori placed a Japanese Bunraku puppet. This is the type of puppetry where the figure is manipulated by two or three puppeteers in plain sight. Mori commented that it is the simple masklike face of the puppet and the movement of its figure that imbues it with life. We know it's a puppet being manipulated and yet we are emotionally drawn in to the story it is enacting. It's not at all real, and yet as we project our perceptions onto it, it seems very real indeed.

I've used Mori's research and other more contemporary studies to show how the fixed masks of Greek tragedy were similarly capable of seeming very real. With a gesture by the actor, they could seem to change their expressions quite profoundly between fear, anger, sadness, joy, surprise, and disgust. In actuality, the mask is not changing at all, but to the spectator it can look completely different when tilted at different angles and accompanied by bodily movements that reflect particular emotional states. Additionally, the mask makes the spectator's experience highly individualistic as each person projects their view of a particular emotion onto the mask. This is an incredible special effect and makes for a deeply personal experience. Think about it: If I go to see Brad Pitt play Achilles and I'm not really a fan, then no amount of emoting on his part is going to draw me deeper into the narrative. But if we put Brad in a mask (and I for one would pay good money to see that), then I am now unaware of the celebrity and only see my version of Achilles. It's not Brad looking mad but the full-on anger of Achilles as I conceive of it. The human brain is still the most fantastic special effects producer we know.

When I stage mask workshops and demonstrate how Greek masks can change their emotions, people see all the "basic" emotions I mentioned previously: fear, anger, sadness, joy, surprise, and disgust. These are the six facially displayed emotional states commonly exhibited across cultures, ages, genders, and generations. I think there is slippage and fluidity between these emotional states, with anger being a resultant state generated by fear, for example. I also believe that different cultures are provoked to these emotions by different things. Yet these six do seem to be universally perceived whenever I have demonstrated them in a mask all over the world.

There are limitations. The mask cannot display some states that we tend to think are emotions like love, jealousy, and guilt. But this is what I love about the arts, how they exploit those little cognitive gaps that make the world seem so beguiling, uncanny, and sometimes even sublime. The cognitive archaeologist Carl Knappett has called the bridging of these gaps "sympathetic magic."[8] This is when the "icon," the thing being represented, say a mask of Achilles, and the "index," or wearer, such as Brad Pitt, fuse together in a strange and compelling way.

A similar perceptual experience can happen in the MCU movies. The breakout success of *Iron Man* has been justifiably credited in large part to the central performance of Robert Downey Jr., and that's certainly true. But there's something else going on that relates to Knappett's theory of sympathetic magic. Most viewers of the movie, even those unfamiliar with the Marvel Comics character, knew of the highly publicized past erratic behavior of the movie's star, and his reputation for taking on roles that played on his public persona as a troubled playboy. Even in the same year the first *Iron Man* was released in 2008, Downey starred in Ben Stiller's *Tropic Thunder* in blackface, another kind of mask with a negative history. Downey's Tony Stark is first presented as an embodiment of this playboy persona, a callous, risk-taking, fast-talking arms dealer. Stark's catharsis comes appropriately enough in a dark cave, where he is forced to confront the reality of the havoc his weapons have wrought. When he bursts out of the cave to confront his terrorist captors, he is fully masked and armored in an early incarnation of the Iron Man suit that will come to define his superhero status.

The snarky, manicured face of Tony Stark is replaced by the steely glare of the Mark 1 Iron Man helmet. This simple visage will soon be discarded once Stark has escaped and inadvertently trashed the Mark 1 by trying to fly. In this moment, free, but laid out in the desert, his creation shattered in pieces around him, the iconic Iron Man suit and the indexical Tony Stark, its puppeteer, are merged. When Stark creates and then wears new, upgraded suits, we are always aware of both the awesome technological power of Iron Man and the somewhat fragile and egotistical personality behind that fearsome-looking mask. It is this constant tension between the two that helps make Iron Man such a compelling character.

We had to wear masks during Covid-19 and as a result, according to a UK study, jurors became better at telling if a witness was being deceptive.[9] Facial expressions are the primary ways people lie. With masks the jurors had to focus far more on what was said to learn the truth. Tony Stark's truth is Iron Man, and when he announces it to the world at the end of the first movie, we feel the impact wearing that mask has had on him. Now the human Stark stands with the same kind of steely resolve that emanates from his artificial mask. In Iron Man's duel with Thanos in *Infinity War*, the mad Titan hammers at Stark's mask until it is shattered and broken, and we see the terrified human face beneath. With one last punch the mask is destroyed and Stark is vulnerable and defeated. It is fitting then that in Stark's death scene at the culmination of *Avengers: Endgame*, the mask is already absent, revealing Stark's unprotected face. Stark's iconic last words "And I am Iron Man" is when index and icon are once again merged in a supreme act of self-sacrifice and pure sympathetic magic. We are relieved, exalted, heartbroken, and mesmerized. The fact that this famous line was improvised in the moment by Downey Jr. strongly suggests that at that time actor and character were fused in a moment of masklike possession.

There is a difference in the way we process the masks presented to us within the graphic pages of comics and how we interact with those same masked characters enlivened in motion on our screens. Although there are certainly profound moments of viewer projection within the comic books, we do have the advantage of experiencing these characters' thoughts and inner dialogues via thought bubbles. Apart from the stream-of-consciousness banter of Deadpool, we don't have this advantage on-screen. We do, however, get the benefit of experiencing the mask in movement. Like those ancient Greek tragedy masks, we project emotional states onto them, which can greatly enhance our cognitive and emotional engagement with the narrative.

If you look closely at images of traditional Japanese Noh drama masks, or the even older representations of Greek theatre masks found on ancient vase paintings and sculptures, you will notice another uncanny feature: these masks have eyes. For most of the masks we encounter today, even our modern version of masks of comedy and tragedy, the eyes are dark holes. If we were to wear one of these then our own eyes fill those sockets, but unless being viewed close-up, these masks still seem to have empty dark eye hollows. In the Marvel comics, the kind of mask worn by Captain America does reveal the eyes, but the corners where we look for expression are obscured, and we only see the pupils glaring through small eyeholes.

In contrast, Spider-Man's mask has distinctive large white eyes, bordered by a thick black line, setting them apart from the dark red background with its distinctive web design. Steve Ditko's Spider-Man mask and all its later variations have become one of the most instantly recognizable in the world. Ditko chose to draw these huge eyes in white, and aside from one frame in the first Spider-Man story, we never see Peter Parker's eyes beneath. That image occurs at the end of "Spider-Man," featured in *Amazing Fantasy #15* in 1962, when Parker realizes the thief that he had allowed to get away earlier in the story went on to murder his beloved uncle. Ditko drew small black dots as pinpoint pupils in the middle of those distinctive eyes to emphasize Parker's shock and the moment he changed into a superhero. "With great power comes great responsibility" reads the final panel, adding "and so a legend is born." We never see Spider-Man's pupils again.

Spider-Man's eyes are all sclera, the area of white around the pupil. Humans are the only mammal to have prominent sclera. Some of our closest genetic cousins in the animal world, chimpanzees, orangutans, and some types of monkeys, have a small amount of white too, but it is not at all as prominent and does not surround the entire pupil and iris. Animals are either predators or prey, so a flash of white in their eyes would serve no purpose for the hunter or hunted. The reason humans developed this trait is for interpersonal nonverbal communication and mutual dependency. We can get some idea about what another is thinking by noticing the direction of their gaze—are they paying attention, distracted, or waiting for a better opportunity? Are they focused on us or something else? Will they attack or retreat? Our eyes communicate an enormous amount silently.

Spider-Man's mask is a mass of sclerae that stares out at us. This is mesmerizing because we are primed to use sclera to track the motion of the pupil and iris. Spider-Man has neither, yet we can't stop looking. It is one of the most active masks I've ever seen. In the many movies Spider-Man's eyes have undergone a series of different transitions. In 2012's *The Amazing Spider-Man*, the sclerae become screens in their own right. Andrew Garfield's Peter Parker constructs them from sunglasses lenses. In other renditions the eyes appear silver rather than pure white or are perforated with hundreds of tiny holes. Sometimes the mask's eyes reflect what Spider-Man is viewing, both in the films and comics.

Eventually in film and animation those big eyes started to move themselves, communicating the emotional state of the young man behind the mask. I think this was a smart idea. The kind of projective capabilities of a three-dimensional mask in a live performance cannot be completely replicated in the two dimensions of a movie screen. In all their various incarnations, these huge eyes compel because we are programmed to use the sclerae of other humans to figure out their intentions based on how their pupil moves within it. But Spider-Man has no pupils, so we just keep looking and searching. A lot like Spider-Man himself.

Studies in the field of cultural neuroscience have shown that people look at faces differently depending on where they were raised. This is also borne out by the masks people respond to. For example, in Japan, Marvel is not the comic powerhouse it has become in the United States and other parts of the world. Japan has its own rich tradition of manga and anime. But there is an exception, and that is the enormous popularity of *Supaidāman,* the Japanese Spider-Man. A licensing deal from Marvel in the late 1970s led to the development of a TV show, which proved a huge hit at the time. Perhaps this was due largely to the mask they used. It was the same basic design as Ditko's original, red with a black web, but the eyes are far smaller. This is not unlike the mask drawn for the comics after Steve Ditko by John Romita Sr., except that with the *Supaidāman* mask we are always aware of the nose and mouth of the actor protruding from beneath. On the Marvel mask the nose is erased, while for *Supaidāman* it is needed for the kind of holistic face processing germane to Japanese culture.

Recently the Marvel Cinematic Universe has become more attuned to these cultural differences. In 2023's *Spider-Man: Across the Spider-Verse* we saw a new Spider-Man mask on our screens worn by Pavitr Prabhakar, the Indian Spider-Man. His large white eyes are more angular, and the web motif that centers the eye on Peter Parker's mask is almost absent here. Instead, we see expressive white lines outlining the upper eyes and cheeks, a plume of real hair, and, between those large white eyes and above the nose, a diamond shaped *Tilaka* mark, which is found at the site of the so-called third eye, the area of the sixth chakra, known as the *Anja*. This is the site of self-realization and understanding, and a reminder of Indian spiritual practice and mythology. It is worn by both Shiva, the creator and protector of the universe, and Buddha.

The main Spider-Man of the *Spider-Verse* films is Miles Morales. Born in Brooklyn, he is the teenage son of a Puerto Rican mother and African American father and debuted in the 2011 comic *Ultimate Fallout #4*, in a scene drawn by Sara Pichelli. Miles is given a brand-new suit by Nick Fury. The mask is distinctive with huge white eyes edged in thick red lines on a reflective dark, almost black, fabric with an open web pattern. When Miles opens the case that holds the suit his face is clearly reflected in both large eyes. In this image mask and hero are merged as one, icon and index once again.

When Miles dons the dark suit and mask in issue 5 of *Ultimate Comics: All New Spider-Man,* Pichelli gives us a dynamic full-page image of this new creation leaping above the city rooftops with the Brooklyn Bridge behind. "You're officially Spider-Man" reads the caption. This mask is as compelling as Ditko's original. The entire suit is shiny and reflective, and the red web pattern brings the focus of our gaze to a point in the center between the eyes, creating a nose-like effect and helping to anthropomorphize the mask. On the cover of the next issue (6) we see Miles, in a classic Peter Parker "half mask" pose, lifting the fabric headpiece over his eyes, a motif that was used a lot by Ditko. It shows the hero's youth and vulnerability, but also his status as an *ephebe*—a boy on the cusp of becoming a man. Like Miles receiving his new suit, when the ancient Greek *ephebe* completed his transition, he was also awarded weapons, armor, and a mask in the form of the distinctive Corinthian helmet.

In the 2018 movie *Spider-Man: Into the Spider-Verse,* Miles is dressed in a store-bought costume with its large eyes hollowed out in the center to allow him to see through. When he meets Peter Parker's Spider-Man, Miles's eyes are huge, like a Japanese anime character, while Spider-Man's are small and narrow. The contrast is striking, and we see the epitome of the student and mentor relationship. For Miles, donning the Spider-Man mask, even a cheap store-bought knockoff, seems to offer a way of exploring his identity by temporarily losing it, what is termed "deindividuation."

Anonymity may be the case with masks that simply act to disguise the face, but the superhero mask stands in a different tradition, a mythic one. Like the West African Igbo elders who become the ancestral spirit protectors and arbiters of their people, the mask transforms the wearer, even helping to elicit a state of possession. We see a supervillain possessed by his mask in Sam Raimi's 2002 movie, where Willem Dafoe, playing the Green Goblin, has a disturbing Jekyll and Hyde–like conversation with himself in a room full of unnerving traditional masks.

Mask performance specialist Margaret Coldiron has noted how traditional Balinese and Japanese masked performance forms are dissociative practices that produce a kind of trance state in the masked actor. This possession is not total, the actor remembers their lines and where to move, but they also feel that they have become the character. It empowers them to be more than human at the moment of the performance. As I watch my nephew dress up in his Spider-Man costume and mask and leap off the sofa, over the coffee table, and onto the living room rug, much to the terror of his parents, I see something very similar. This boy was "possessed" by the mask and emboldened to push physical boundaries, defy the norms of behavior, and fly through the air to stop a villain and save the world.

Andrew Garfield's Spider-Man was lauded for its physical expressiveness. The mask cannot do the work on its own, and Garfield's background in gymnastics and his theatre training shone through when he put on that mask. In his 2012 movie *The Amazing Spider-Man* there is a heart-stopping moment set on the Williamsburg Bridge. A crashed car dangles off the bridge high over the East River with a small boy inside. Spider-Man swings into action to save him. But the child is petrified, and as the car bursts into flames he refuses to move, frozen in terror. Parker removes his mask to show the boy he is friendly. Then he hands it to him and tells the boy to wear it so he won't feel afraid. It's a wonderful moment of filmmaking in a surprisingly emotionally affecting movie, and this scene brilliantly captures the possessive and empowering spirit of the mask.

Masks are one of the most mythic elements of the Marvel universe. They connect us cognitively and viscerally to the ancient traditions of mythic performance that are found in all our cultures. Masks transport, transform, and take hold of us in ways that sometimes seem to defy explanation. The masked face of Spider-Man launched an entirely new kind of comic-book hero: vulnerable, searching, angsty, relatable, and *human*. The artists of Marvel inherently knew we all have a masked hero or a hidden villain inside of us. As Oscar Wilde once wrote, "Man is least himself when he talks in his own person, give him a mask and he will tell you the truth."[10]

CHAPTER 9

SCARY MONSTERS AND SUPERCRIPS

He only wants to be like his father—his hero. His father was a New York City prizefighter who above all else wouldn't stay down. So, one day in New York's Hell's Kitchen when the boy sees an old man about to walk in front of a speeding truck on a busy avenue, he reacts. Without thinking about his own safety, he jumps in the road and pushes the man out of the way. Instead, the truck hits the boy, and he is hurt. Barrels of toxic sludge the truck was hauling have spilled and splashed the young Matt Murdock in the face. Now he is blind.

Stan Lee introduced *Daredevil* in 1964, when Hell's Kitchen was far from the expensive mid-Manhattan area it has since become. The comic book shows the young Matt dealing with his new disability by studying hard during the day and training to fight like his father at night. Lee has created a new kind of superpower—the toxic sludge from the accident imbues Matt with incredible, heightened sensory perception. He develops the phenomenon of sensory compensation, when one sense is damaged or lost, into a form of perceptual strength. Matt also develops heightened auditory abilities, meaning he can hear cries for help blocks away. He can feel everything around him, including the heartbeats of other people. He has an incredible sense of proprioception, the impression of where his body is in relation to what is around him. Matt Murdock doesn't just overcome his disability, he uses it to become a new kind of crime fighter—lawyer to the little guy by day, and the fearless Daredevil at night.

Daredevil is one of several beloved Marvel characters with a disability. Among them is the paraplegic Professor X who teaches and leads the mutant X-Men; one of Daredevil's enemies, Echo, is deaf, and in her TV incarnation is also an amputee; the Avenger Hawkeye is also deaf; Dr. Strange has hand paralysis after a car accident; and Bucky Barnes as the Winter Soldier has a prosthetic arm. There are others, such as Tony Stark, who needs an artificial heart to live, and many more who are depicted with severe psychological disorders such as Bruce Banner (Hulk), Frank Castle (Punisher), Logan (Wolverine), Wade Wilson (Deadpool), and Natasha Romanoff (Black Widow), to name but a few.

Daredevil encapsulates the trope of the "supercrip," a term used in disability studies to describe a superhero character whose powers are derived from their disability. Supercrips can be viewed positively as mythic representations of disabled people. One example is the neurodiversity of Rick Riordan's Percy Jackson. His learning disabilities and ADHD are framed as hidden superpowers, and his dyslexia is explained as the brain of a demigod being wired to read ancient Greek rather than English. There is no doubt that the huge popularity of the Percy Jackson books has been in part due to many young readers relating to this aspect of the character. However, some have seen the valorization of disability in figures such as Daredevil as diminishing the disability itself. By having such a superpower, their disability becomes surmountable, in Daredevil's case through determination, training, and mentorship. This runs the risk of cultivating the idea that any disability can be overcome or even turned into an advantage, rather than accepted and accommodated.

In mythology such supercrips are often depicted as healers, as if the embodiment of their disabilities gives them an insight into how to soothe the ailments of others. In the West African Yoruba mythology, we find the orisha (god) known as Ossain, who was often depicted as missing a leg, an arm, and an eye. Ossain, also called Osanyin or Ossanha, was the god of plants and their healing properties. In Greek mythology the healing deity is Asclepius who was depicted as leaning on a walking stick with a snake wrapped around it, still a medical symbol today. Asclepius was said to have been trained by the centaur Chiron, who suffered from a chronic injury from a wound that would not heal, despite his own considerable medical skills.

Healers and healing also surround Daredevil: as a child he is depicted tending to his father's wounds after a boxing match. His relationship with Claire Temple, the New York nurse, is primarily based on his need to receive treatment for the substantial injuries he sustains in pursuit of his concept of justice. Claire's last name hints at a sacred aspect to the care that she brings. In antiquity there was often a connection between characters with disabilities and their roles as healers.

In Norse mythology we find several supercrips. There is the one-eyed Odin, and his son Hodr, who is blind. The warrior-god Tyr has his hand bitten off by the great wolf Fenrir. In Hopi culture the trickster god Kokopelli is depicted with a spinal curvature. In Hindu myth Shani, the god of karma and justice, has his foot permanently damaged by his brother Yama, the god of death. And then there is the amazing water goddess Khodiyar, whose name means "she with injured foot." She transcends earth and water and comes to those who are injured or disabled.

Khodiyar was depicted standing on a crocodile and holding a trident, and her shrines were placed at springs and wells. She was prayed to at times of plague and sickness as a healer. She is a localized Gujarati version of the Hindu mother goddess figure, Akhilandeshwari Ma, a version of the supreme deity of Shaktism, the branch of Hinduism that venerates goddesses. Her name means "she who is never not broken."

Khodiyar's disabled foot is a physical manifestation of the idea of universal brokenness. If we accept this premise, that we are all always broken, then the very idea of disability is viewed quite differently. Not as a medical condition or an impairment, but as an aspect of the varied experiences of humanity. Of course, attitudes toward the disabled in ancient India were not at all dissimilar to what we find in other ancient cultures. Although not medicalized, disabilities were placed on a spectrum of whether the individual could still take part in social, cultural, and work-related tasks. However, as in Greek mythology, disabilities could sometimes be seen as sent by the gods as a punishment for impiety.

We see this in the story of Ashtavakra, the legendary Vedic philosopher who was born with eight disabilities, because his father made the same number of mistakes when chanting the sacred mantras and was too arrogant to correct them. Then there is Dhritrashtra, who in the *Mahabharata* is a king born blind with the strength of one hundred elephants. He was offered the gift of "second sight" but was unwilling to foresee the carnage of the war to come, so he gave it instead to his charioteer. This only increased Dhritrashtra's psychological torments as the charioteer told him of the coming death of ninety-nine of his one hundred sons in battle.

Like Dhritrashtra, Daredevil's strengths are sometimes compromised by his psychological challenges. He struggles over his feelings of guilt and anger because of the death of his father. Jack Murdock wanted nothing more than for his son to feel proud of him, especially after the accident. Jack wants his son to know that Murdocks refuse to stay down, so he defies an order to throw a big fight. This leads to his murder ordered by "the Fixer" (played by Roscoe Sweeney in the MCU). In season 3 of the *Daredevil* TV series, Matt returns to Fogwell's Gym where Jack trained, and is haunted by a vision of his dead father. Jack tells him that Matt's mother left them both "because she knew we got the devil inside." In this hallucination Jack tells his son to face up to why he puts on the Daredevil mask—it lets him feel all right with who he really is, and it gives him permission to hurt other people. Then the vision shifts to the supervillain crime boss Kingpin (aka Wilson Fisk) who tells Matt he is the son of a crooked boxer trying to convince himself he is better than his criminal father. At the scene's climax Fisk rants, "You were born from nothing—you remain nothing!" Matt snaps, his pent-up anger and violence flooding out as he attacks Fisk and imagines snapping his neck.

The psychological turmoil of Daredevil reminds us that "we are all always broken." Matt's relationship to his father, his blindness, and his complex struggle with identity places him within a much older mythic tradition. This is the ancient Greek story of Oedipus, who unknowingly killed his father and had children with his mother. We know Oedipus primarily through three tragic plays created by the ancient Athenian playwright Sophocles. Known as the Theban Trilogy after the city where Oedipus rules, the three plays, *Oedipus the Tyrant* (often erroneously called "the King"), *Oedipus at Colonus,* and *Antigone,* are usually viewed as a trilogy but were produced some forty years apart.[1] Like Daredevil, Oedipus becomes blind, but unlike the Marvel hero, his blindness is self-induced. He is willfully blind to the reality of his situation, and when he sees the consequences of his actions, he blinds himself by viciously gouging out his eyes.

Oedipus was born disabled and his name, which plays on the Greek word *oida,* "to know," also means "clubfoot." What Oedipus does not know or *want* to know is that he was adopted. His father, the king of Thebes, received a prophecy that his new son would kill him, so the infant Oedipus was sent to be slain. But the baby survived and ended up being raised in Corinth instead. Later Oedipus hears the prophecy and leaves, distraught, not wanting to kill the man who he thinks is his father. On the road to Thebes, he is forced out of the way by a group of men, and in the fight that follows he kills them.

When Oedipus arrives in Thebes, the city is in a state of emergency. A malevolent sphinx has inflicted a plague that will only be lifted if someone can solve a riddle. The king went to Apollo's shrine at Delphi for help and has disappeared. Oedipus hears the riddle of the sphinx: "What creature walks on four legs in the morning, two in the afternoon, and three in the evening?" Because of his damaged foot, Oedipus walks with a stick, a vestige of this practice of postnatal abortion in Greece, where babies were pegged out by their feet to die of exposure. His disability inspires his answer, "Humans." They crawl on all fours as children, walk upright on two legs as adults, and walk with sticks in old age. The Sphinx leaves and the problems of the city seem solved. Oedipus is celebrated and welcomed. He marries the queen and has four children with her. Oedipus has seemingly saved Thebes, and he becomes a *tyrannos*, a populist leader.

The problem with being a populist is one must stay popular and be seen to solve the people's problems. When the plague returns years later because the city is harboring an unknown cursed person, Oedipus must step up again. He publicly vows to root out the evildoer even if it is a member of his own family. But Oedipus's tyranny is based on a cult of his personality, and he is blind to what is really going on. As the story unfolds, the themes of blindness and knowledge make us question what it really means to see.

In the Oedipus story it is a blind man with the superpower of prophecy who finally tells Oedipus the truth. The man is Tiresias, the most famous prophet in Greek mythology. Tiresias was said to have had the benefit of living as both a man and woman when he was recruited by the gods to settle a dispute between Zeus and Hera. The question was simple—who enjoyed sex more, a man or a woman? After seven years living as a woman, Tiresias dutifully reported back—women enjoy sex ten times more than men. A furious Hera struck him blind, but Zeus enhanced his hearing and other senses so he could know the songs of birds and be able to interpret the future.

Tiresias says what he can see: Oedipus is the curse that has infected Thebes. His wife, Jocasta, is really his mother, and the man he killed on the road to Thebes was his biological father, the king. But Oedipus cannot see. Instead he sees a conspiracy against him and becomes increasingly paranoid. Oedipus ridicules Tiresias's blindness and rejects his prophecy, something even the gods did not do. So, the blind seer tells him, "Your eyes cannot see your own corruption or where you live and who you sleep with . . . do you even know your parents?" As Tiresias leaves, he makes one last prophecy, "He bred in his father's bed and his father's blood he shed!"[2]

Daredevil is also depicted as being in denial about the harm he inflicts on people, including sometimes killing them. After suppressing New York criminals one night, Matt goes to confession, wracked by guilt and trying to justify his use of violence. The priest responds, "Men who succumb to violence, no matter the justification, can grow to crave it."[3] Matt is on a precipice, and he rushes from the church in turmoil. This is the moral tension of Daredevil that makes him such a captivating and rich character. Like Oedipus he tries but cannot escape who he is.

In one compelling graphic rendition, *Daredevil #508* (2010), Matt has become a tyrant himself, taking over the supervillain organization called the Hand and policing Hell's Kitchen with fear, violence, and death. *Daredevil* is constantly examining the psychological makeup that created this masked superhero. It asks us to consider just how far the person who takes a solitary stand can really go before they become the kind of figure they originally set out to fight.

The final scene of *Oedipus the Tyrant* is devastating. When she learns the truth, his wife (and mother) Jocasta hangs herself and Oedipus emerges from his house with his eyes gouged out and rails against the gods.

Perhaps the most impactful rendition of Oedipus's curse I have seen was in a 2007 hip-hop stage version of the story by Will Power that used hip-hop, rap, funk, R&B, and African American spirituals. This Oedipus was presented as an old school 1970s Mack Daddy, "pimped out" with a wide brimmed fedora hat, dark glasses, and a flashy suit. Oedipus's stick was a sharp, gold-handled cane, and when he came out on stage this Oedipus bought the house down with his opening shout—"Mother Fuckers!"

Oedipus as the OG Mother Fucker worked well enough, but what he said next to his two sons, born of incest, drove home the essential, enduring truth of the Oedipus myth: "I'm gonna fuck you up, cuz my Daddy fucked me up!" And there it was in all its harsh simplicity: the curse of Oedipus handed down generation after generation as the psychological trauma of the parent is passed on to the child. This is why in many ways the moral dichotomies and generational trauma of *Daredevil* make it one of the Marvel stories closest to the myths found in a Greek tragedy.

In Greek mythology the most prevalent disability is psychological trauma, and this is the scariest of monsters that confront its many heroes. If we want proof, just look at the first word we have in Western literature—"Rage." It is from the opening of Homer's *Iliad*, "Rage—sing goddess of Achilles' rage, that devastated the Greeks and sent so many heroic souls to Hades, as feasts for dogs and birds." The *Iliad* shows us the cost of this kind of psychological break—destruction, loss, isolation, and emotional numbness.

Greek myths do not shy away from showing us heroes struggling with what we might now call combat trauma or posttraumatic stress disorder. Other times and other wars have called the same kind of psychological state soldier's heart, shell shock, or battle fatigue. It has only been since 1980 that this serious condition has come to be medically recognized and treated. The Greeks came to use their myths as a form of emotional healing called catharsis, especially in the theatre of the fifth century BCE, a time of almost constant war. Greek drama has been described by the former Veterans Administration psychologist Jonathan Shay as theatre written by combat veterans, performed by combat veterans, for an audience of combat veterans. In classical Greece, everybody was involved in war, and many were traumatized.

One of the oldest Greek performances we know about was an enactment of the return of Hephaestus, the god of the forge and creator of all matter of wondrous inventions. For all his substantial technological skills, Zeus hated Hephaestus, who was the son of Hera and was born without a father. His presence so enraged Zeus that he threw him off Olympus and he landed hard on the volcanic island of Lemnos, injuring his leg and becoming permanently disabled. His resentment at Zeus meant that he refused to return to Olympus, and the gods found themselves bereft of the technologies they had come to rely on. Eventually Dionysus was dispatched to bring Hephaestus back by plying him with wine, surrounding him with hilarious songs and dances, and seating him on a donkey to take him home, a cathartic healing by a comic performance.

Catharsis was the concept of purgation and cleansing that the Greeks believed was essential to the health of everything. They saw their world in terms of what was harmful and tainted as opposed to what had been cleansed. This affected how they thought about medicine, believing that the body contained four humors (blood, yellow bile, black bile, and phlegm) that needed to be purged to bring things into balance. Our words "sanguine," "choleric," "melancholic," and "phlegmatic" come from these categories, which stayed in medical orthodoxy until the seventeenth century. Catharsis was as much a psychological treatment as a bodily one, involving experiencing an event, having a moment of deep and sudden recognition and self-realization, and then coming to an understanding of what it meant. If this seems hard to grasp, catharsis is probably one of the most debated words in ancient Greek! But it means far more than the feeling you get after having had a good cry.

The best way to demonstrate catharsis is to look at how it is presented in Greek myths. There is a poignant example in Homer's *Odyssey*, which is a story about the long journey home from war of a combat veteran. After Odysseus leaves the isle of Calypso, where he has been languishing for seven years, Poseidon, angry that Odysseus blinded his son the Cyclops, destroys his makeshift raft with a great swell. Odysseus finds himself washed up on the island of Scheria, the place that some people think is Atlantis (it's not). He is found by Nausicaa, the daughter of the Phaeacian king, and is welcomed, although he hides his identity. The king and queen make this stranger their honored guest, and a bard called Demodocus, who is blind, is invited to perform for all gathered in the great hall. He sings of the recent Trojan War, the heroes who died there, and the wooden horse and great victory planned by Odysseus. But this song does not cheer the disguised guest, instead he weeps. These are not muffled, quiet tears. Odysseus cries like a Trojan woman mourning her dead husband as she is prodded by the butt of a spear into slavery.

Demodocus's song provokes in Odysseus an image of the trauma of war, not the glory of his victory. The Phaeacian king asks why the stranger is so distraught. "Because I am Odysseus," he replies. This is a heart-stopping moment: the song of the bard has produced a moment of catharsis—an emotional epiphany, as Odysseus reveals his truth. The Phaeacians are stunned and implore Odysseus to tell his story. This is where we hear of his famous travels, the monsters, the sorcerers, the descent to Hades, and the song of the Sirens. While they listen, the Phaeacians have their own moment of collective catharsis. They are so moved by Odysseus's story that they resolve to sail him to Ithaka so that he may at long last return home.

Does Marvel, working in a similar way, present stories of its heroes that provoke healing? That's certainly not the aim of the material, but nevertheless the feeling of recognition and identification with a character's struggles can still provide a form of cathartic reaction, even if this is unintended. Part of what makes Daredevil such a compelling character has been the ways in which his story lines have tackled his depression and posttraumatic stress disorder, resulting from the violence he had endured and the murder of his father.

We also see mental illness in other Marvel characters such as the Winter Soldier. His survivor guilt and PTSD have been presented alongside his search for redemption to atone for his past wrongs as a supervillain. Even so, we learn that he was acting involuntarily, prompted by HYDRA's psychological manipulation. Bucky's healing begins when he is received as a guest by the people who once hated him the most. The Wakandans thought he had killed their king, and it is in Wakanda where Bucky will find peace, be deprogrammed, and be healed. So, is the heroic impulse sometimes born from trauma?

The Greeks seemed to think so. They had a very different attitude to mental illness, and it can make their myths sometimes hard to understand. One example is the Athenian playwright Euripides's portrayal of Herakles (Hercules) in his play of the same name. Herakles is the mortal son of Zeus and in every way a superhuman. He has great strength, cunning, and bravery, and when he is sent to perform his famous twelve labors, he completes these seemingly impossible tasks with confidence and bravado. And yet for all his heroic achievements, Herakles is despised by Hera, the queen of Olympus. Not because he is the offspring of one of Zeus's many affairs, but rather because he represents unbridled male conquest. He aggressively tames wild elements, bringing animals, rivers, Amazons, Titans, and even Cerberus, the hellhound of Hades, to heel.

Hera views Herakles as a threat to the Olympian male-female cosmic balance and so she denies him the human element she presides over—a family. How she does this is terrifying and not at all the Disney version of the story. In the Euripides play, Herakles returns to his wife, Megara, after his final labor in the underworld and is driven insane at Hera's command. In this frenetic, altered state, he kills Megara and their children, shooting them with his arrows and bringing his famous great club crashing down on their heads.

When Herakles comes to his senses, he cannot comprehend what he has done. His mortal stepfather, Amphitryon, tells him he has brought an unnatural war home to his family. Herakles sits in a catatonic state, his cloak pulled over his head so no one else might become infected by his evil—the Greek concept of the evil eye. Then his former comrade, the legendary Athenian king Theseus, approaches. He removes Herakles's veil and looks directly at him. He says that his love for his friend is far more powerful than the evil act he has committed. Theseus reminds Herakles that his insanity was sent by the gods, and it was not his fault—Herakles in his right mind would never do such a thing. Then, like the Winter Soldier being sent to Wakanda, Theseus tells his old friend that there is a home for him in Athens, where he will find catharsis. He leads him away to a new role as the protective hero of Theseus's city.

I had the privilege of working on a stage production of *Herakles* with American veterans who had served in Vietnam, Iraq, and Afghanistan. When we started to work on the messenger scene when the carnage of Herakles's extreme violent episode was revealed, the room fell silent and became very tense. Many of the men and women in this project related to this harrowing scene and began to tell their own stories of children killed and maimed by war. These could sometimes be a result of their own inadvertent actions—a mortar round that hit a home where children were sheltering, schoolchildren accidently fired on from helicopters, the broken bodies of infants brought to the base gates by distraught relatives after a bombardment or firefight. For these veterans the retelling of the Herakles myth evoked something palpably real and deeply traumatic that each of them had personally experienced in different ways.

The veterans were prompted to tell their traumatic recollections because they identified with the themes of an ancient one. These experiences are shared across the ages and can then bring the telling of new stories. This can create a community of empathy. It is the telling of a story of trauma that is often the first step toward healing. This is the therapeutic power of myths.

Marvel has a plethora of characters who are veterans, including Captain America, Bucky Barnes, Carol Danvers (Captain Marvel), Nick Fury, Professor X, Deadpool, and Wolverine. But there is one notable former military character who is narratively interconnected with Daredevil and whose personal trauma defines his role as an avenging vigilante. Unlike Daredevil, he has no qualms about killing the criminals he pursues. This is the Punisher, or Frank Castle, and he served for five years in Vietnam and was a highly decorated Marine. Like Herakles, his family was also destroyed, not by his hand, but by a New York crime syndicate that accidentally came upon them in Central Park. Frank survives but is racked by guilt and anger and becomes the uncompromising assassin known as the Punisher in response.

The Punisher is perhaps Marvel's most subversively popular and controversial character. Originally created as a supervillain sniper engaged to assassinate Spider-Man, Frank Castle develops into the distraught former Marine tortured by the death of his family and determined for revenge. In the 1970s and '80s this trope of the individual revenge vigilante who took matters into their own hands when law enforcement seemed to have failed was popularized by movies, including Charles Bronson's *Death Wish* films and the Dirty Harry series starring Clint Eastwood. The Punisher took this to a whole new level with a maniacal zeal, his expert military training, and a complete disregard for any kind of legal or judicial process. The Punisher just savagely and effectively killed anyone he thought deserved to die. This was a mode of operation that brought him into frequent conflict with Marvel superheroes such as Captain America and Daredevil.

Here was a Marvel hero, albeit an antihero, who questioned the very idea of the superhero. The Punisher is a figure that acts outside the confines of the usual justice system and in so doing exposes the entire concept as deeply flawed and highly problematic. On his chest he wears a symbol of what he represented as a harbinger of death—a large skull with a disturbing elongated mouth. This is the very last thing his victims would see. Frank Castle was never supposed to be held up as a paragon of anything except the nihilism of revenge and the isolation of a man broken by trauma. Surely then not a character anyone would want to emulate.

Like the Punisher and the Winter Soldier, Herakles often went outside of the confines of ethical behavior. He was viewed as reckless, craven, and even gluttonous, led by his desires and ego rather than good sense. The Athenians in the classical period at the time of their democracy often saw him as a mythic metaphor for a man not moderated by the female. In Euripides's version of the myth of Herakles, we hear how he brutally killed his wife and children in a fit of god-sent madness. However, he believed he was killing the family of his enemy, Eurystheus, the king who sent him on his labors. Is this really any better? The sane Herakles was still a massive destructive instrument, very much like the Winter Soldier in his deranged altered state, but in his right mind he shared much with the Punisher.

In the 2000s the Punisher and his instantly recognizable skull became a new potent symbol. Some people saw Frank Castle, with his lonely, violent quest, as somehow standing up for their own situations and ideals. The character was rebooted in film and on the graphic page, as a veteran of the wars in Iraq and Afghanistan and a former Special Forces operator. In the real Iraq and Afghanistan wars, the Punisher's distinctive death's-head symbol was adopted by Navy Seal units who sported it on unit patches. They spray-painted it on their body armor, vehicles, and even buildings as a warning to enemy fighters. Then the symbol was adopted by militia groups, white supremacists, and far-right activists who resonated with the Punisher's extrajudicial individual actions. It even found its way to some police departments, and was worn on uniforms and police cruisers, and filled in with the blue, black, and gray stripes of the "Blue Lives Matter" movement. It was seen on some flags during the January 6 insurrection at the US Capitol in 2021. As a result, Punisher cocreator Gerry Conway denounced the skull use, saying that these groups had misunderstood the character he helped develop.

Myths and the symbols associated with them are still some of the most effective communication devices we know. The death's head skull, known to the Nazis and the Hussars before them as the *Totenkopf,* has a long history in world mythology, stretching back to 9000 BCE Jericho, where human skulls covered in plaster were buried in the floors of homes as a form of ancestor worship or for apotropaic (warding-off) purposes. Like Frank Castle and the Special Forces operators in Iraq and Afghanistan, warriors have used skulls, severed and shrunken heads, and images of skull-like creatures for generations. They place them on their helmets, armor, and shields to invoke fear in their enemies and ward off any harm that might come to them in battle.

For ancient Greek warriors, their apotropaic battle symbol was the head of the Gorgon Medusa, whose snake hair, fanged teeth, and piercing eyes could petrify the viewer. They were literally turned to stone in fear. Herakles had a Gorgon painted on his great shield with its piercing eyes, snake hair, terrifying grimace, and protruding tongue. We see the Gorgon face again and again on shields of Greek infantry soldiers in the classical period. It was also worn on the mantle of Athena so that mortals never forgot that even this most reasonable of gods could obliterate them in the mere blink of an eye. A reminder that the justice of Zeus she presided over was supported by fear.

A Greek hero who fought at Troy often depicted with a terrifying Gorgon's head on his shield was Ajax. He was the cousin of Achilles who came from the island of Salamis, near Athens. Ajax was admired as a fearsome warrior, but he was a loose cannon, preferring to fight on his own rather than standing in line with his comrades. The Punisher reflects many of the same qualities as Ajax, positive and negative. He also prefers to fight on his own and stands outside of a system he believes has failed him. This seemingly uncomplicated and uncompromising ultra-individuality of these kinds of heroes is appealing to those who sport the Punisher skull today, but their stories are far more complex and disturbing.

The Punisher takes justice into his own hands, and this is a big theme for mythological content in fifth-century Athens. This was a new democracy where every male citizen fully took part, and every government position was filled by selection, like juries are chosen today, except for generals who were elected. The playwright Sophocles was one such general, and his experiences inform the seven complete plays of his that we have. In his play *Ajax*, the great warrior snaps after ten years of fighting at Troy. The catalyst was a vote by the Greek lords over who should get the armor of the recently killed Achilles. They decide on Odysseus, the master of strategy. Ajax is infuriated by what he perceives as a diminishment of his service by those around him. He is unable to understand a world where collective action is valued over individual achievement. This perceived rejection sends him over the edge, and he sets out to kill his fellow Greek commanders in a night attack.

Athena thwarts Ajax by deluding his eyes so he kills, captures, and tortures livestock instead of men. When he awakes, covered in the blood of these animals and surrounded by their butchered corpses, he realizes what he has done, and he kills himself by falling on a sword. Ajax could be said to suffer from combat trauma, and many of the veterans I have worked with on the play have very strong feelings about his suicide. At one special performance of the veteran's group in the Obama White House, a former Airborne soldier and veteran of several tours in Iraq and Afghanistan reenacted that scene while staring intently into the eyes of the Pentagon brass seated in the front row. In the follow-up discussion a former Marine sergeant told us how he was once proud to have brought his entire unit back from Iraq but then learned of the deaths of several by suicide in the years after they returned. Trauma takes a terrible toll.

As Marvel's Punisher developed, his trauma was expanded to encompass not only the death of his family at the hands of the mob but his experiences in combat. On a New York rooftop in season 2 of *Daredevil,* Matt Murdock and Frank Castle have an intense exchange that gets to the heart of what is driving the Punisher. Matt cannot condone how Castle seems to have no qualms about killing and says that he is still fighting some kind of war. This is like the unnatural war Herakles waged on his family in Euripides's play. Frank answers that he does what he does out of necessity. Matt says that it is not their right to decide who lives and who dies, and Frank responds forcibly, calling him no hero and a half measure who is afraid to finish the job. To the Punisher, Daredevil's moral prevarications are the acts of a coward.

It is the certainty of the Punisher that is perhaps most attractive to modern authoritarians. Many who line up behind such extremist positions are also seeking clarity. But the myths constantly show us that life is always far more complicated. The Athenian democracy nearly faltered early on because the aristocrats could not abide the complexities of more equal power sharing. The bulwark against anarchy and self-service was to have a system of justice that all could believe in. At a time of deep division in Athens, on the brink of civil war, an old warrior-poet Aeschylus, who had fought against the Persians, produced his masterwork, the Oresteia trilogy. This tells how the ancient House of Atreus is cursed with generation upon generation of revenge killing. Agamemnon destroys Troy but returns home to pay the price of sacrificing his daughter by being murdered by his wife, Clytemnestra. She is killed seven years later by their son Orestes, who is then punished by infernal female spirits called the Furies who avenge those who have spilled the blood of kin.

Who is right and who is wrong? Democratic Athens will decide. Aeschylus staged the world's first courtroom drama where the Furies prosecuting Orestes go up against Apollo representing Olympus. It was the old matrifocal gods versus the new patriarchy of Zeus, and the jury is split right down the middle. Athena casts the deciding vote for Orestes, but she also recognizes the Furies' case and their ancient rights. So, like Herakles, they are given a new home in Athens where they will become the sacred goddesses. Aeschylus shows us with this myth that the trauma of violence and the cycle of revenge it spawns can be averted by a democratic due process shared among the people. The testimony heard in court and the stories told by witnesses are not dissimilar to how stories of trauma told can help alleviate psychological suffering.

Frank Castle continues to suffer. Ultimately the violent, arbitrary acts of the Punisher bring him no peace. In the TV show Frank is depicted briefly speaking at the veteran group therapy session led by his former comrade and admitting to being scared of having no war to fight (season 1, episode 13). Frank has barely even started on his cathartic journey toward healing from all that he has suffered. Every time he becomes the Punisher, that prospect moves further away. That death's-head symbol he wears to intimidate his victims is really a sign of his total isolation and nihilism. The Punisher is one of the most disabled characters in the entire Marvel Universe.

CHAPTER 10

MARVEL JESUS

"I am the messiah. I am . . . Marvel Jesus." So exclaims Deadpool, the most meta of all Marvel superheroes, in the MCU's 2024 summer blockbuster *Deadpool & Wolverine*. He is given the chance to become a selfless hero among heroes who will save an entire world. The narcissistic "Merc with a (foul) Mouth" opts to sacrifice himself by creating an antimatter circuit with a McGuffin machine called the Time Ripper. As he locks Wolverine out of the chamber, effectively taking his place, Deadpool repeats his messianic mantra, "I'm Marvel Jesus . . . or Spock . . . hard to say." Why Spock? A reference to an iconic moment in the 1982 movie *Star Trek II: The Wrath of Khan*, when the loyal first officer of the USS *Enterprise* sacrifices himself to save his crewmates.

The concept of self-sacrifice is deeply embedded in Marvel. In the MCU, Deadpool takes a bullet in *Deadpool 2* to prove his loyalty to the young mutant boy Russel Collins and prevent him from committing a murder that leads him to becoming a serial killer. Wolverine also sacrifices himself at the end of *Logan* to save another young mutant named Laura. Then there's Vision who dies (or deactivates) to help stop the world-destroying Thanos in *Avengers: Infinity War*. In *Age of Ultron* Pietro (Quicksilver) gives his life to save the Avengers. One of the most memorable self-sacrifices is the space pirate Yondu, who dies to save his mentee, Peter Quill (Star-lord), in *Guardians of the Galaxy Vol. 2*. In *Captain America: The First Avenger,* Steve Rogers pilots the HYDRA bomber into the icy waters of the Northern Atlantic to save New York from destruction. Then, of course, *Endgame* is propelled by the sacrifices of Black Widow and Iron Man. These are just a few examples. There are many more. What's this obsession with sacrifice all about, and why is it so prevalent in Marvel?

In my Mythology class at NYU, I start the discussion on human sacrifice by asking how many of the two hundred or so students enrolled have ever practiced some form of real or representational human sacrifice. I raise my hand, but nobody else does—confusion. Then I ask another question: how many of us have taken part in a Christian, Islamic, or Jewish religious ceremony? (Although human sacrifices have been attested in some Hindu-affiliated cults, it is not part of mainstream Hindu practice.) Now many students raise their hands, even more baffled. I explain: In a Christian church what is the most prominent symbol? A human figure being put to death on a cross. And what rites are commonly performed before this symbol? The act of communion where this figure's blood is drunk and his body eaten.

At its most basic form this Christian communion rite is an overt representation of a human sacrifice. A sacrifice in which the congregants pretend to consume the victim to communicate with their supreme being. As for Judaism and Islam, the ancestral founder of those traditions (and Christianity) is Abraham. His faith is tested by his willingness to offer the life of his own son Isaac to his god. He would have gone through with it too, if not prevented in the nick of time by the intervention of an angel of God. In one form or another many people in the modern world are still acknowledging the power of human sacrifice.

Deadpool's giddy excitement over becoming what he calls "Marvel Jesus" taps into the cultural persistence of the sacrificial motif. The main way most ancient people interacted with the divine was through blood sacrifice. By the time of the Roman Empire, these sacrifices were of animals. Afterward they were usually butchered, cooked, and shared among the congregants. Meat was not a staple for most people in antiquity, so eating it at a religious carnival ("day of meat") was a highlight. Animal sacrifices were performed by state-sanctioned priests and were highly regulated with strict stipulations about how they should be carried out.

One of the attractions of early Christianity in the ancient world was that it reversed the act of sacrifice—now any adherent, rich or poor, free or enslaved, male or female, citizen or foreigner, could personally benefit from the moment of communion with the divine without going through a priest or a king. This was nothing less than a popular revolution in religious thought and cult practice.

The sacrificial rite of early Christianity was heavily influenced by one of the most popular secret cults in the Mediterranean, the Eleusinian Mysteries. These ancient rites to the Earth goddess Demeter and her daughter Persephone can be traced back to the Greek Bronze Age. By the classical period, the mysteries had grown to exert an enormous influence over Greek culture. Famous initiates possibly included Socrates, Plato, Julius Caesar, and the emperor Marcus Aurelius.

The entire cult of Eleusis was based on the sacrifice of Persephone, who was seized by Hades and dragged down into the underworld to be lost forever. But this was an unwilling sacrifice, and one not sanctioned by her mother, Demeter, who would not rest until she had found her lost child. When she discovered that Persephone had been married to death in the guise of Hades, she went ballistic, rejecting this fate and refusing to let anything grow on Earth. This proved to be an existential problem for the Olympians—humans were starving, and without them the gods would not be worshipped nor receive their sacrifice. A compromise was reached: Persephone would spend half the year with Hades and half with her mother on earth. A myth constructed to explain the seasons is framed with the concept of sacrifice.

Initiation into the Eleusinian Mysteries' secret cult was a long process involving selection, education, and participation in a nine-day procession from Athens. We do not know how people were selected to be initiated or if they could apply. We do know that they were assigned a guide who was already initiated to prepare them for the rites. These involved all kinds of altered-state practices such as trance from dancing, vagus nerve stimulation through chanting, fasting, alcohol consumption, and emotional contagion through the participation in collective performance rites and being scared half to death. At its culmination, the initiates might have ingested a psychotropic drug called ergot derived from barley mold, although archaeologists are still divided on this. Then they entered a dark theatre space where they encountered some form of incredible light and masked priests. Whatever they did in there, it was a mind-blowing experience and completely changed their lives. It was as if they had sacrificed a part of themselves to inherit what they called "the blessed life and death."

Deadpool's actions in willingly offering himself up to die to save others, even fighting off Wolverine for the privilege, adheres closely to the ritual script of ancient sacrificial rites. These were explained by the anthropologist and classicist Walter Burkert in his work on the subject entitled *Homo Necans* (Man the Killer). A sacrificial victim, human or animal, must seem to willingly consent to its own death, otherwise the sacrifice would be tainted and ineffective. Really, very few people consent to their own deaths. Even when the myths say they do. We have many stories of the victims trying to back out once the time draws near.

The Vikings were said to have practiced mass human sacrifice. Christian writers were commenting on them as late as the eleventh century CE. We must take these accounts with a large pinch of salt, though. At this time there was a great deal of animosity toward what were considered the old pagan ways. However, archaeologists have discovered signs of human sacrifice in Norway from this period at Trelleborg, where both human and animal remains were purposely deposited in ancient wells, which were considered sacred.

The Islamic traveler Ahmad Ibn Fadlan documented the sacrifice of an enslaved girl by the Viking Rus in 922 CE. He wrote that she originally consented to die, but when the time drew near, she panicked and refused. Her end was grisly, resulting in her brutal rape and killing at the hands of her sacrificers. For Burkert, this would count as a corrupted sacrifice and one that would not sit well with those witnessing it or the gods. He suggested that from the time humans began to consume animals they created rituals to counter the violence of the killing. He called this the "comedy of innocence" where the sacrificial victim is led to their death by a great procession and honored by the community. The victim then agrees to its own death by visibly assenting. In the case of an animal, honey cakes would be placed on the altar so that it would reach in to eat them and seem to offer its neck to be severed by the sacrificial blade. Or water would be sprinkled on the head of the animal so it would seem to nod in assent as it shook off the droplets.

In many ways the entire plot of *Deadpool & Wolverine* can be seen as an elaborate comedy of innocence. Wade Wilson's humdrum existence as a used car salesperson is only made bearable to him by the small group of friends he has gathered around him. He wants to find a deeper meaning and is at once attracted to the offer from the Time Variance Authority (TVA) to save his universe and friends. For all its potty-mouthed parody, ironic moments, and metatheatrical self-referentiality, the movie delivers an emotional climax with Wade's self-sacrifice. He tries desperately to reach the other pole of the Time Ripper and is failing. Deadpool's moment of superhero transfiguration is slipping away. That is until Wolverine clasps his hand at the last minute, makes the connection, and the two heroes destroy the machine together, thus saving the universe. Yes, it's a cliché but one that is so well executed to the epic strains of Madonna's "Like a Prayer" that the viewer must be very hard-hearted not to be moved.

Here Marvel is tapping into something very ancient indeed. Richard Schechner, a performance theorist and my NYU colleague, says that the sacrificial procession is one of the first forms of theatre practiced by humans. The victim is led in a place of honor through the streets accompanied by a parade of music, dance, and song. Every now and then the procession halts and a spontaneous little performance erupts. The viewers form a circle and watch and even join in. Then the procession sets off again toward its destination, the place where the sacrifice will occur and, more important, be witnessed. Both the procession and the act of sacrifice itself were intended to form a bridge of communion with the gods. They would take delight in mortals celebrating them in the open, and then when the sacrifice was made they received it with what the Greeks called *charis*—good grace (where we get the word "charity").

Deadpool's sacrificial act was ultimately thwarted, even though he achieved his aim, to save his friends and the world they lived in. Wade survives. The prior battle between him and Logan for who would be "the one" parallels another famous Marvel sacrifice, that of Black Widow (Natasha Romanoff) in *Endgame*. Here Hawkeye (Clint Barton) fights with Natasha to be the one to die to obtain the Soul Stone. Clint, having lost his family to Thanos's purge, wants to find some meaning after living the previous five years as a vigilante. If he gives his life, it will at least help to bring his family back. Natasha, who has been helming the Avengers, feels that it is her duty.

This has been her sole responsibility for the past five years. Natasha wins the fight at the cliff's edge and pushes herself off the rock wall, freeing herself from Clint's grip, and falls to her death below. When Clint returns without her, the other Avengers grieve. They look for meaning in her death. Captain America says, "We have to make it worth it," knowing that another epic existential battle with Thanos is coming.

Natasha's sacrifice is a modern cinematic version of the sacrifice of the innocent before a conflict. Natasha's experience defies the usual innocent sacrifice, which is often a young girl, and she makes it by choice, believing that her death will save Clint and unite the Avengers to defeat Thanos. In this scene she fulfills the role of what the Greeks called the *protelia*, or the "pre-sacrifice." This is a reciprocal act, a life for a life. It occurs before the hunt or battle. Burkert explains the *protelia* as a way of butchering and feeding the hunters high-value protein in the form of a slaughtered domestic animal so they will have the energy to go after much bigger game to feed the community. Later the *protelia* became a means of forging resolve and unity before combat. We see this trope used time and time again to create the will to go to war. This is the idea of the sacrifice of the innocent: it is a passionate call to arms when unarmed or unwitting people are attacked and killed.

When Chris Hedges, the *New York Times* war correspondent, returned from Iraq and Bosnia, he wrote a book called *War Is a Force That Gives Us Meaning* in the year following the 9/11 terrorist attack on the World Trade Center. He noted how the death of the innocents is frequently a prelude to war. He cites the sinking of the passenger ship *Lusitania* by Germany that helped persuade the USA to join World War I, the unprovoked attack on Pearl Harbor prior to World War II, and the Gulf of Tonkin attack prior to the war in Vietnam that might have been manipulated to create a "sacrifice of innocents" incident. It is the mark of a good person to want to protect the innocent and repel unprovoked attacks, and the *protelia* sacrifice taps into this urge. Hedges also thinks that the desire to self-sacrifice in recompense is connected to Freud's death drive, that people seek meaning in life by courting and even embracing death. Freud named this after the Greek spirit of death—Thanatos.

For our hunter-gatherer ancestors, killing a domestic animal provided them with energy. It also acted as a death of an innocent to steel the hunters to the act of killing a wild animal. Now, most of us never experience the slaughtering of animals and obtain our meats already butchered and shrink-wrapped at a supermarket. It is hard to understand the sacredness of killing an animal to eat its meat.

I know a story from my younger days with the Royal Marines. Inductees on survival courses had to survive on nettles, roots, and the occasional small berry in some very hostile environments. On one such field exercise, a small rabbit was caught after a few days, when the participants were almost hallucinating with hunger. They said that it was amazing how that small amount of meat distributed among the four people completely changed their physiology. It was as if the power of the animal had temporally transferred into their bodies. They could think more clearly; they had more energy and felt warmer and stronger. They could then forage effectively and gather foodstuffs and firewood.

Yet, in killing, skinning, and butchering that small rabbit, they knew something was off. When they came back to their makeshift camp, they saw the skin and bones sucked clean, strewn around a firepit, and do you know what? They felt a sense of guilt. Yes, they had benefited greatly from the small feast the rabbit provided, but they had also killed an innocent creature. But they didn't all feel this way. One member of the small group thought the others were being ridiculously sentimental as the bones were collected, wrapped in the skin, and an attempt made to reconstitute the little rabbit. "Should we say anything?" one of the guys asked. "Here lies Flopsy, may she rest in fucking peace!" replied one cynical group member.

It was not until years later, after I had read Burkert as a classical scholar, that I understood that these Marines had unknowingly taken part in one of the oldest sacred rites known to humanity. A sacrifice was performed, followed by a resurrection of the remains, before sending her to a rabbit afterlife. Even the cynical group member took part by naming the corpse and in so doing imbuing what was once a meal with a persona.

On a practical level ancient sacrificial rites created a method of sorting, butchering, cooking, and dividing meat, then disposing of the remains so they did not make the community sick. The Greeks had a myth about this called the "Trick at Mekone." Prometheus was a Titan who, although allied to the Olympians against the other Titans, did not want their power to go unchecked. So, he stole a spark of Zeus's divine fire from Olympus and gave it to humanity. He taught people how to sacrifice and cook animals. He told them that once butchered the meat should all be heaped up in a pile on one side. Then the bones and the *splagmata*—a wonderfully onomatopoeic ancient Greek word for guts (say it a few times to get the gist)—should be wrapped up in the skin of the dead animal and placed on the other.

Prometheus asked Zeus to decide what he wanted—the rather unsightly pile of uncooked slabs of meat, or what seemed to be the whole animal. Zeus chose the latter, and the skin, bones, and guts were burned on the altar with the smoke trailing up to Olympus to "feed" the gods. Meanwhile the humans had a nice barbecue, grilling the meat on spits: souvlaki and gyros for all! The Greeks placed so much value on their meat kebabs roasted on metal spits that their word for them, *obol*, became the name of a Greek coin. Six spits (*obols*) made up a *drachma* ("handful"), which was the official currency of Greece until supplanted by the Euro in 2002. The value of sacrifice transfers its importance even to money.

So, why did Natasha die in *Endgame* and not Clint? Here, Marvel has been most influenced by the Greeks, where in many myths it is the blood of a young virgin woman that must be spilled as the *protelia*. This may be an extension of the concept of the innocent victim, but it is more likely that these myths present the virgin sacrifice as the highest value offering that can be made. The Greeks had a name for this type of sacrifice, one that was not eaten, and instead the entire animal is burned—a *holokaustos* from *olos*, "whole," and *kaustos*, "burned." These types of sacrifices were tremendously expensive, particularly if it was a cow or bull, and were made to propitiate specific gods or heroes. In myths the costliest sacrifice was a female virgin, and the most extreme version of that would be the sacrificer's own daughter.

The virgin sacrifice was linked to marriage exchange networks in ancient Greece. A young bride had enormous value and was wed with a significant dowry. Her marriage forged alliances and political ties, building the wealth of her family. This was why Paris absconding with Menelaus's wife, Helen, was such a big deal that it launched the Trojan War. His act obliterated the rules and therefore the value of bridal exchange. Many virgin sacrifices in Greek myth were presented as if they were symbolic marriages.

The sacrifice of Natasha must also be viewed alongside its equivalent in *Infinity War*: Thanos's sacrifice of his adopted daughter Gamora. This occurs in the same place as Natasha's death, in a different point of the multiversal timeline, the bleak planet Vormir. "A soul for a soul" is the provision offered by Red Skull. This is the essence of reciprocal sacrifice. In Greek culture this was usually offered to Artemis, the virgin goddess of the hunt, protector of all wild animals, and one of the most remorseless of all the Olympians. Artemis imposed the same kind of reciprocal sacrificial demand on

Greek mythology's human version of Thanos, the commander of the Greeks and destroyer of Troy, Agamemnon.

Like Thanos, Agamemnon believes he is pursuing a war for the greater good and to uphold the laws of Zeus. Paris abused the sacred codes of hospitality by absconding with Helen when he was a guest in the house of Menelaus. In Bronze Age society, marriage was the main way alliances were formed, diplomatic ties were established, and communication between states was maintained. Kings across the Bronze Age world were connected to one another by these interstate marriages. In Greek myth, one of the most famous of these were the marriages of Agamemnon and Menelaus, the boys from Mycenae, with Clytemnestra and Helen, the girls from Sparta. Joining these two southern Greek states created a new regional military and trade power.

There was fierce competition for the hand of Helen, though. She was a daughter of Zeus, who had come to her mother, Leda, in the guise of a swan and impregnated her on the same night her mortal husband, Tyndareus, slept with her (classic Zeus behavior). Subsequently, Leda birthed two mortal children—Clytemnestra and her brother Cleobis—and two semidivine children from an egg—Helen and her brother Biton (the brothers are also known as Castor and Pollux). All the lords of Greece proposed marriage to Helen, as she was famed for her beauty and divine parentage. When Menelaus was chosen, they all swore a scared oath to uphold this new political power marriage.

So, Menelaus and Helen lived in Sparta, and Agamemnon and Clytemnestra in Mycenae. All seemed well until the day a handsome young prince of Troy came to visit Sparta, and all hell broke loose.

Paris had grown up in exile from Troy. His parents received a prophecy that he would destroy the city, so he was sent away to die as a baby. But like Oedipus, he did not perish but was raised as a shepherd-boy ignorant of his true origins. That is, until he was suddenly visited by three goddesses: Hera, Athena, and Aphrodite, who thought that this innocent young man would be able to honestly settle a dispute—which of these three divinities was the most beautiful? Each offered Paris gifts if he should choose them. Hera promised untold power, and Athena an incredible intellect; Aphrodite pledged that he would have the most beautiful woman in the world. Look, he's a sixteen-year-old boy who has been living with goats, what do you think he chose? Aphrodite was declared the winner.

So, a few years later he reunites with his Trojan royal family who took his survival and the divine visitation as a miracle. Now here he is at dinner in Sparta staring hard at Helen. Some people thought it was Aphrodite's fault, others that Helen took it as an opportunity to escape an unhappy union; either way she secretly left with Paris and was welcomed in Troy.

Menelaus was distraught, but Agamemnon was enraged. This was an affront against the codes of bridal exchange and hospitality. There must be war, a sacred war, and those lords who swore to uphold the marriage, they would all have to join and bring their armies. And so, the greatest military force the Greek world had ever assembled gathered in ships in the bay of Aulis in central Greece ready to sail on Troy.

But things did not go well. A massive storm raged for days and days. Food and water were running out and men were starting to starve and die. Nothing the Greeks could do seemed to help, until a prophet reading the birds in the sky told them that Artemis was angry. She knew that this mighty force was setting out to destroy an entire city. And so, the greatest war ever fought demanded the greatest sacrifice, and it was decided that this should be Agamemnon's daughter, Iphigenia. She was sent for under the premise that she would be marrying Achilles. Iphigenia is sacrificed by her father, just as Gamora is thrown off the cliffs of Vormir by her father Thanos. "You must lose what you love, a soul for a soul."

Thanos is distraught at the thought of sacrificing his beloved Gamora. When Agamemnon learns what he must do, he cries out in anguish and beats the ground with his scepter, the symbol of his office. If he saves his daughter his soldiers will die. But the sacrifice will stop the storm. Agamemnon feels he must act for the good of his men. When Iphigenia learns her fate, she pleads with her father and the other Greek lords whom she had sung to when they were guests at her house. They gag her to stifle her cries that will curse the rites, then bind her like a goat and hold her face down over the altar as Agamemnon slits her throat. The storm passes and the campaign against Troy resumes. But from that moment on Agamemnon was forever changed, his mind darkened. Nothing would stop him from destroying Troy.

What do these sacrificial myths mean? For Thanos and Agamemnon, the act of destroying their daughters, what they cherish most in the world, shows their extreme commitment to their causes. It proves to their subordinates the tremendous lengths they are prepared to go to win. Agamemnon may not be the best fighter at Troy—Achilles could easily defeat him one-on-one—but his ruthlessness is such that it creates a mythic aura around him, which forces others to fall in line. This is why Natasha dies; the Avengers need a sacrifice of equal significance to them to steel themselves against the near-impossible task of defeating Thanos. And of the original six MCU Avengers, she was the only woman.

Another meaning is perhaps more human. The sacrifice of a beloved family member to set off for war stands for the concept of duty to others over personal concerns. This is something every serviceperson wrestles with each time they are deployed. They must leave their loved ones to go on a mission they may never return from.

Agamemnon's and Thanos's sacrificial acts are extreme versions of this, to be sure, but they nevertheless strike a chord with anyone who has had to make the same kind of choice between service to the state and their family. This is why we still call the loss of a loved one in war the supreme sacrifice. Thanos kills his daughter because in his own twisted way he thinks he is saving the universe. Agamemnon does the same, believing that he is saving the army and assuring the rightful destruction of Troy. After making the terrible decision to kill their daughters, nothing will stop both Thanos and Agamemnon from achieving their goals—except, that is, another sacrifice.

The climax of the MCU's "Infinity Saga" is the self-sacrifice of Tony Stark in order to defeat Thanos. What makes this scene even more poignant is that Stark knows it needs to happen. Dr. Strange calculated 14,000,605 possible outcomes, this being the only one with a chance. Iron Man knew going into the fight what he needed to do. This is not the only time Tony Stark dies in the wider Marvel Universe, and they all carry the same element of sacrifice. The most striking occurs in the 2018 Marvel comic *Thanos Wins*, where Stark is gruesomely ripped apart by Thanos, his guts spilling out of his protective suit in vivid, disturbing detail. This is nothing less than a modern *sparagmos*, the ritualistic tearing apart of a body found in several ancient cult traditions including the rites of Orpheus, Dionysus, and Isis.

In the Egyptian myth Osiris is torn apart by Seth and his body parts scattered far and wide. In a representation of the sacrificial resurrection and Egyptian burial customs, Isis collects the parts of her brother, brings him back to life for one day, and copulates with him to birth Horus, the first Pharaoh. One Dionysian myth tells how he is torn apart by the Titans, except for his heart, which is swallowed by Zeus—who then sleeps with the mortal Semele and produces the "twice born" Dionysus. Orpheus, who charmed the gods with his song and was the figurehead of the Orphic mystery cult, was also torn apart by the female followers of Dionysus who threw his head into the sea, where it continued to sing.

For Thanos and Agamemnon there is no restoration. Thanos undergoes his own *sparagmos*, disintegrating into dust as he is destroyed along with his army by the Infinity Gauntlet wielded by the dying Iron Man. Agamemnon returns home to be butchered in his bath by his wife with three strikes of a huge sacrificial axe. These sacrifices are also reciprocal, and they prove that despite what Thanos says, nothing is inevitable, except that is, death.

The final defeat of Thanos in *Endgame* is the triumph of the humane forces of friendship, mutual trust, international cooperation, and the shared values of individual human rights. All of this is arrayed against an authoritarian tyrant who uses mass sacrifice to turn the universe into his singular vision, whatever the cost. This is not without historical precedent: Maya, Toltec, and Aztec cultures regularly performed human sacrifice. At times of social stress, such as natural disasters, wars, and invasions, those sacrifices increased. When the Spanish marched into what is now Mexico City in 1519, they justified its destruction based on the thousands of skulls they reported seeing heaped up on massive racks, some of these which have now been uncovered by archaeologists.

Human sacrifice in one form or another has been attested at different times throughout the world. It does still occur, always against the law, and usually in recognition of an extreme religious position or local superstition. It was outlawed in India in 1830, although the practice still occasionally occurs and is usually performed on young, female victims. In 2020 the Ugandan government passed a law criminalizing human sacrifice, which was reported to be on the increase. Some of the most iconic cultural monuments in Europe have also recently been associated with human sacrifice. For instance, remains of a young man showing signs of a ritual death have been found at Stonehenge. Scholars view Roman acts of *devotio*—when a commander offered to die for the state—as a willing self-sacrifice. My colleague Joan Connelly has argued that the most famous of ancient Greek artworks, the Parthenon Frieze on the Athenian acropolis, depicts the sacrifice of the daughters of King Erechtheus to save Athens.

Does this mean that the ancient Greeks, those rational, philosophizing, democracy-building, theatre-producing, exquisite artwork makers, practiced real human sacrifice? Their myths are certainly full of them, and recently there have been several sensational archaeological finds that point to real practices occurring in the Bronze Age. These include the remains of child sacrifice on Minoan Crete, and the offering of a headless body found in the center of the Altar of Zeus on Mt. Lykaion in mainland Greece. We also hear how three Persian boys were sacrificed by the Athenian commander Themistocles in 480 BCE before the naval battle of Salamis. Occasionally human sacrifice was also carried out by the Romans, with gladiatorial contests originally being established as a martial form of human ritual bloodletting. This puts a different spin on the famous prefight proclamation "Those who are about to die, we salute you!"

Marvel is also reflecting something far deeper in some parts of our culture. This is the idea that there will always be a savior who was themselves a victim of some form of sacrifice. They are resurrected and empowered, then deliver a solution. This concept of victimhood runs deep in many parts of society. Rather than the people who feel they have been "defeated" becoming resigned to their perceived loss and seeking other paths, they keep the idea that they have been somehow sacrificed. Some believe that their cause will be resurrected by a messianic figure, and this can stir up feelings of deep resentment and hostility against what they perceive as the wrong side. The victims will "rise again" and things will be set right, even if that means severe repercussions against those that they perceive as the victimizers. This is the negative application of sacrifice and what was so devastatingly practiced by Thanos.

One of the most well-known Greek mythological heroes, Odysseus, learns a hard reality about the limits of self-sacrifice. In Homer's *Odyssey*, when our hero leaves the island of the brilliant sorcerer Circe, he must journey to the edge of the underworld to receive a prophecy about his fate. He sacrifices two rams and instead of burning their corpses to Olympus he collects their blood in a ritual pit. When the shades of the dead start to gather, he allows some of them to drink the blood, and they become temporarily revived so he can speak with them. This is like a chthonic (underworld) sacrifice to the dead when the animal's blood falls on the ground and is soaked up by the earth.

In Hades, Odysseus sees his dead comrades from the Trojan War. Agamemnon tells him about his death at the hands of his wife and that he should be careful returning home. The soul of the great warrior Ajax turns his back, still aggrieved that Odysseus received the armor of Achilles and not him. Then he meets Achilles and, as we saw in Chapter One, receives a jolting shock. "Surely you, Achilles, must now be happy? You have the fame you always wanted." A solemn Achilles looks at him and says, "I would rather be a living servant than lord of the dead." Wow! Everything these Homeric heroes believed in, blown up in one moment. Even Achilles, of all people, thinks that his self-sacrifice wasn't worth it. Odysseus, who thought he knew how to die, now must find a new way to *live*.

So, did Black Widow and Iron Man need to die to save our world? We can agree that a character initially presented as one of the most self-obsessed in Marvel, Tony Stark, offering himself up in an act of supreme sacrifice makes for compelling drama. But does it also show something darker in our human psyches that lurks in so many of our ancient myths? Or are these sacrificial moments what occasionally raise Marvel into the realm of semispiritual experience or pop-culture quasi religion? There was no doubt that for many, me included, movies like *Black Panther* and *Endgame* were kind of cathartic. Even the last ten minutes of *Deadpool & Wolverine,* where two buddies are prepared to die for each other and the good of humanity, put a lump in this often overly critical professor's throat.

Perhaps then, it is the idea that we too could be prepared to sacrifice something, even everything, of ourselves for a higher cause that makes us seem superhuman.

EPILOGUE

THE POST-CREDITS SCENE

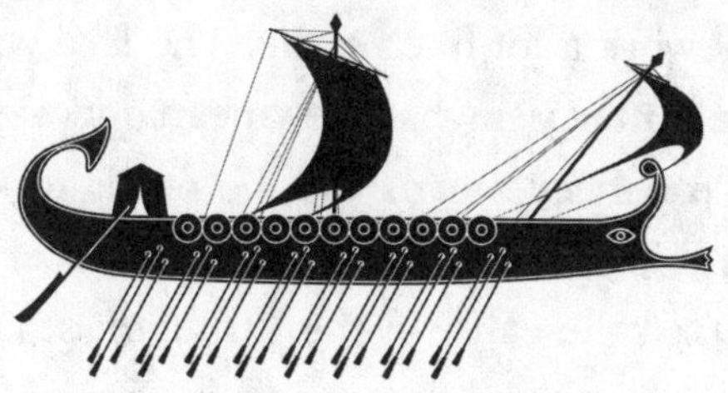

A lonely traveler beaches his small boat on a deserted shore. He hauls in the sail and pulls in the oars, except one, which he slides out of the oar lock and places across his back. He sets off inland until he can no longer see the sea. He spies smoke rising in the distance, and a small village comes into view. He hasn't had a hot meal for a week, so he props his oar up against the wall of a large hut and enters, giving a gesture of friendship. The people there offer him a plate of food. It tastes different, unseasoned, there is no salt. As the traveler leaves, he picks up his oar once again. An old man asks why he is carrying a winnowing fan—the harvest time has passed. There is no wheat to be threshed. The traveler smiles, offers a prayer to his god, climbs a nearby hill, and plants the oar upright in the ground. Now he can finally live in peace.

If the *Odyssey* were a Marvel movie, this would be the post-credits scene. In Homer, it is told as a prophecy to Odysseus by Tiresias, the blind seer, when he is in the underworld. Odysseus does make it home to Ithaka. He kills the suitors alongside his son and reunites with his wife, Penelope. Then Athena appears and calls for peace. But is this the end of Odysseus's journey?

Scholars argue over what the prophecy means, but the best oracles are always vague and open to interpretation. That's the point of prophecies; they work a lot like myths. The free will of the person hearing them will interpret what they mean one way or another. For me, Odysseus's prophecy means that he needs to see others in his world as equals. He must accept their differences to receive their hospitality and find the calm in the turbulent seas. The people he meets think his oar is a paddle used for scooping up the harvested crops and letting the wind separate the wheat from the chaff. The act also points to the Eleusinian Mysteries, where the implements of threshing wheat were used to represent the separating of the good from the bad that led to the cleansing of catharsis. Odysseus now knows that the kernel of his life is his family, not fame or glory won by violence, plunder, and war. Odysseus is purging himself and making peace with Poseidon.

The psychotherapist and author Ed Tick, who has led healing pilgrimages to Greece for many years, writes in his forthcoming book, *Passage to Poros: In the Sanctuary of the Sea God*, "Poseidon is a repository of primitive, instinctual energies, and passions, and these are of nature, the earth, and the animal parts of humanity." When Odysseus plants his oar he knows that by telling his story he has come to terms with the spirit of Poseidon that lives in him. Odysseus's myths of mystical witches, terrifying monsters, and god-sent storms have helped him understand what it means to be human.

I have spent a year on my odyssey through the Marvel universe, and like many of my students who first come to my Greek and Roman Mythology class having read Percy Jackson or an illustrated story book of the *Odyssey*, I initially thought that the material was stories for kids, expensive summer blockbuster fare, all special effects and bluster with not much depth. I agreed with the director Martin Scorsese that the MCU was the theme park ride of American cinema.

But in my odyssey through what was unfamiliar territory, I have found something far more profound. At its best, Marvel is a large part of our modern American mythology, and it looks back at the past, reflects the present, and opens the doors to our future. Marvel's famous characters are ancient archetypes, and its multiverse is a metaphysical playground of infinite possibilities, although sometimes at the expense of the myths themselves. Its masks project the emotions of our age, its myths reflect potent contemporary issues, and even its violence and dysfunctions help us see who we really are, even the ugly parts.

I've particularly loved getting to know the comics and their exquisite artwork and often intricate story lines. I can see how anyone who read the stories as a child continues to hold them in high esteem and care deeply about the characters they grew up with. Although I do not profess to be any kind of expert on Marvel, I do know a good mythical tradition when I see one, and in Marvel this abounds. So, while not a Marvel specialist, I have now become a fan.

I've also tried to open up the fascinating realms of ancient mythology. I wanted to show how many of the things we thought we knew about the ancient world were seen quite differently thousands of years ago. Myths get retold, hijacked, co-opted, and used for both good and ill, but it is always within myths where we find meaning, even if sometimes those meanings are hateful or wrong. The premise of this book is the same as what I try to teach my students. This is to break down myths and see them for what they are—stories that have been structured to suit a particular purpose. If they learn how to do that, then they will at least have the tools to see the incredible parts of the human experience they convey. They will hopefully also be able to better see through the bullshit, lies, political manipulations, and paranoid conspiracy theories that ping on our screens every day—the destructive side of mythology. In our internet age, with the exponential growth of artificial intelligence, people need these skills now more than ever.

As for my pop-culture odyssey, I'm not sure I'm ready to plant my myth-seeking oar just yet. There are certainly a lot more ancient stories in our modern world yet to explore.

ACKNOWLEDGMENTS

This book is dedicated to all my past and future students at New York University, Princeton, and the University of South Carolina, where I have had the privilege to teach over the past twenty-nine years. But it would not have been possible without the guidance, encouragement, and expertise of the brilliant agent Sam Birmingham and my wonderfully creative and supportive editors at William Morrow, Mauro DiPreta and Allie Johnston, as well as Evangelos Vasilakis and Mark Steven Long. I also need to extend my thanks to Sian-Ashleigh Edwards at WME and the incredible Rose Schwartz for their help in guiding me through the process. My wonderful wife and partner, Desiree Sanchez, has been with me every step of the way, listening to all my ideas, showing me new avenues of inquiry and sharing my lifelong love of these ancient works. My daughters, Sofia Estrella and Marina Hippolyta, were the sounding board for these stories, at bedtime, around the fire, on epic trips to Greece and Italy, at the movie theatre, and in our living room. They introduced me to the fantastic world of Marvel and the sheer delight of telling a story because there's always a story worth telling.

NOTES

PROLOGUE: THE NEW ANCIENT MYTHOLOGY

1. Jef Rouner, "Stan Lee's Immortal Message About Politics in Pop Art," *Houston Press*, November 13, 2018, https://www.houstonpress.com/news/what-stan-lee-had-to-say-about-politics-in-comics-11035025, accessed June 20, 2025.

CHAPTER 1: THE ETHOS OF MARVEL

1. Aristotle, *Poetics* 1454a 16–17.

2. Rand Hoppe, "Jack Kirby Interview," *The Kirby Effect*, 2002, https://kirbymuseum.org/blogs/effect/2012/06/27/19900413-interview/.

3. Shawn Snow, "Captain America-clad Marine Vet Squares off at Unite the Right 2 Rally in Washington," *Marine Corps Times*, August 14, 2018.

4. Homer, *Odyssey* 11.482–92.

5. Aristotle, *Nicomachean Ethics* 1175b, 24–26.

CHAPTER 2: TONY STARK: POLYTECHNES

1. Andy Clark, *Natural-Born Cyborgs* (Oxford: Oxford University Press, 2003).

2. Sophocles, *Antigone*, trans. Paul Woodruff (Indianapolis: Hackett Pub. Co., 2001), 333–75.

3. E. Schatzberg, *Technology: Critical History of a Concept* (Chicago: University of Chicago Press, 2018), 22.

4. E. Cline, *1177: The Year Civilization Collapsed* (Princeton: Princeton University Press, 2014).

5. Homer, *Odyssey*, 9.387–95, adapted from the translation by Stanley Lombardo (Indianapolis: Hackett Pub. Co., 2000), 72–73.

6. Homer, *Odyssey*, 12, 279–80, trans. Stanley Lombardo (Indianapolis: Hackett Pub. Co., 2000), 123.

7. Apollonius of Rhodes, *Argonautica* or *Jason and the Argonauts*, trans. Benjamin Acosta-Hughes (London: Penguin Classics, 2014).

CHAPTER 3: BLACK WIDOW: AMAZONIAN QUEEN

1. Aeschylus, *Oresteia*, trans. Peter Meineck (Indianapolis: Hackett Pub. Co., 1998).

2. Homer, *Iliad* 8.189–90.

3. Herodotus, *Histories* 4.110–17.

4. Photius, *Bibliotheca* 72.3.

5. Aeschylus, *Suppliants* 286–87.

6. Xenophon, *Anabasis* 4.4.17.

7. Isocrates, *Panathenaicus* 12.193–94.

8. Aeschylus, *Eumenides* 685–90.

9. Arctinus of Miletus, *The "Aethiopis" Fragment* 1.

10. Scholia on Sophocles's *Philoctetes* 454.

11. Quintus Smyrnaeus, *The Fall of Troy* 1.891.

12. Pausanias, *Guide to Greece* 2.20.8–9.

13. Aeschylus, *Eumenides* 681–99.

CHAPTER 4: THE MADNESS OF THE MULTIVERSE

1. Euripides, *Helen* 1140–42.

2. Euripides, *Helen* 40.

3. Mike Grell (writer), "Shining Iron," *The Invincible Iron Man Vol. 3 #59*, Marvel, November 2002.

4. Killian Fox, "Cosmologist Laura Mersini-Houghton: 'Our Universe Is One Tiny Grain of Dust in a Beautiful Cosmos,'" *The Guardian*, August 27, 2022.

5. Bhagavad Gita 10.11.

6. Euripides, *Helen* 1137–39.

7. Mark Waid (writer), "Hereafter Part 3," *Fantastic Four #511*, Marvel, May 2004.

8. For an explanation of the MCU "phases" visit the webpage https://thedirect.com/article/marvel-phases-explained, accessed June 16, 2025.

9. Aristotle, *Poetics* 1452a, 2–5.

10. Cullen Bunn (writer), "Part IV," *Deadpool Kills the Marvel Universe #4*, Marvel, October 2012.

11. Aristotle, *Poetics* 1455a, 34.

CHAPTER 5: PLATO'S BLACK PANTHER

1. Plato, *Timaeus* 20d–25d; Plato, *Critias* 108d–121c.

2. Plato, *Laws* 3.701–702.

3. Herodotus, *Histories* 2.169–71.

4. Aristotle, *Politics* 1327b.

5. S. O. Y. Keita, "Ancient Egyptian 'Origins' and 'Identity,'" in *Ancient Egyptian Society: Challenging Assumptions, Exploring Approaches*, ed. Danielle Candelora, Nadia Ben-Marzouk, and Kathlyn M. Cooney (New York and Abingdon: Routledge, 2022), 111–121: 121.

6. Matt Miller, "Stan Lee's Powerful 1968 Essay About the Evils of Racism Is Still Necessary Today," *Esquire*, November 12, 2018, https://www.esquire.com/entertainment/movies/a25022397/stan-lee-marvel-racism-1968-essay/, accessed June 20, 2025.

7. Roy Thomas (writer), "Three Stood Together!," *Fantastic Four #119*, February 1972.

8. Caitlin Tyrell, "Ryan Coogler Explains Why *Black Panther 2* Based Talokan on the Americas," *Screen Rant*, November 4, 2022.

9. Pseudo-Apollodorus, *Library* 2.1.4.

10. Pausanias, *Guide to Greece* 4.35.2.

11. Aeschylus, *Suppliants* 295–99.

CHAPTER 6: MEDEA MAXIMOFF

1. Attic Red Figure Kylix attributed to the Douris Painter, 500–450 BCE, Vatican City, Gregorian Etruscan Museum, Vatican 1645.

2. For a pretty nasty 1999 takedown of Gimbutas's work see Bruce Thornton, "The False Goddess and Her Lost Paradise," *Arion: A Journal of the Humanities and Classics* 7, no. 1 (1999): 72–97. The DNA evidence collected from the past ten years has since proven Thornton wrong about the Kurgan (Yamnaya) migrations.

3. J. Chapman, "The Impact of Modern Invasions and Migrations on Archaeological Explanation: A Biographical Sketch of Marija Gimbutas," in *Excavating Women*, ed. Margarita Díaz-Andreu García and Marie Louise Stig Sørensen (New York and Abingdon: Routledge, 1998), 295–314. Also, A. Carta, "Who's Afraid of the Goddess? Leopard's Tale, Menopausal Syndrome: Terms of Debate within Archaeology," *Studia Mythologica Slavica* 25 (2002): 245–71.

4. N. A. Ring, N. M. McHugh, B. B. Reed, et al., "Healers and Midwives Accused of Witchcraft (1563–1736)," *Nurse Education Today*, 133 (2024): 106026.

5. A. Nove, P. ten Hoope-Bender, M. Boyce, et al., "The State of the World's Midwifery 2021 Report: Findings to Drive Global Policy and Practice," *Human Resources for Health* 19 (2021): 1–7.

6. Plato, *Theaetetus* 149a.

7. Wolfgang Haak et al., "Massive Migration from the Steppe Was a Source for Indo-European Languages in Europe," *Nature* 522, no. 7555 (2015): 207–11.

8. Euripides, *Medea*, trans. Celia Luschnig (Indianopolis: Hackett Pub. Co., 2008): lines 35–38.

CHAPTER 7: WOLVERINE'S WILD WEST

1. A. Takeuchi, T. L. Ahern, and S. O. Henderson, "Excited Delirium," *Western Journal of Emergency Medicine* 12, no. 1 (2011): 77–83.

2. Jonathan Shay, *Achilles in Vietnam* (New York: Atheneum, 1994), 98.

3. *Rigveda* 2.33.11.

4. *Atharvaveda* 11.2.30–31.

5. Homer, *Iliad* 16.155–63.

6. This and other Canadian indigenous wolf-transformation rituals are collected by Hammerson Peters in "Native Werewolf Legends from Western and Northern Canada," *Mysteries of Canada*, March 2, 2024, https://mysteriesofcanada.com/canada/native-werewolf-legends-from-western-and-northern-canada, accessed June 21, 2024.

7. Dorcas R. Brown, David W. Anthony, and B. A. Olsen, "Late Bronze Age Midwinter Dog Sacrifices and Warrior Initiations at Krasnosamarskoe, Russia," in *Tracing the Indo-Europeans: New Evidence for Archaeology and Historical Linguistics*, ed. Birgit Anette Olsen, Thomas Olander, and Kristian Kristiansen (Oxford, UK: Oxbow Books, 2019), 97–122.

8. William Shakespeare, *Julius Caesar*, act 1, scene 2.

9. Julius Caesar, *The Gallic Wars* 4.24.

10. Virgil, *Aeneid*, trans. A. S. Kline (Oxford: Poetry in Translation, 2018), lines 2.355–57.

CHAPTER 8: THE HERO WITH A THOUSAND (OTHER) FACES

1. Juan Sebastian De Vivo, "The Memory of Greek Battle: Material Culture and/as Narrative of Combat," in *Combat Trauma and the Ancient Greeks*, ed. Peter Meineck and David Konstan (New York: Palgrave Macmillan, 2014), 163–184: 170.

2. Car Buckley, "Tom Hiddleston Playing Hank Wiliams," *New York Times*, September 12, 2015.

3. Marius V. Peelen, Anthony P. Atkinson, and Patrik Vuilleumier, "Supramodal representations of perceived emotions in the human brain," *Journal of Neuroscience* 30, no. 30 (2010): 10127–10134.

4. Peter Meineck, "The Neuroscience of the Tragic Mask," *Arion: A Journal of Humanities and the Classics* 19, no. 1 (2011): 113–58.

5. J. Parvizi, C. Jacques, B. L. Foster, et al., "Electrical Stimulation of Human Fusiform Face-Selective Regions Distorts Face Perception," *Journal of Neuroscience* 32, no. 43 (2012): 14915–20.

6. Aristotle, *Poetics* 1450b1.

7. Mike Russell, "Interview with James Cameron on 'Avatar' re-release, BP oil spill—and much more," *The Oregonian*, August 26, 2010, https://www.oregonlive.com/movies/2010/08/interview_with_james_cameron_o.html.

8. Carl Knappett, "Photographs, skeuomorphs and marionettes: some thoughts on mind, agency and object," *Journal of material culture* 7, no. 1, (2002): 97–117.

9. A. Vrigj and M. Hartwig, "Deception and Lie Detection in the Courtroom: The Effect of Defendants Wearing Medical Face Masks," *Journal of Applied Research in Memory and Cognition* 10, no. 3 (2021): 392–99.

10. Oscar Wilde, *Intentions: The Decay of Lying; Pen, Pencil and Poison; The Truth of Masks* (London: James R. Osgood, McIlvaine and Company, 1891), 182.

CHAPTER 9: SCARY MONSTERS AND SUPERCRIPS

1. In fifth-century Athens most plays had only one performance. Sophocles's *Antigone* was staged in 441 BCE, his *Oedipus Tyrant* around 425 BCE, and his *Oedipus at Colonus* in 401 BCE, after his death in 405 BCE.

2. Sophocles, *Oedipus Tyrannus* 297–462.

3. Chip Zdarsky (writer), "Know Fear, Part 1," *Daredevil #1*, April 2019.

FURTHER READING

A FEW SUGGESTIONS TO DELVE A BIT DEEPER

THE NEW ANCIENT MYTHOLOGY

Buxton, Richard. *Greek Myths That Shape The Way We Think*. London: Thames and Hudson, 2022.

Leeming, David. *The Oxford Companion to World Mythology*. Oxford: Oxford University Press, 2005.

March, Jennifer, *The Penguin Book of Classical Myths*. London: Penguin UK, 2009.

Parker, Robert. *On Greek Religion*. Ithaca, NY: Cornell University Press, 2011.

1. CAPTAIN AMERICA: THE ETHOS OF MARVEL

González, Marta González. *Achilles*. New York and Abingdon: Routledge, 2017.

Helle, Sophus. *Gilgamesh: A New Translation of the Ancient Epic*. New Haven, CT: Yale University Press, 2021.

Homer, *Iliad*. Translated by Stanley Lombardo. Indianapolis: Hackett Publishing Company, 1997.

Nagy, Gregory. *The Ancient Greek Hero in 24 Hours*. Cambridge, MA: Harvard University Press, 2019.

2. TONY STARK: POLYTECHNES

Cave, Stephen, Kanta Dihal, and Sarah Dillon, eds. *AI Narratives: A History of Imaginative Thinking about Intelligent Machines.* Oxford: Oxford University Press, 2020.

Currier, Richard. *Unbound: How Eight Technologies Made Us Human and Brought Our World to the Brink.* New York: Simon and Schuster, 2017.

Homer, *The Odyssey.* Translated by Emily Wilson. New York: WW Norton & Company, 2017.

Oleson, J.P., ed., *The Oxford Handbook of Engineering and Technology in the Classical World.* Oxford: Oxford University Press, 2009.

3. BLACK WIDOW: AMAZONIAN QUEEN

Budin, Stephanie Lynn, and Jean MacIntosh Turfa, eds. *Women in Antiquity: Real Women across the Ancient World.* New York and Abingdon: Routledge, 2016.

Fabre-Serris, Jacqueline, and Alison Keith, eds. *Women and War in Antiquity.* Baltimore: JHU Press, 2015.

Mayor, Adrienne. *The Amazons: Lives and Legends of Warrior Women across the Ancient World.* Princeton: Princeton University Press, 2014.

McCarter, Stephanie. *Women in Power: Classical Myths and Stories, from the Amazons to Cleopatra.* London: Penguin 2024.

4. THE MADNESS OF THE MULTIVERSE

Hesiod, *Work and Days & Theogony.* Translated by Stanley Lombardo. Indianapolis: Hackett Publishing, 1993.

López-Ruiz, Carolina. *Greek Mythology: From Creation to First Humans.* Oxford: Oxford University Press, 2025.

Soyinka, Wole. *Myth, Literature and the African World.* Cambridge: Cambridge University Press, 1990.

Sproul, Barbara. *Primal Myths: Creation Myths Around the World.* San Franciso: HarperOne, 2013.

5. PLATO'S BLACK PANTHER

Chapoutot, Johann. *Greeks, Romans, Germans: How the Nazis Usurped Europe's Classical Past.* Oakland, CA: University of California Press, 2016.

Derbew, Sarah F. *Untangling Blackness in Greek Antiquity.* Cambridge: Cambridge University Press, 2022.

Fagan, Garrett G., ed. *Archaeological Fantasies: How pseudoarchaeology misrepresents the past and misleads the public.* New York and Abingdon: Psychology Press, 2006.

Plato. *Timaeus and Critias.* Translated by Thomas Kjeller Johansen. London: Penguin UK, 2008.

6. MEDEA MAXIMOFF

Gimbutas, Marija. *The Living Goddesses.* Oakland, CA: University of California Press, 2001.

Mallory, J.P. *The Indo-Europeans Rediscovered: How a Scientific Revolution is Rewriting Their Story.* London: Thames and Hudson, 2025.

Reich, David. *Who We Are and How We Got Gere: Ancient DNA and the New Science of the Human Past.* Oxford: Oxford University Press, 2018.

Euripides. *Medea.* Translated by Diane Arnson Svarlien. Indianapolis: Hackett Publishing, 2008.

7. WOLVERINE'S WILD WEST

Anthony, David W. *The Horse, the Wheel, and Language.* Princeton: Princeton University Press, 2010.

Lindow, John. *Norse Mythology: A Guide to Gods, Heroes, Rituals, and Beliefs.* Oxford: Oxford University Press, 2002.

Neel, Jaclyn, ed. *Early Rome: Myth and Society.* Hoboken, NJ: John Wiley & Sons, 2017.

Shay, Jonathan. *Achilles in Vietnam: Combat Trauma and the Undoing of Character.* New York: Simon and Schuster, 2010.

8. THE HERO WITH A THOUSAND (OTHER) FACES

Meineck, Peter. "The Neuroscience of the Tragic Mask." *Arion: A Journal of the Humanities and the Classics* 19, no. 1. (2011): 113–58.

Njoku, Raphael Chijioke. *West African Masking Traditions and Diaspora Masquerade Carnivals: History, Memory, and Transnationalism*. Martlesham, UK: Boydell & Brewer, 2020.

Ridley, Susan, ed. *The Expressive Use of Masks Across Cultures and Healing Arts*. New York and Abingdon: Taylor & Francis, 2024.

Wiles, David. *Mask and Performance in Greek Tragedy: From Ancient Festival to Modern Experimentation*. Cambridge: Cambridge University Press, 2007.

9. SCARY MONSTERS AND SUPERCRIPS

Laes, Christian, ed. *Disability in Antiquity*. New York and Abingdon: Taylor & Francis, 2016.

Meagher, R. "Herakles Gone Mad." In *Rethinking Heroism in an Age of Endless War*. Northhampton, MA: Olive Branch Press, 2006.

Meineck, Peter, and David Konstan, eds. *Combat Trauma and the Ancient Greeks*. New York: Springer, 2014.

Sophocles. *Theban Plays*. Translated by Peter Meineck and Paul Woodruff. Indianapolis: Hackett Publishing, 2003.

10. MARVEL JESUS

Aeschylus. *Oresteia*. Translated by Peter Meineck. Indianapolis: Hackett Publishing, 1998.

Burkert, Walter. *Homo Necans: The Anthropology of Ancient Greek Sacrificial Ritual and Myth*. Oakland, CA: University of California Press, 1983.

Naiden, Fred S. *Smoke Signals for the Gods: Ancient Greek Sacrifice from the Archaic through Roman Periods*. Oxford: Oxford University Press, 2012.

Recht, Laerke. *Human Sacrifice: Archaeological Perspectives from around the World*. Cambridge: Cambridge University Press, 2018.

THE POST-CREDITS SCENE

Cavafy. *Poems*. Translated by Daniel Mendelsohn. London and New York: Everyman's Library Pocket Poets Series, 2014.

Cline, Eric H. *The Trojan War: A Very Short Introduction*. Oxford: Oxford University Press, 2013.

Hall, Edith. *The Return of Ulysses: A Cultural History of Homer's Odyssey*. London: I.B Tauris, 2008.

Shay, Jonathan. *Odysseus in America: Combat Trauma and the Trials of Homecoming*. New York: Simon and Schuster, 2003.

ABOUT THE AUTHOR

Peter Meineck, PhD, holds the endowed chair of professor of Classics in the Modern World at New York University. He has authored several translations of Greek drama and published widely on ancient performance. He has been teaching mythology, classical drama, and literature for nearly thirty years. Originally from South London, Peter trained with the Royal Marines and later discovered the theater, working as a technician, designer, producer, and director, from rooms above pubs to the Royal National Theatre. He founded Aquila Theatre to mount bold new stagings of the classics, and has presented plays in New York, London, Athens, across the United States, Canada, and Europe. His theater work includes national public programs that work with veterans, which have been presented at the Bush and Obama White Houses. Peter also serves as a volunteer firefighter, emergency medical technician, and specialist rescue operator in New York. www.aquilatheatre.com